ON THE ORIGINS OF LANGUAGE

The Evolution of Primate Behavior
Alison Jolly

The Ascent of Man
David Pilbeam

Primate Evolution
Elwyn L. Simons

The Macmillan Series in Physical Anthropology
Elwyn L. Simons and David Pilbeam, editors
other volumes in preparation

Philip Lieberman

BROWN UNIVERSITY

ON THE ORIGINS OF LANGUAGE

AN INTRODUCTION TO THE EVOLUTION OF HUMAN SPEECH

The Macmillan Series in Physical Anthropology

MACMILLAN PUBLISHING CO., INC.
New York

COLLIER MACMILLAN PUBLISHERS
London

Macmillan Publishing Co., Inc.
866 Third Avenue, New York, New York 10022

Collier-Macmillan Canada, Ltd.

Library of Congress Cataloging in Publication Data

Lieberman, Philip.
   On the origins of language.

   (The Macmillan series in physical anthropology)
   Bibliography: p.
   1. Language and languages—Origin.   I. Title.
P131.L5   401'.9   74-5720
ISBN 0-02-370690-2

Printing: 1 2 3 4 5 6 7 8   Year: 5 6 7 8 9 0

Preface

"Presumption is our natural and original malady. The most vulnerable and frail of all creatures is man, and at the same time the most arrogant. He feels and sees himself lodged here, amid the mire and dung of the world . . . , and in his imagination he goes planting himself above the circle of the moon, and bringing the sky beneath his feet. It is by the vanity of this same imagination that he equals himself to God, attributes to himself divine characteristics, picks himself out and separates himself from the horde of other creatures, carves out their shares to his fellows and companions the animals, and distributes to themselves such portions of faculties and powers as he sees fit. How does he know, by the force of his intelligence, the secret internal stirrings of animals? By what comparison between them and us does he infer the stupidity that he attributes to them?

"When I play with my cat, who knows if I am not a pastime to her more than she is to me?"

So wrote Michel Eyquem de Montaigne in 1580. Montaigne's philosophical stance is especially appropriate for the study of the evolution of human language. Perhaps no other aspect of human behavior has been so closely linked to the supposed "special" status of human beings. I will discuss a number of factors that seem to be relevant to the evolution of language. One of these factors, human speech, is "unique" insofar as *Homo sapiens* is the only living animal that can produce it. Human speech shapes human language. Human speech, however, is not the only factor that is necessary in the evolution of language. We share these factors with other living animals to a greater or lesser degree. I will therefore discuss the communications of living nonhuman animals as much as my interpretation of the fossil record of hominid evolution. We really don't know very much about the communications of other animals, not even of our nearest living relatives, the apes. Didactic statements about the presumed absence of "language" in these animals, as Montaigne pointed out, are evidence of our presumption rather than our knowledge.

My interpretation of the data is my own, and any disagreements that the reader may have should be directed to me alone. However, I could not have written this book without the crucial reconstructions of the speech-producing anatomy of various fossil hominids that are the work of Edmund S. Crelin of the Yale University School of Medicine. Crelin's reconstructions are the result of his years of careful observation of the anatomy of adult and newborn *Homo sapiens.* The insights and comments of Kenneth N. Stevens, Alvin M. Liberman, Paul Rozin, William S. Laughlin, and David M. Pilbeam have all been very helpful; those of my coauthors of the papers on this topic, especially Dennis H. Klatt, have been essential. The support of Haskins Laboratories under the able and understanding direction of Franklin S. Cooper also has been an essential element. Mary Ellen Elwell's efficient typing and proofreading were of great assistance, as were the efforts of Ken Scott, Ray Schultz, and Ron Harris of Macmillan. I would also like to thank Rony Inderbinen, Bergführer of Zermatt. The thought of climbing with him in the summer helped me to sustain my labors.

Nothing, however, would have happened if my wife, Marcia, had not first pointed out this problem, that of the evolution of language, to me. Marcia is now engaged in a different struggle that bears on human evolution—the lifting of the sexist barriers that keep us "amid the mire and dung of the world." This book is thus dedicated to Marcia and her sisters.

P.L.

Contents

Introduction

Any book that approaches the evolution of human language must necessarily take account of issues and phenomena that are seemingly disparate. Human language is not a phenomenon that can be completely divorced from other aspects of human behavior and human life. Language affects and indeed structures virtually all aspects of human behavior. It is almost impossible to think of any aspect of human culture or human behavior that would be unchanged if language did not exist. Human language could have evolved only in relation to the total human condition. There would have been no selective advantage for retention of the mutations that gradually resulted in the evolution of human language if language had not been of use in what Darwin in 1859 termed the "struggle for existence." Darwin was aware of the complexity of life and the interrelated nature of the factors that may play a role in the evolution of a particular species or even of a particular attribute of a species. In discussing the nature of the evolutionary process, Darwin says:

Owing to this struggle for life, any variation, however slight and from whatever cause proceeding, if it be in any degree profitable for an individual of any species, in its infinitely complex relations to other organic beings and to external nature, will tend to the preservation of that individual, and will generally be inherited by its offspring. The offspring, also, will thus have a better chance of surviving, for of the many individuals of any species which are periodically born but a small number can survive. I have called this principle, by which each slight variation if useful is preserved, by the term of Natural Selection. (1859, p. 61)

Darwin's version of the struggle for existence is *not* the vision of "Nature red in tooth and claw" conjured up by Tennyson. Evolution to Darwin is not a process in which violence and aggression are the dominant factors insuring success. Rabbits are still with us; saber-toothed tigers are not. Natural selection furthermore doesn't necessarily have to follow from startling major changes in an organism or its environment. Darwin throughout *On the Origin of Species* makes the same point:

Nor do I believe that any great physical change, as of climate, or any unusual degree of isolation to check immigration, is actually necessary to produce new and unoccupied places for natural selection to fill up by modifying and improving some of the varying inhabitants. For as all the inhabitants of each country are struggling together with nicely balanced forces, extremely slight modifications in the structure or habits of one inhabitant would often give it an advantage over others; and still further modifications of the same kind would often still further increase the advantage. (1859, p. 82)

Darwin has been quoted because we shall operate within the framework that he established. We will discuss, in some detail, comparative, ontogenetic, and evolutionary studies of one factor that appears to be uniquely human, that is, the production and perception of human speech. However, this single factor would in itself, be meaningless if we did not also consider other aspects of human language, as well as other aspects of human and nonhuman behavior. We therefore will discuss, among other things, studies of cognitive behavior in nonhuman primates, the neural bases of auditory perception in humans and other animals, play activity in rhesus monkeys, and stone-tool-making techniques. In short, we will attempt to synthesize a great deal of data into a coherent theory. The theory hopefully is a useful approach to the study of the evolution of human language. Like all theories, it won't account for everything, but it does appear to "explain" and relate a number of phenomena that otherwise appear to be quite unrelated and moreover it appears to point to a coherent evolutionary process that relates the communication systems of other animals to human language. It most importantly points out a number of questions that can be resolved through controlled experiments and careful observations.

We have to draw on a number of seemingly disparate ethological, anatomical, psychological, and anthropological sources because there is no single factor that is, in itself, responsible for the evolution of human language. Evolution is, as Darwin recognized, a complex process that inherently involves all aspects of the life cycle and environment of a species and its relationships to other species. Though particular factors such as gestural communication undoubtedly had an important role in the evolution of language, no one of them can provide the "key" to the puzzle. Everything depends on everything else, and the interaction through natural selection is the "crucial" factor if anything is. Note that we're not stating that we cannot analyze the factors that underlie the evolution of language. We are instead proposing that the process involved many interrelated factors. We will show that particular factors that result in a selective advantage in one aspect of behavior, e.g., hunting or toolmaking, carry over into language. The same factor may have also a selective advantage in language, and natural selection may again produce "further modifications of the same kind." More effective language, for example, will further enhance the survival of the species by making hunting and toolmaking more effective. In short, we will apply Darwin's theory of natural selection to the study of the evolution of human language.

A Darwinian approach to the study of language of course involves more than the application of the theory of natural selection. We will, for example, make use of the principle of "preadaption," that is, natural selection channeling development in a new direction because of previous modifications for some other role. This principle is extremely important, for it demonstrates how natural selection operating in small steps can effect radical changes in behavior. Darwin's comments on the evolution of the lung from the swim bladder make the principle clear:

> The illustration of the swim bladder in fish is a good one, because it shows us clearly the highly important fact that an organ originally constructed for one purpose, namely flotation, may be converted into one for a wholly different purpose, namely respiration. (1859, p. 190)

We'll also make use of the concept of "the affinities of extinct species to each other, and to living forms" (p. 329) when we apply inferences from the anatomy, physiology, and behavior of living primates to fossil hominids. We'll also make extensive use of the observations noted in the section on embryology (pp. 439–449) in drawing inferences from the relationship of the skeletal structure of human newborns to that of Neandertal man. The relationship we want to show between human newborns and various fossil hominids is that noted by Darwin, rather than the "law" attributed to Haeckel (1866).[1] We'll also discuss our findings with reference to Darwin's views on speciation and extinction. Perhaps the most important lesson that we'll try to draw from Darwin is his method. As Mayr (1964) notes, Darwin introduced "a method novel then but now perhaps the prevailing method of science. Expressed in modern terms, it is the testing of a model developed on the basis of prior observations."

[1]The German Darwinist Haeckel formulated a "law" wherein he claimed that the ontogenetic development of living animals mirrors the phylogenetic development of the species. In other words, past stages that were typical of various "ancestral" forms can be seen as an organism evolves from its foetal to its adult form. Haeckel did not claim that every stage in the phylogenetic evolution of a species will be manifested in the course of its growth and development. His "law," however, tends to elicit a great deal of controversy since it often is interpreted as though *every* stage in the evolution of a species must be manifested in the course of its onto-genetic development. Darwin took note of the same facts as Haeckel but he did not formulate a "law." He simply noted that the foetal and infantile forms of various closely related species resembled each other more than was the case for the adult forms.

Cognitive and Communicative Factors Underlying Language

2

We can start the discussion of the evolution of language by listing some of the factors that are involved. The list is not intended as an inclusive list of all the factors that might have played a role in the evolution of human language, but we'll start with the hypothesis that these are the central ones. We'll order these factors according to their probable role in differentiating the language of modern *Homo sapiens* from that of progressively earlier hominids and other animals. In other words, we'll first list the factors that may have been most important in the late stages of human evolution and proceed to those that were probably more relevant in earlier stages. It is important to note at this point that we will not categorically differentiate human language, i.e., the language of present-day *Homo sapiens*, from other languages, e.g., the possible language of present-day chimpanzees. Evolution proceeds in small steps, and the only reason that human language appears to be so disjoint from animal communication systems is that the hominids who possessed "intermediate" languages are all dead.

Linguists have been somewhat anthropocentric in defining language to be necessarily human language. We will instead propose an operational definition of language. *A language is a communications system that is capable of transmitting new information.* In other words, we're operationally defining a language as a communication system that places no inherent restriction on the nature or quality of the information transmitted. It is obvious that this definition does not require that all languages have all of the properties of human language. It isn't very profitable to define language in terms of a "set" of properties or "design features" (Hockett and Ascher, 1964) that purportedly characterize human language. Linguists simply do not know what properties in fact do characterize human languages. Even if a list of "language universals" could be found that applied to all human languages, we would have to be able to assess the functional value of each "universal" before we could assess the status of a communication system that lacked a particular feature. For example, if we found that all human languages had relative clauses, we might still want to state that the communication system of the little green men who had just arrived in their flying saucer was a "language," though it lacked relative clauses.

FACTOR 1:
SPEECH ENCODING AND DECODING

Human language achieves a high rate of speed and overcomes the limits of memory span by the process of encoding. Encoding takes place at two levels, in the production of speech and in the transformational syntax of human language. The encoding of speech appears to be the more recent factor in the evolution of human language. The encoding that takes place in the *transformational syntax* of human language is formally similar, but it's not as specialized a process and probably was present in hominids who differed in significant ways from modern *Homo sapiens.* We'll start by briefly discussing the encoding of speech. A full appreciation of speech encoding and the neural decoding of speech requires the background material of Chapters 4, 5, and 6, so we'll simply sketch out the general outline of the process here.

Modern human speech communication achieves a high rate of speed by a process of speech encoding and a complementary process of decoding. The rate at which meaningful sound distinctions are transmitted in human speech is about 20 to 30 segments per second. That is, phonetic distinctions that differentiate meaningful words, e.g., the sound symbolized by the symbols [b], [æ], and [t] in the word *bat,*[1] are transmitted, identified, and stored at a rate of 20 to 30 segments per second. It is obvious that human listeners

[1]The brackets indicate that the letters are being used as phonetic symbols.

cannot transmit and identify these sound distinctions as separate entities. The fastest rate at which sounds can be identified is about 7 to 9 segments per second (Liberman, 1970). Sounds transmitted at a rate of 20 per second merge into an undifferentiable "tone." That's why high-fidelity amplifiers and loudspeakers generally have an advertised lower frequency limit of 20 cycles per second (20 Hz).[2] The human auditory system simply cannot temporally resolve auditory events that occur at a rate of 20 per second. The human visual system incidentally can't work any faster; motion pictures work because the projector presents individual still frames at rates in excess of 16 frames per second. The linguist's traditional conception of phonetic elements comprising a set of "beads on a string" clearly is not correct at the acoustic level. How, then, is speech transmitted and perceived?

The answer to this question comes from work that was originally directed at making a reading machine for the blind. The machine was to identify alphabetic characters in printed texts and convert these symbols into sounds that a blind person could listen to. It isn't too difficult to devise a print-reading device, though such would not be necessary if the machine's use were to be restricted to the "reading" of new books and publications. At some stage in the preparation of a publication a machine with a keyboard is used. The talking machine could be connected to the keyboard so that it produced simply a different sound, or combination of sounds, for each typewriter or linotype key. The sequence of sounds could then be tape-recorded, and blind people could listen to the tape recordings after the tapes were perhaps slowed down and edited to eliminate pauses, errors, and so on. A number of different systems were developed. They all were useless because listeners had to slow the tapes down to rates that were about one tenth that of normal human speech. The blind "readers" would forget what a sentence was about before they heard its end. It didn't matter what sorts of sounds were connected to the typewriter keys; they all were equally bad. The basic rate of transmission, the inherent difficulty of these systems, was about the same as that of the traditional "dots" and "dashes" of the telegrapher's Morse Code. The systems worked, but they were very, very slow.

The obvious solution to this problem seemed to rest in making machines that would "glue" the phonetic elements of speech together to make words. As already mentioned, linguists had traditionally thought of phonetic segments as "beads on a string." There seemed to be no inherent problem if the beads were isolated, collected, and then appropriately strung together. The medium of tape recording seemed to be the solution. Speakers could be recorded while they carefully pronounced "test" words. The phonetic elements of these words could then be isolated by cutting up the

---

[2] These terms are defined in Chapter 4. It's impossible to discuss the acoustics of speech without using the appropriate terminology. Readers who don't understand what we mean by the term *frequency* should refer to Chapter 4 at this point.

magnetic tape (preferably by segmenting the tape with the electronic equivalent of a pair of scissors). A speaker, for example, would record a list of words that included *pet, bat, cat, hat,* and so on. The experimenters would then theoretically be able to "isolate" the sounds [p], [b], [h], [k], [e], [æ]. The isolated sounds would be stored in a machine that could put them together in different patterns to form new words, for example, *get* and *pat.* The list of possible permutations would, of course, increase as the vocabulary of isolated stored phonetic elements increased. Systems of this sort were implemented at great expense and with enormous efforts (Peterson et al., 1958). Surprisingly, they produced speech that was scarcely intelligible. Despite many attempts to improve the technique by changing the methods used in isolating the phonetic elements, the systems proved to be completely useless.

Though these studies failed to produce a useful "reading machine" they demonstrated that phonetic elements could not be regarded as beads on a string. It was, in fact, impossible to isolate a consonant like [b] or [t] without also hearing the vowels that either preceded or followed it because such "stop" consonants cannot be produced without pronouncing a vowel. The smallest segment of speech that can be pronounced is the syllable. If you try to "say" the sound [b] you'll discover that it's impossible. You can say [bi], [bu], [bʊ], [ba], [bɪ], [bæ], [bɪt], [bɪd], and so on, but you can't produce an isolated [b]. The results of the past 20 years of research on the production of speech by humans demonstrate that individual sounds like [b], [ɪ], and [d] are encoded, i.e., "squashed together," into a single unit when we produce the syllable-sized unit [bɪt] (the phonetic transcription of the English word *bit*). A human speaker in producing this syllable starts with his supralaryngeal vocal tract, i.e., his tongue, lips, velum, and so on, in the positions characteristic of [b]. However, he does not maintain this articulatory configuration but instead moves his articulators toward the positions that would be attained if he were instructed to maintain an isolated, steady [ɪ]. He never reaches these positions, because he starts toward the articulatory configuration characteristic of [t] before he ever reaches the "steady-state" (isolated and sustained) vowel [ɪ]. The articulatory gestures that would be characteristic of each isolated "sound" are never attained. Instead the articulatory gestures are melded together into a composite, characteristic of the syllable.

The sound pattern that results from this encoding process is itself an indivisible composite. Just as there is no way of separating with absolute certainty the [b] articulatory gestures from the [ɪ] gestures (you can't tell exactly when the [b] ends and the [ɪ] begins), there is no way of separating the acoustic cues that are generated by these articulatory maneuvers. The isolated sounds have a psychological status as motor control or "programming" instructions for the speech-producing apparatus.[3] The sound pattern that results

---

[3]Lesions in Broca's area of the brain disturb these "programs." We'll discuss the neurological aspects of speech perception in the pages that follow.

is a composite, and the acoustic cues for the initial and final consonants are largely transmitted as modulations imposed on the vowel. The process is, in effect, a time-compressing system. The acoustic cues that characterize the initial and final consonants are transmitted in the time slot that would have been necessary to transmit a single isolated [ɪ] vowel.

The human brain decodes, i.e., "unscrambles," the acoustic signal in terms of the articulatory maneuvers that were put together to generate the syllable. The individual consonants [b] and [t], though they have no independent acoustic status, are perceived as discrete entities. The process of human speech perception inherently requires "knowledge" of the acoustic consequences of the possible range of human supralaryngeal vocal tract speech articulation (Liberman et al., 1967; Lieberman, 1970, 1972). The coding and decoding of speech in terms of syllables is an essential aspect of human linguistic ability. Children who have severe reading "disabilities" can, for example, be taught to read with 3 to 6 hours of tutoring by making use of a syllabic notation (Rozin et al., 1971). Traditional methods of teaching reading essentially assume that the phonemic level of language is basic (roughly the alphabetic level). Much of the difficulty in teaching children to read can be overcome if intermediate units, representing syllables, are used to introduce reading.

The special link between human speech and human language was recognized in the pioneering nineteenth-century studies of Broca (1861) and Wernicke (1874). Broca found that lesions in a small area of the brain situated near the motor cortex in the left, dominant hemisphere of the brain impaired speech production and writing. The victims of the "aphasia" could still move their tongues, lips, and so on, and in some instances they could sing, but they had difficulty when they either spoke or wrote. Lesions in the area of the brain that has come to be known as Broca's area essentially interfere with the organization of the articulatory maneuvers that produce speech, the "programs," as well as the written symbols that represent speech. Wernicke in 1874 described and localized the complementary aspect of aphasia. He located an area of the brain near the auditory centers of the left, dominant hemisphere where lesions produced an aphasia in which the victim either left out words, used the wrong syntax, or "lost" the proper phonetic "spellings" of words. The victim of a lesion in Wernicke's area might use the words "Bolivian shovel" when he meant to say "nickel," or he might instead invent a new word "yipfoo" that would be used when he meant to say "nickel." These people essentially lose part of the "dictionary" and the grammar that every human carries about in his (or her) head. Both of these areas of the brain can be regarded as evolved additions to parts of the brain that deal with the production of sounds (Broca's area) and the perception of sounds (Wernicke's area). Lesions in Wernicke's area clearly involve much more than the mere perception of sound, just as lesions in Broca's area involve much more than the ability to simply move the tongue, lips, jaw, and so on. The total linguistic ability of the victim is impaired. The siting of these areas near the parts of the brain that are directly concerned with auditory signals suggests that special neural mechanisms evolved matched to, and as a consequence of, vocal communication.

The studies of Broca and Wernicke have been replicated and extended through the systematic study of brain lesions. We know that modern *Homo sapiens* has language-specific neural devices sited in the dominant (usually the left) hemisphere of the brain (Geschwind, 1970). The results of psycho-acoustic experiments focused on the process of speech perception also demonstrate that special processing is involved that appears to crucially involve the dominant hemisphere of the human brain (Kimura, 1964, 1973; Shankweiler and Studdert-Kennedy, 1967; Liberman et al., 1967). We will discuss in detail the process of human speech perception as it is related to the anatomy of the human vocal tract. For the moment, we will note that the special neural devices necessary for the "decoding" of human speech may be comparatively recent evolutionary acquisitions.

FACTOR 2:
SPECIAL SUPRALARYNGEAL
VOCAL TRACT ANATOMY

Modern man's speech-producing apparatus is quite different from the comparable systems of living nonhuman primates (Lieberman, 1968; Lieberman et al., 1969, 1972b). Nonhuman primates have supralaryngeal vocal tracts in which the larynx exits directly into the oral cavity (Negus, 1949). In the adult human the larynx exits into the pharynx. The only function for which the adult human supralaryngeal vocal tract appears to be better adapted is speech production. Understanding the anatomical basis of human speech requires that we briefly review the *source-filter theory of speech production* (Chiba and Kajiyama, 1958; Fant, 1960).[4] Human speech is the result of a source, or sources, of acoustic energy being filtered by the supralaryngeal vocal tract. For voiced sounds, e.g., sounds like the English vowels, the source of energy is the periodic sequence of puffs of air that pass through the larynx as the vocal cords (folds) rapidly open and shut. The rate at which the vocal cords open and close determines the fundamental frequency of phonation. Acoustic energy is present at the fundamental frequency and at higher harmonics. The fundamental frequency of phonation can vary from about 80 Hz for adult males to about 500 Hz for children and some adult females. Significant acoustic energy is present in the har-

---

[4] We will discuss the source-filter theory of speech production in detail in Chapter 5. This discussion should be regarded as a prefatory "overview" of one of the central features of the theory that we will develop. If you can't follow the discussion here, don't despair; it ought to become clearer as you read on!

monics of fundamental frequency to at least 3 kHz (kilohertz; 3 kHz is 3000 Hz). The fundamental frequency of phonation is, within wide limits, under the control of the speaker, who can produce controlled variations by varying either pulmonary air pressure or the tension of the laryngeal muscles (Lieberman, 1967). Linguistically significant information can be transmitted by means of these variations in fundamental frequency as, for example, in Chinese, where these variations are used to differentiate words.

However, the main source of phonetic differentiation in human language arises from the dynamic properties of the supralaryngeal vocal tract acting as an acoustic filter. The length and shape of the supralaryngeal vocal tract determine the frequencies at which maximum energy will be transmitted from the laryngeal source to the air adjacent to the speaker's lips. These frequencies, at which maximum acoustic energy will be transmitted, are known as formant frequencies. A speaker can vary the formant frequencies by changing the length and shape of his supralaryngeal vocal tract. He can, for example, drastically alter the shape of the airway formed by the posterior margin of his tongue body in his pharynx. He can raise or lower the upper boundary of his tongue in his oral cavity. He can raise or lower his larynx and retract or extend his lips. He can open or close his nasal cavity to the rest of the supralaryngeal vocal tract by lowering or raising his velum. The speaker can, in short, continually vary the formant frequencies generated by his supralaryngeal vocal tract. For example, the acoustic properties that differentiate the vowels [a] and [i] are determined solely by the shape and length differences that the speaker's supralaryngeal vocal tract assumes in articulating them. The situation is analogous to the musical properties of a pipe organ, where the length and type (open or closed end) of pipe determine the musical quality of each note. The damped resonances of the human supralaryngeal vocal tract are, in effect, the formant frequencies. The length and shape (more precisely the cross-sectional area as a function of distance from the laryngeal source) determine the formant frequencies.

The situation is similar for unvoiced sounds, where the vocal cords do not open and close at a rapid rate releasing quasiperiodic puffs of air. The source of acoustic energy in these instances is the turbulence generated by air rushing through a constriction in the vocal tract. The vocal tract still acts as an acoustic filter, but the acoustic source may not be at the level of the larynx as, for example, in the sound [s], where the source is the turbulence generated near the speaker's teeth.

The anatomy of the adult human supralaryngeal vocal tract permits modern man to generate supralaryngeal vocal tract configurations that involve abrupt discontinuities at its midpoint. These particular vocal tract shapes produce vowels like [a], [i], and [u], which have unique acoustic properties. The acoustic properties of these sounds will be discussed in detail, but for the moment we will simply note that they are sounds that minimize the problems of precise articulatory control. A speaker can produce about the same formant frequencies for an [i] while he varies the position of the midpoint area function discontinuity by 1 or 2 centimeters (Stevens, 1972). The vowels [a], [i], and [u] are also maximally distinct acoustically as well as being sounds that a human listener can efficiently use to establish the size of the supralaryngeal vocal tract that he is listening to. This last property relates to Factor 1, the specialized speech encoding and decoding that characterizes human language. The reconstructions of the supralaryngeal vocal tracts of various fossil hominids that Edmund S. Crelin has made indicate that some extinct hominids lacked the anatomical basis for producing these sounds whereas others appear to have had the requisite anatomical specializations for human speech. We will, of course, return to this topic, which is central to our theory.

FACTOR 3:
SYNTACTIC ENCODING AND DECODING

There are three interrelated aspects to the neural mechanisms that underly language: *syntactic encoding and decoding, automatization,* and *cognitive ability.* Syntactic encoding and decoding obviously involve the presence of neural mechanisms. However, we don't know very much about the workings of the brain except for certain very general facts derived from studies like those of lesions in Wernicke's area. We'll discuss some further aspects of neural organization and the evolution of the brain in Chapter 11, but we don't have to know *how* the brain works to know *what* it does. A *transformational grammar* (Chomsky, 1957, 1964, 1968) is, among other things, a formal description of the syntactic encoding characteristic of human language. Encoding in a more general sense seems to be a characteristic of other forms of human behavior.[5]

A grammar to a linguist is not a set of prescriptive "rules" that tells how to write sentences. A grammar is instead a formal description of some aspect of linguistic behavior. As Chomsky puts it,

> Syntactic investigation of a given language has as its goal the construction of a grammar that can be viewed as a device of some sort for producing sentences of the language under analysis. More generally, linguists have been concerned with the problem of determining the fundamental underlying properties of successful grammars. (1957, p. 11)

The fundamental property of grammar that Chomsky revealed is its *transformational syntax.* Chomsky demonstrated that language

[5]We'll later discuss some of the evidence suggesting that earlier hominids, who lacked fully developed human language, may have developed toolmaking techniques that must formally be described by a transformational grammar.

must be viewed as a two-level process. Underlying the sequence of words that constitutes a normal, grammatical sentence is a "deep phrase marker" (Chomsky, 1964), which is closer to the logical level of analysis necessary for the semantic interpretation of a sentence. The transformational syntax is the "device" that restructures the "deep," underlying level of language that is suited for semantic analysis into the actual sentence that a person writes or speaks. It is impossible to present a comprehensive discussion of the principles of transformational syntax here; we will return to this topic in Chapter 11, but the interested reader should consult one of the many introductory texts on this subject. The aspect of transformational syntax that we want to stress is its encoding property, which is formally similar to the process of speech encoding (Liberman, 1970).

Figure 2-1 is a diagram essentially similar to the "parsing" or "constituent analysis" (Bloomfield, 1933) of traditional grammarians. The symbol S stands for the word *sentence*, NP for *noun phrase*, VP for *verb phrase*, V for *verb*, N for *noun*, and T for *article*. The diagram shows the syntactic relationships that exist between the words of the sentence *The man is old*. The words *the man*, for example, constitute a noun phrase; the words *is old* constitute a verb phrase, which in turn is made up of a verb plus a second noun phrase. The word *old* constitutes the second noun phrase (the article of the second noun phrase reduces to an implied article). Diagrams of this sort are quite traditional. The first noun phrase could be called the subject of the sentence, the second noun phrase the object or predicate, and so on. Semantic relationships are often "explained" by means of diagrams of this sort. The "actor–object" relationship, for example, is apparent in the diagram of the sentence *Joe hit the man* (Figure 2-2). The actor is the noun that precedes the verb, the object the noun that follows the verb.

We have simplified these diagrams, and many of the details that a grammarian might find essential have been eliminated, but the essential facts and "explanatory" power of these diagrams have been preserved. Parsing is a "device" that formally "explains" some aspects of semantics; that is, it reduces semantic analysis to a mechanical procedure. The noun to the left of the verb is the actor,

Figure 2-1 Syntactic relationships in *The man is old.*

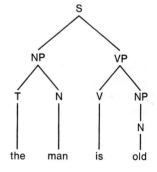

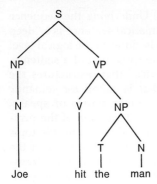

Figure 2-2 Syntactic relationships in *Joe hit the man.*

that to the right of the verb is the object, i.e., the noun acted on. The interesting thing about human language is that no one ever really utters sentences like *Joe hit the man* and *The man is old* when he wants to convey the information in the sentence *Joe hit the old man.* The two "underlying," "deep phrase markers" that would result in the "simple" sentences *The man is old* and *Joe hit the man* are encoded, i.e., "scrambled" together, into one, more complex sentence. The process is general and pervasive. The sentence *Joe hit the dirty old man who was wearing the red hat* would have underlying it a set of deep phrase markers that could have resulted in the sentences *Joe hit the man, The man is old, The man is dirty, The man was wearing a hat, The hat is red.* It's much faster to utter the single complex sentence than the set of "simpler" sentences that underlie it. The listener also doesn't have to keep track of the semantic referents and remember that the speaker is talking about the same man in the first four simple sentences. All four repetitions of the word *man* are collapsed into a single *man* in the complex sentence. The two repetitions of the word *hat* are collapsed into a single *hat.* The complex sentence has fewer words and doesn't require keeping track of the semantic referents of the five "simple" sentences.

The transformational syntax is the device that rearranges, deletes, and adds words to form the sentences of human language. The transformational syntax is the device that makes it possible to mechanically sort out the semantic relationships of the words of complex sentences by using traditional sentence parsing. The "actor–acted on" relationship, for example, is semantically equivalent in the sentences *Joe hit Bill* and *Bill was hit by Joe,* though the words are on opposite sides of the verb. There are a number of reasons why traditional constituent grammars are not, in themselves, able to account for the properties of human languages (Chomsky, 1957, 1964; Postal, 1968), but it's enough to point out that they cannot account for the syntactic encoding that is characteristic of human language and the complementary "decoding" that must take place when a listener or reader interprets a sentence (Fodor et al., 1974).

FACTOR 4:
AUTOMATIZATION

Human language involves rapidly executing complex sequences of articulatory movements or making equally complex perceptual decisions regarding the identity of particular sound segments. At a higher level, complex syntactic relationships must be determined. None of these processes is, however, what the speaker or listener is directly concerned with. The semantic content of the message is the primary concern of the speaker or listener. The sending and receiving processes are essentially automatic. No conscious thought is expended in the process of speech production, speech perception, or any of the syntactic stages that may intervene between the semantic content of the message and the acoustic signal. It is clear that "automatized" skills are not unique to human language. Other aspects of human activity, dance, for example, involve similar phenomena. The novice dancer must learn the particular steps and movements that characterize a particular dance form. Once the steps have been learned, they become automatized. The dance itself involves the complex sequences. Playing the violin, skiing, and driving a car all involve automatized behavior.

The bases for the automatized behavior that is a necessary condition for human language may reside in cross-modal transfers from other systems of hominid and primate behavior. Tool use, for example, requires a high degree of automatization. You can't stop to think how to use a hammer every time you drive a nail in. Hunting is perhaps a still stronger case. A successful hunter must be able to thrust a spear or throw a stone without pausing to think about the mechanics of spear thrusting or stone throwing. Natural selection would quickly favor the retention of superior automatization. Automatized behavior pervades all aspects of culture. Indeed a cultural response is, to a degree, a special case of automatized behavior. Electrophysiological data derived from study of the rhesus monkey (*Maccaca mulatta*) demonstrate that automatization in primates involves establishing special pathways in the animal's motor cortex as the animal "learns" to perform a task (Evarts, 1973). Evarts observed the electrical activity of motor cortex neurons and the muscles during the performance of learned hand movements. The animal's muscular activity when it learned to perform the task was extremely rapid. Its muscles acted within 30 to 40 msec (milliseconds; 1 msec is one thousandth of a second), about twice as fast as the animal could have responded if it had to "think about" the task. Short response times usually are associated with "reflex" actions, but these were the result of the animal's automatizing a response. The "learned" automatized responses of simpler animals generally are not taken as tokens of the animal's "culture," but they nonetheless exist. The function of "play" in animals may indeed be to learn various patterns of automatized behavior that are germane to the animal's "culture." Dogs spend a lot of time staging mock battles when they're pups, kittens stalk, and so on. It wouldn't be difficult to devise appropriate experiments to explore the possible connection between play and automatization.

A special factor that may be involved in automatized behavior is a "critical" period, when it is comparatively easier to shape behavior. Afterward, it is either impossible or more difficult to "learn" the automatized behavior. Puppies thus can be trained more readily than adult dogs. We're just beginning to appreciate some of the "critical" periods involved in "learning" various activities. Human newborns, for example, can be trained to walk alone about 2 months earlier than they normally do if we take advantage of a "critical" period. Brief daily exercise of the walking reflexes that exist in human newborns leads to an earlier onset of walking alone (Zelazo et al., 1972). If a newborn infant is held under his arms and his bare feet are permitted to touch a flat surface, he will perform well-coordinated walking movements similar to those of an adult. This reflex normally disappears after about 8 weeks. If the infant is actively exercised throughout this period, the reflex can be transferred intact to a volitional action. Critical periods are quite important in the acquisition of human language (Lenneberg, 1967). All humans can readily learn different languages in their youth, apparently retaining this ability to at least age 12 (Sachs et al., 1973). However, most adult humans can learn a foreign, i.e. unfamiliar, language only with great difficulty (or not at all). There are, of course, exceptions to this rule, and some adults are quite fortunate insofar as they retain the ability to learn new languages with great facility. The same comments probably apply to learning to play the violin, tightrope walking, and so on, though no definitive studies have yet been made.

FACTOR 5:
COGNITIVE ABILITY

Cognitive ability is a necessary factor in human language. Linguists often tend to assume that cognitive ability *is* linguistic ability. Indeed, since the time of Descartes the absence of human language in other animals has been cited as a "proof" of man's special status and the lack of cognitive ability in all other species. Human language has been assumed to be a necessary condition for human thought; conversely, its absence has been assumed to be evidence of the lack of all cognitive ability.

It is clear that cognitive, i.e., logical, abilities can be demonstrated or observed in many animals. For example, behavioral conditioning, which can be applied with great success to pigeons and rats, can itself be viewed as a demonstration of logical ability on the part of the "conditioned" animal. Behavioral conditioning simply involves rewarding an animal when it performs the desired activity and/or punishing it when it performs some other activity. The techniques are very general and work with very simple animals such as the mollusk *Pleurobranchaea californica*, where the learned responses can be observed in the animal's isolated nervous system (Mpitsos and Davis, 1973). The technique used in "teaching" mollusks is similar to that employed by Pavlov, who, in his classic experiments, "conditioned" dogs to salivate when they heard the sound of the bell that was rung when they were fed. The dogs learned that the sound of the bell signified the presence of food, as their anticipatory salivation indicated. They had learned to make the association between the sound of the bell and food. The sound of a bell can in no way be regarded as an "image" or "icon" of food; it is essentially an abstract *symbol* that stands in the same regard to dog food as the word *steak* stands to its semantic referent. Pavlov's dogs had to make a *logical* association between the bell and food. Calling the animals' response a "conditioned reflex" obscures this fact. The same "conditioned" response often can be observed as a human gourmet regards the menu. In both cases cognitive ability must interpose between the token of the food that is anticipated and the observed physiological response. The human gourmet is hopefully more flexible, adaptive, and discriminating than Pavlov's dogs, but the basic process is similar.[6] In *Homo sapiens* the cognitive abilities that underlie this particular aspect of behavior are simply more complex than is the case for *Canis familiaris*. However, the difference is quantitative rather than qualitative.

The cognitive abilities that have traditionally been associated with presumably "unique" human behavioral patterns like tool use and toolmaking have been observed in a number of different animals. Chimpanzees have often been observed making and using tools (Goodall, 1971). Beck (in press) reviews much of the evidence that shows tool use in other primates in their natural settings. Tool use has also been carefully documented in sea otters (Kenyon, 1969). Sea otters float on their backs and use stones as anvils against which they break the shells of crustaceans; they will hold onto stones that are suitable anvils, tucking one under a flipper as they swim between meals. A sea otter thus not only uses a stone tool but also preserves it for future anticipated applications.

[6]The distinction between the "conditioned reflex" of Pavlov's dogs and the response of human gourmets is essentially that of the nature and generality of the physiological response and the "tutorial" process. Many trials are needed to teach a dog to associate the sound of a bell and food and thereby elicit a physiological response. Humans need far fewer trials or experiences to learn the meaning of a new word. Humans also can demonstrate that they "know" the meaning of a word without making an obvious physical response. When humans are forced to act as though they were dogs, it also takes a fairly long time to establish a "conditioned" reflex. The appropriate parallel with the Pavlovian situation for humans is that of an Army drill sergeant and his recruits. It's a long, hard process before the recruits automatically execute an order, though from the beginning they have known the meaning of the words.

Tool use and toolmaking under less natural conditions have even been observed in birds. Laboratory-raised northern blue jays (*Cyanocitta cristata*) have been observed tearing pieces from pages of newspapers and using them as tools to rake in food pellets that were otherwise out of reach (Jones and Kamil, 1973). The toolmaking techniques that can be observed in living nonhuman animals are rather simple; however, the stone tools associated with the earliest known fossil hominids are also rather simple. We'll discuss the cognitive implications of different toolmaking techniques in Chapter 11, but it is clear that the tool-using and toolmaking behavior of many living animals is a reasonable approximation to the initial base on which natural selection acted in the gradual evolution of hominid behavior.

The linguistic ability of present-day chimpanzees also is evidence of the cognitive "base" that is present in living nonhuman animals. Chimpanzees do not have the speech-producing anatomy of modern *Homo sapiens*. We'll discuss their phonetic limitations in detail in Chapters 8 and 9. They could not produce human speech even if they had the neural devices, localized in Broca's area, that organize the complex articulatory gestures of human speech. However, chimpanzees can be taught to use a modified version of American Sign Language. American Sign Language is not a method of "finger-spelling" English words. It is instead a system that makes use of gestures that each correspond to complete words, morphemes (e.g., past tense), or phrases (Stokoe, 1960). It has a different grammar than standard English and really is a different language that has its own linguistic history. Chimpanzees, when they are taught this sign language, communicate in a linguistic mode with human interlocutors (Gardner and Gardner, 1969; Fouts, 1973). They also can be observed communicating with other chimpanzees through sign language (Fouts, 1973). Other experimenters have taught chimpanzees to communicate with humans by means of plastic symbols (Premack, 1972) and by means of a computer keyboard (Rumbaugh, 1973). These experiments and observations also demonstrate that chimpanzees can communicate in a linguistic mode. For example, they are aware of what constitutes a "grammatical" syntactic construction (Rumbaugh, 1973). They can conjoin words to form sentences, e.g., *I want apples and bananas,* and can understand the principle of negation (Premack, 1972). They generalize the use of words, categorize in terms of semantic attributes, and use syntactic and logical constructs like conditional sentences, e.g., *Lucy read book if Roger tickle Lucy* (Fouts, 1973). Chimpanzees' cognitive linguistic abilities are, at worst, restricted to some subset of the cognitive abilities available to humans. Chimpanzees may lack the syntactic encoding that must be formally described by a transformational syntax in human language. Definitive experiments investigating the syntax of chimpanzee communications using sign language have yet to be done, and we don't really know whether their sentences are syntactically encoded. The difference at the cognitive level may, however, be quantitative rather than qualitative.

It is important to note, at this point, that quantitative functional abilities can be the bases of behavioral patterns that are qualitatively different. I think that this fact is sometimes not appreciated in discussions of gradual versus abrupt change. A modern electronic desk calculator and a large general-purpose digital computer, for example, may be constructed using similar electronic logical devices and similar magnetic memories. The large general-purpose machine will, however, have 1,000 to 10,000,000 times as many logical and memory devices. The structural differences between the desk calculator and general-purpose machine may thus simply be quantitative rather than qualitative, although the "behavioral" consequence of this quantitative difference can be qualitative. The types of problems that one can solve on the general-purpose machine will differ in kind, as well as in size, from those suited to the desk calculator. The inherent cognitive abilities of humans and chimpanzees thus could be quantitative and still have qualitative behavioral consequences.

The cognitive abilities that are typically associated with human language may have their immediate origins in the complex patterns of hominid behavior associated with tool use, toolmaking, hunting, and the cultural complex that supports these activities. The evolution of activities like toolmaking that necessitate learning complex skills places a selective advantage on social organizations that encourage the transmission of knowledge. Enhanced linguistic ability would have a high selective value in these cultural settings. Hewes (1973) makes a convincing case for the role of gestural communication in the earliest forms of hominid language and associates language with the transference of cognitive ability from these complex behavioral patterns. However, the earliest hominid languages probably were not exclusively gestural, nor can the cognitive abilities that underlie language be restricted to hominids. Tool use and hunting certainly are not exclusively hominid patterns of behavior.

We can get some insights on the neural abilities that nonhuman primates possess by taking note of the phylogenetic evolution of the peripheral systems involved in information gathering and communication. For example, the acute color vision of primates would have had no selective advantage if it had not been coupled with matching cognitive processes. Gestural communication is consistent with the evolution and retention of increasingly complex facial musculature in the phylogenetic order of primates. It is likewise unlikely that gestural communication was at any stage of hominid evolution the *sole* "phonetic" medium. Negus (1949), by the methods of comparative anatomy, demonstrates that the larynges of nonhuman primates are adapted for phonation at the expense of respiratory efficiency. The far simpler larynx of the lungfish is better adapted for respiration and protecting the lungs. Clearly, mutations that decreased respiratory efficiency would not have been retained over a phylogenetic order unless they had some selective advantage. The cognitive skills that underlie linguistic ability in hominids thus probably evolved from cognitive facilities that have functional roles in the social behavior and communications of other animals. Like automatization, these skills would appear to be part of the biological endowment of many species, and their continued development in "higher" species is concomitant with behavioral complexity. The transference of these cognitive skills to human language could be viewed as yet another instance of "preadaptation," the use of cognitive processes that originally evolved because of the selective advantages conferred on activities like hunting, evading natural enemies, food gathering, and social organization.

The Comparative Method in the Study of Communication: Darwin and Negus

3

Charles Darwin, in *The Expression of Emotion in Man and Animals* (1872), laid the foundation for most subsequent studies of the communications of animals. In this comprehensive work, he again makes use of the comparative method that worked so well in *On the Origin of Species* but, rather oddly, fails to make full use of the principle of natural selection and the concomitant principle that evolution proceeds in small steps. Darwin essentially accepts the Cartesian theory that human language is disjoint from animal communication and that it is in some sense uniquely human. To Descartes, human language was a proof that man was unique. Supposedly only man possessed a soul, which provided the basis of language (Descartes, 1955). Darwin may or may not have believed in the existence of the human soul, but he does not really attempt, through evolutionary process, to connect human language with the communications of other animals.

Darwin instead assumes that animals "express" emotions and that humans both "express" emotions and communicate by means of language. To Darwin, the expression of emotions is quite different from human language. For example, it has no syntax. A gesture or sound thus stands in a one-to-one relationship with an "emotion." Expressions are innately determined; they are not subject to environmental or cultural modification. Darwin furthermore tends to see the gestural and vocal patterns that serve as the vehicles for the expression of emotion in *Homo sapiens* as surviving fragments of behavioral patterns that once were functional in man's animal-like ancestors. The anatomical mechanisms that are involved in the expression of emotion in *Homo sapiens* therefore are *not* the result of natural selection for mechanisms that would enhance the power of expression. They instead essentially constitute a grab-bag of old bits and pieces of muscular activity left over from former days. Darwin indeed seems to see no particular adaptive value in the expression of emotion. This is, of course, consistent with his basic underlying premise—that human language is disjoint from the expression of emotion. Modern research on the paralinguistic communication of humans demonstrates that the boundary between the communication of supposedly "emotional" information and that of linguistic information is very fuzzy (Markel, in press; Lieberman, 1973). People rarely communicate "innately" determined emotional states analogous to the "agonized death-bellow of the cattle" that Darwin discusses (p. 84). Instead, most of our so-called emotional information is stylized and culture bound.

DARWIN AND THE STUDY OF GESTURE

Darwin does take account of the constraints of the muscles and anatomy that structure the expression of emotion in man, but these constraints are not his primary focus. Discussion of their role is indeed not a novel element in Darwin's book. Charles Bell, the Scottish anatomist, had in the period between 1806 and 1844 published three revised versions of his *Anatomy and Philosophy of Expression,* in which he developed the hypothesis that many of the muscles of the human face are "purely instrumental in expression" or are a "special provision" (1844, pp. 98, 121) for the communication of emotion. Darwin's primary focus in *The Expression of Emotion in Man and Animals* is in attempting to show how the expression of emotion in man is linked to animal behavior and how particular acts of "expression" have evolved. For example, he derives the facial expression that he associates with sneering from the hypothesis that "our semi-human progenitors" bared their canine teeth before battle:

The expression here considered, whether that of a playful sneer or ferocious snarl, is one of the most curious which occurs in man. It reveals his animal descent; for no one, even if rolling on the ground in a deadly grapple with an enemy, and attempting to bite him, would try to use his canine teeth more than his other teeth. We may readily believe from our affinity to the anthropomorphous apes that our male semi-human progenitors possessed great canine teeth. . . . We may further suspect, notwithstanding that we have no support from analogy, that our semi-human progenitors uncovered their canine teeth when prepared for battle, as we still do when feeling ferocious, or when merely sneering at or defying some one, without any real intention of making a real attack with our teeth. (1872, p. 252)

This quotation is consistent with Darwin's prevailing view that all human "expressions" are innately determined.

Some of Darwin's examples almost read as attempts at parody. In the discussion of "Shrugging the Shoulders" (pp. 264–266) he relates how this gesture appears in the children of a family living in a cultural setting in which shrugging of the shoulders "never" occurs, i.e., an upper-middle- or upper-class Victorian family. He argues that this gesture is genetically transmitted. The argument is roughly as follows:

1. "Englishmen are much less demonstrative than the men of most other European nations, and they shrug their shoulders far less frequently and energetically than Frenchmen and Italians do."
2. "I have never seen very young English children shrug their shoulders. . . ."
3. A child one of whose grandparents was Parisian, the remainder being British or Scottish, "was observed to shrug her shoulders at the age of between sixteen and eighteen months" though she was reared in a shrug-free environment; i.e., "the nursemaid is a thorough Englishwoman, who has never been seen to shrug her shoulders."
4. The child, "it may be added, resembles her Parisian grandfather in countenance to an almost absurd degree."

The shrug-free state of England thus is seemingly genetically conditioned.

The main deficiency in Darwin's analysis of gestural communication is, however, the almost complete lack of any concept equivalent to that of syntax. Though Darwin notes some "dialectical" variations in the expression of emotion in humans (for example, in the discussion of "anger" on pp. 246 and 247), he never makes use of the concept of a syntax. A particular gestural pattern or facial expression always stands directly for some "emotion." If Darwin were successful in his analysis, he would have derived a long list of "expressions" that would each signify some "emotion." There might be some alternatives available that would typify particular groups, e.g., Englishmen versus Frenchmen and Italians. However, each group could communicate by means of a "formal grammar" that had the complexity and significance of the linguistic theory proposed by Swift in *Gulliver's Travels,* where each word refers to one particular item.

The syntax of human language is a productive device. The individual words of a human language almost never have a single semantic referent. For example, the word *bank* can function as a noun or a verb, and it can have at least two distinct meanings as a noun. It can refer to a place where financial transactions are conducted, or it can refer to the side of a river or canal. The "meaning" of the word *bank* is, however, clear in the sentence *He got five dollars at the bank.* The syntax of English enables the reader to interrelate the set of semantic referents that are entered in his internalized "dictionary" for each word. Without the syntax, the sentence would be incomprehensible. Syntax, in other words, is an essential, functional attribute of human language. It allows humans to associate many meanings with each phonetic entry of their internal dictionary. Traditional dictionaries have intuitively recognized this attribute of language by listing the different meanings of each phonetic form, i.e., each "word," rather than doing it the other way, the different phonetic forms of each "meaning."

This property of language is related to the fact that humans can generalize the "meaning" of particular words to suit the changing requirements of human culture. A single page of any comprehensive dictionary that takes note of historical changes will reveal how the "meaning" of words changes and how rarely particular words have a specific, invariant meaning. In most cases, new words have to be invented when we want to convey some precise meaning, as is the case for "technical" terms. The studies of the gestural communication of chimpanzees who have been taught American Sign Language show that they, like humans, "generalize" the meaning of particular words. Fouts (1973), for example, describes how a chimpanzee who was taught the sign for *dirty,* where the initial semantic referent was soiling from defecation, used it as an insult in the context *dirty cat* when it was angry at a monkey (whom it called a cat, a second generalized insult because it knew the distinction between cats and monkeys). The chimpanzee went on to use the sign in a later communication *dirty Roger* when it was angry with its handler, Roger Fouts. Neither the monkey nor Fouts exhibited any of the qualities associated with the semantic referent of the sign *dirty* as it was initially taught to the chimpanzee; the chimpanzee had obviously generalized the semantic referent of the sign *dirty.* There were at least two semantic referents, i.e., "meanings," associated with the sign in the chimpanzee's internal mental "dictionary" and the chimpanzee had to be making productive use of at least a primitive syntax to differentiate these meanings.

Darwin did not consider the role of syntax in animal communication, and unfortunately this is still the case for most contemporary studies of animal communication. Modern ethological studies of animal communication typically assume, as Darwin did, that particular gestures or particular vocalizations convey particular invariant "meanings." This assumption, which is often implicit, structures the procedures that may be employed. Ethologists, for example, often attempt to determine the "meaning" of a particular gesture by studying all the behavioral situations in which the gesture may occur and looking for the element of "meaning" that is common to all of these situations. This procedure would be valid only if we knew in advance that the animal's communication system had no syntax. If we applied this technique to human speech, we would be completely misled. The words *sat, mat,* and *bat,* for example, all make use of the same vowel sound, but they have different meanings. The only element of commonality in the probable association of these different words with different behavioral situations might be that at least two human speakers were present (if we ignored soliloquies, tape recorders, telephones, TV sets, and so on). If we looked for the common "meaning" that could be associated with most human vocal communications we would have to conclude that speech perhaps was a means whereby humans located each other—in other words, that one human made noise and the other human made a return noise.

Animal languages may, in fact, lack anything comparable to human syntax, but we won't know if this is the case if our procedures guarantee a negative result. The evidence derived from chimpanzees using American Sign Language, as we've noted, suggests that they have the cognitive ability that would allow them to use a language with a productive syntax. It is most unlikely that the natural "language" of chimpanzees does not make use of a syntax, and we're simply wasting a lot of valuable time and money in analyzing ethological data as though no animal other than *Homo sapiens* had syntax. We'll return to this topic in Chapter 11.

VOCAL COMMUNICATION

Darwin's emphasis on gestural communication was quite natural. Whereas the relationship between facial musculature and expression is reasonably clear, the physical basis of speech production was, at best, imperfectly understood. The source-filter theory of speech production that we've already mentioned and that we'll discuss in Chapter 5 was proposed by Johannes Müller in 1848 and was elaborated by Helmholtz in 1863. Darwin really did not make use of this theory, though he cites Helmholtz. His discussion of the differing sound quality of vowels is thus the usual confused account of different "pitches" and the "vibrating apparatus of the human larynx" (1872, p. 90). The larynx has long been wrongly identified as the principal anatomical mechanism involved in human speech, and the famous eighteenth-century Dutch anatomist Camper (1779) dissected the larynx of the orangutan to find out why it could not talk. The larynx still continues to be the focus of anatomical studies that attempt to isolate the "uniqueness" of human speech (Kelemen, 1969; Wind, 1970).

The larynx is in fact *not* the "crucial" anatomical structure that differentiates human speech from the vocalizations of other animals. Anatomical studies of the larynx therefore cannot demonstrate that a chimpanzee could, or could not, produce the range of sounds necessary for human speech. This doesn't mean that comparative studies of the anatomy and physiology of the larynx have no value. For example, the comparative studies of Negus (1949) demonstrate that gestural language probably was never the sole medium of communication in the evolution of human language.

Negus, in his systematic *The Comparative Anatomy and Physiology of the Larynx* (1949), which is itself a condensed and revised version of his earlier work, *The Mechanism of the Larynx* (1929), explores the evolution and the function of the larynx. His title is somewhat misleading because he actually compares many different types of larynges with respect to the adaptive value of particular anatomical characteristics. Negus considers different aspects of laryngeal anatomy with respect to the physiology of respiration, deglutition (swallowing), olefaction, and phonation and the protection of the lungs. These factors don't all have equal selective value in all animals. Negus, therefore, adopts the comparative method in effect, looking at nature's anatomical experiments and correlating the anatomical specializations of the larynx with the different behavior of each species.

The adaptive value of the larynx of *Homo sapiens* can be inferred from Negus's demonstration of what it is *not* adapted for. Negus's methods are quite simple. Medical texts, for example, often state that the "function" of the human larynx is to protect the lungs from the intrusion of harmful substances. This is certainly true, but is the protection of the lungs the only function that had a selective advantage in the evolution of the human larynx? This is not a trivial question, because the human larynx is a very complex structure compared to that of the Australian mud fish (*Neoceratodus*), a fish that can survive out of water. Are the anatomical complexities distinguishing the human larynx from the mud fish's larynx specializations that are the result of natural selection that enhanced the ability of the human larynx to seal off the lungs? The answer is that the human larynx actually is not as efficient a device for sealing the lungs as the simple fish larynx is. We can't, for example, swim very long under water with our mouths open. The fish larynx can withstand the pressure exerted by water at great depths; ours can't.

Once we know that the human larynx is not optimally designed for protecting the lungs, we can pose another question. Is its complex anatomy the result of adaptions for more efficient respiration? Negus again answers the question negatively. He first notes that "The trachea of such fast-running animals as Horses and Antelopes is very wide" (p. 31). This is, of course, what we would expect in animals that have adapted to run rapidly for long distances. The trachea is simply the air "tube" that goes between the larynx and the lungs. A wider tube has less resistance to the air flow through it. The larynx essentially sits on top of the trachea. Negus looked at the maximum opening of the larynx during respiration in the horse (*Equus caballus*) and found that it is slightly greater than the diameter of the horse trachea. The horse's larynx thus doesn't present any additional resistance to the flow of air through the respiratory system. In contrast, the diameter of the human larynx, open to its maximum respiratory position, is only half as large as the diameter of the human trachea. The human larynx thus impedes the flow of air to the lungs. It is not as efficient for respiration as the larynx of the horse.

The relative respiratory inefficiency of the human larynx compared to the horse larynx is a consequence of an adaptation for phonation. The process of phonation, which we'll discuss in Chapter 5, involves the rapid motion of the vocal cords of the larynx. The horse larynx has relatively long arytenoid cartilages that allow it to open wide and has short vocal cords that don't move very efficiently because they're stiffened by the rigid arytenoid cartilages. The human larynx has relatively short arytenoid cartilages and long vocal cords that easily move in and out during phonation. The human larynx is thus adapted for efficient phonation at the expense of respiratory efficiency. The horse larynx is the result of an opposite pattern of natural selection. Negus shows that the larynges of animals such as cats, dogs, and lions are also better adapted for phonation than respiration (1949, pp. 40–42). It therefore is most unlikely that gestures were ever the sole means of communication in hominids when all primates and many mammals have larynges that bear the traces of natural selection adapted to phonation.

Negus makes similar arguments concerning olefaction and swallowing. The position of the human larynx in relation to the mouth and pharynx makes the human respiratory system less effective for olefaction and also more susceptible to blockage during swallowing. These relative deficiencies of the adult human respiratory system will become apparent after we discuss the anatomy of the human supralaryngeal vocal tract. The human vocal tract in a sense represents the most recent stage of a long evolutionary process in which various anatomical specializations have been added to the respiratory system making it a more effective instrument for communication.

4

Basic
Acoustics

The principles that underlie the process of speech production and speech perception are difficult to discuss without using the physical concepts of wave motion, periodicity, frequency, and amplitude. These concepts are, fortunately, fairly simple and straightforward. We will also discuss the use and the physical meaning of graphs as they relate to the description of physical measurements, and we will conclude with an elementary description of the frequency analysis of acoustic signals and the properties of filters. Readers who have appropriate backgrounds in the physical sciences, mathematics, or engineering will undoubtedly find this chapter superfluous, because we will introduce and explain these concepts by means of simple everyday examples, using a minimum of mathematical formalism.

GRAPHS AND PHYSICAL MEASUREMENTS

Let's start by considering the topic of graphs and their inter-pretation. Suppose that you were asked to read the temperature from a thermometer mounted in the shade on the back of your house at 4-hour intervals. You could record the temperature that you read at each interval in the form of a list. The list might look like that in Table 4-1 for the 3-day period August 7 to August 9. An equivalent way of recording this temperature information would be to make a graph. The graph of Figure 4-1 is equivalent to Table 4-1.

The graph is organized as follows: The vertical scale records the temperature registered on the thermometer. The horizontal scale records the time and date when the reading was made. The first observation of temperature of the graph of Figure 4-1 therefore must be interpreted as indicating a temperature of 80 degrees Fahrenheit at 9 A.M. on August 7. The observation is marked by means of the black dot, which lines up with 80 degrees on the vertical scales of the graph and with 9 A.M., August 7, on the horizontal scale. This fact is, of course, recorded in Table 4-1, which also indicates that the temperature at 9 A.M. on August 7 was 80 degrees. The next black dot on the graph indicates that the temper-ature was 90 degrees at 1 P.M. This fact is again indicated by the information in Table 4-1. The graph thus loses none of the infor-mation recorded in Table 4-1. If the graph did no more than display the information recorded in Table 4-1 in a different manner, there would be little point in bothering to make it. The graph, however, does much more. It allows us to make interpretations derived from the temperature readings that are not as apparent when we view the data in Table 4-1.

The first interpretation of the data of Table 4-1 implicit in the graph is that the temperature changed gradually between each observation. The black dots that mark the actual temperature read-ings that were recorded are connected by a line, and we, for exam-ple, would estimate that the temperature at 10 A.M. on August 7 was probably 82 degrees. Note that we did not read the temperature at 10 A.M.; we have derived this estimate of the temperature from the graph. We could have made the same estimate from the data of Table 4-1, but it's more apparent in the graph. The graph directly presents this "interpolation" between the actual temperature read-ings taken at 9 A.M. and at 1 P.M.

Waveforms and periodicity

The visual pattern of this graph where we have plotted temperature as a *function of time* also throws other interpretations of the tempera-ture observations into relief. The terminology "function of time" implies that there is a dependency between the temperature read-ings and time. This is obviously true, because the temperature

TABLE 4-1 LIST OF TEMPERATURES RECORDED AT 4-HOUR INTERVALS FOR 3 DAYS	
Temperature (°F)	**Time**
80	9 A.M. August 7
90	1 P.M.
95	5 P.M.
80	9 P.M.
70	1 A.M. August 8
60	5 A.M.
82	9 A.M.
88	1 P.M.
94	5 P.M.
75	9 P.M.
60	1 A.M. August 9
55	5 A.M.
80	9 A.M.

readings were taken at 4-hr intervals. It is also true in a deeper sense, because there is an overall relationship or pattern between the temperature readings and the time of day. This is quite apparent from the shape, i.e., the "form," of the graph of Figure 4-1. Note that the temperature goes up to a peak value at about 5 P.M. each day and then descends to a minimum value at about 5 A.M.

Figure 4-1 Graph of temperature plotted from data in Table 4-1.

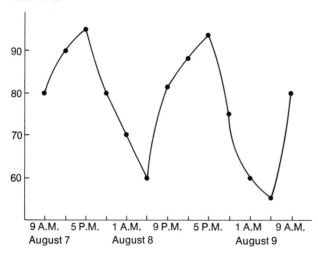

The temperature readings are not identical for the same hour of each day, but the pattern is quite consistent. We can see from the graph that the temperature pattern over this interval of 3 days is *quasiperiodic*. A periodic event is one that repeats itself. The temperature record is almost periodic, i.e., quasiperiodic, over this 3-day interval. The periodicity or period of the temperature cycle is 24 hr. In other words, the temperature variations tend to repeat themselves every 24 hr. It's obvious temperature variations are periodic, with a period of 24 hr, because the sun rises and sets each day. We don't need a graph to tell us this. However, the graph makes the periodicity quite obvious. The periodicity of the temperature variations tends to be buried in the data of Table 4-1.

Frequency

We can make graphs that present virtually any measurement. Graphs allow us to readily "see" periodic relationships. For example, we could record the height of the water as it was measured against a ruler nailed to the side of one of the posts supporting the end of a pier at the Atlantic City beach. We could, in principle, record the height of the water every second and plot, i.e., record, it on a graph. Figure 4-2 is a graph of these hypothetical measurements. Note that the height of the water *at this fixed point in space—the end of the pier—*is plotted as a function of time. The period of the *waveform* refers to the interval during which the plotted data on the graph tends to repeat itself. The period is 10 sec, because the waveform repeats itself every 10 sec. A complete cycle from maximum to minimum back to maximum height occurs every 10 sec. In 1 minute the waveform would repeat itself six times. If we wanted to note how often this waveform repeated itself, we could say that it had a period of 10 sec or we could alternately say that it repeated itself with a frequency of 6 cycles per minute. The term *frequency* thus refers to the number of times that a periodic event repeats itself for some standard interval of time. An ocean wave that had a period of 30 sec, that is, $\frac{1}{2}$ min, would have a frequency of 2 cycles per minute. An ocean wave that had a period of $\frac{1}{4}$ min would have a frequency of 4 cycles per minute.

Figure 4-2 Graph of water height showing 10-sec period of the waveform.

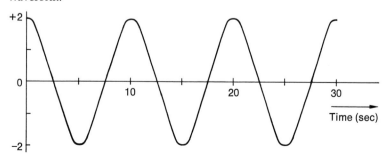

Algebraically, periodicity and frequency have the relationship:

$$f = \frac{1}{T}$$

where f is the frequency and T is the duration of the period. An event that had a period of $\frac{1}{50}$ of a second would have a frequency of 50 cycles per second, an event that had a period of 0.01 sec ($\frac{1}{100}$ of a second in decimal notation) would have a frequency of 100 cycles per second. We will encounter the term *Hertz* (abbreviated Hz) as a measure of frequency when we discuss sound waves. A frequency of 1 Hz is, by definition, equal to 1 cycle per second, 50 Hz to 50 cycles per second, and so on.

Amplitude—sinusoidal waves

Note that the vertical scale on the waveform plotted in Figure 4-2 has both positive and negative values. The value "0" in this particular graph corresponds to the height of the water in the absence of any waves. The positive values thus represent water heights above this zero line, whereas negative values represent water levels below the zero line. Note that the high and low points for each cycle of the waveform in Figure 4-2 have the same numerical value, 2 ft. The waveform plotted in Figure 4-2 is a sinusoidal waveform. Its *amplitude,* i.e., the deviation of each maximum and minimum from the zero line, is 2 ft. The amplitude of a wave essentially is a measure of its size, and it is independent of the frequency of the wave. The greater the amplitude, the "bigger" the wave. Either a big or a small ocean wave can come toward the beach at the same frequency.

The waveform plotted in Figure 4-2 is, as we have noted, *sinusoidal.* Sinusoidal waves, which always have this smooth shape, are extremely important mathematical constructs, because it is possible to analyze any complex periodic waveform in terms of a set of sinusoidal waveforms. The behavior of devices like organ pipes or the human vocal tract can be calculated for sinusoidal sound sources. Because we can analyze any complex periodic wave in terms of sinusoids, we can predict the response of a device like the human vocal tract to any periodic waveform. We will discuss these procedures later in this chapter. For the moment we will simply note that a sinusoidal waveform can be completely specified by noting its frequency, amplitude, and phase. We won't discuss phase, because it is of secondary importance in the perception and production of speech.

Wave motion—propagation velocity

Wave motions are characterized by the transfer of energy. It's obvious that energy is transmitted by an ocean wave when it hits you. The motion of an ocean wave can easily be observed as it sweeps in toward the beach. The crest of the wave moves in with a certain speed, called the *propagation velocity* of the wave. The propagation velocity of an ocean wave could be determined by observing its crest. In Figure 4-3 is sketched the crest of an ocean wave at two instants of time separated by 10 sec. We could have obtained these data by taking two flash pictures of the wave at night. The horizontal scale in these pictures, which are really graphs of the height of the water as a function of *distance,* is the distance measured in feet from the edge of the beach. The vertical scale is the height of the wave. Note that the crest that is at distance 10 ft in Figure 4-3A is at distance 0 ft in Figure 4-3B. The velocity of propagation is therefore 1 ft per second.

The fact that the crest has moved 10 ft in the 10 sec that separates the graphs of Figures 4-3A and 4-3B does not mean that any molecule of water actually moved 10 ft toward the beach. The energy in the wave has moved forward through the medium of the water. For example, the wave that hits you at the beach at Atlantic City, New Jersey, may have started from the coast of Portugal, but no molecule of "Portuguese" water will touch you.

It's fairly simple to see the distinction between the transfer of energy in a wave and the motion of the particles of the medium. One traditional demonstration makes use of three coins placed on a table. If the coins are placed in a row and the coin on one end of the row is flicked against the center coin, the energy of the collision will be transmitted to the coin on the other end of the line. The center coin won't move very far. The first coin obviously won't move around the center coin; however, the energy derived from the motion of the first coin will be transmitted through the middle coin to the last coin.

The transmission of energy in a sound wave is rather like the transmission of energy through the row of coins. The molecules of gas that form the atmosphere transmit forces as they collide with each other. The sound that you hear has been transmitted by a wave that has exerted a pressure on your eardrum. In a near vac-

Figure 4-3 Propagation of an ocean wave. *A:* At first measurement. *B:* Ten seconds later.

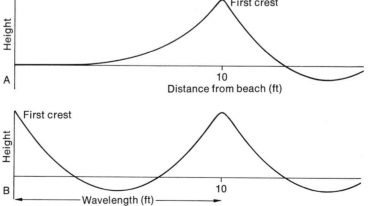

uum, as in outer space or on the moon, where there aren't any gas molecules, sound cannot be transmitted.

In Figure 4-3B the crest of a second cycle of the wave is also drawn. Note that the distance between the two crests of the periodic wave motion is 10 ft. The *wavelength* of the periodic wave is thus 10 ft. The wavelength is, by definition, the distance between recurring events in a wave motion distributed over distance. The wavelength is *not* the same as the period. The wavelength can be seen when a waveform is plotted as a function of distance *at some particular instant of time*. The period can be seen when a waveform is plotted as a function of time *at some particular location*. Wavelength, frequency, and the propagation velocity are all related. Algebraically the following relationship holds:

$$\lambda f = c$$

where λ is the wavelength, f is the frequency of the wave, and c is the propagation velocity.

The relationship between wavelength, frequency, and the propagation velocity is not difficult to visualize if we return to the simple case of ocean waves. If the wavelength in Figure 4-3B is 10 ft and the velocity of propagation is 1 ft per second, then a person standing at a fixed point, e.g., the edge of the beach at the waterline, will be hit by the crest of a new wave at 10-sec intervals. The periodicity of the wave motion as noted by the observer standing at this fixed location therefore will be 10 sec. The frequency of the wave motion will be equal to $\frac{1}{10}$ sec or 0.1 Hz. We would arrive at the same frequency if we solved for it using the equation $f = c/\lambda$. This is, of course, to be expected, because the algebraic equation is a formal statement that describes the physical world.

It's important to remember that the wavelength and period of a wave are quite different quantities. Much confusion can arise because the period of a wave is measured along the horizontal scale of a graph when a wave is plotted *as a function of time*. The wavelength also is measured along the horizontal scale of a graph when a wave is plotted *as a function of distance*. In one case the horizontal axis is measuring the course of time at a fixed location. In the other case the horizontal scale is measuring the amplitude of the wave along the dimension of distance for a particular instant of time.

COMPLEX AND SINUSOIDAL WAVEFORMS—FOURIER ANALYSIS

At first glance there would appear to be very little in common between sinusoidal waveforms like that plotted in Figure 4-2 and the "sawtooth" crested waveform plotted in Figure 4-3. A fundamental principle of mathematics, however, shows that it is always possible to analyze a "complex" periodic waveform like that of

Figure 4-3 into a set of sinusoidal waveforms. Any periodic waveform, no matter how complex it is, can be closely approximated by adding together a number of sinusoidal waveforms. The mathematical procedure of *Fourier analysis* tells us what particular set of sinusoids go together to make up a particular complex waveform. We won't go into the details of Fourier analysis except to note the important fact that the set of sinusoids that one adds together to approximate a particular complex waveform are harmonically related. What does this mean?

Fundamental frequency

In Figure 4-4 are plotted a complex waveform and its first two sinusoidal Fourier components. All three graphs have the same horizontal time scale and same vertical amplitude scale. The complex waveform could, for example, be the sound waveform recorded by a microphone monitoring a loudspeaker. Note that the complex waveform is *not* sinusoidal; for example, its leading edge rises sharply, and it has a flat top. It is, however, a periodic waveform, and the duration of its period is, as Figure 4-4 shows, 10 msec. A millisecond (abbreviated msec) is by definition equal to one thousandth of a second. Milliseconds are convenient units for the measurement of the periods of audible sound waves. The first two sinusoidal components are plotted beneath the complex waveform. The first component's period, T_0, is equal to the period, T, of the

Figure 4-4   A complex waveform (A) and its first two sinusoidal Fourier components (B and C).

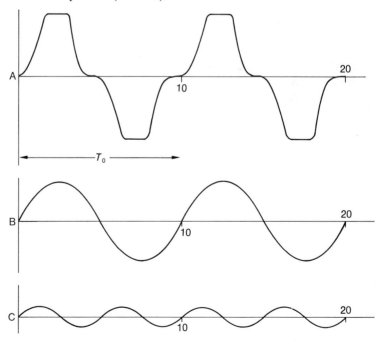

complex waveform. This is always the case. This period, which is the time that it takes for the complex waveform to repeat itself, is called the *fundamental period*. The frequency of the first component is called the *fundamental frequency*. The symbol f_0 is usually used to represent the fundamental frequency. Algebraically,

$$f_0 = \frac{1}{T_0} = \frac{1}{T}$$

Harmonics

The period of the next possible component is always equal to one half of the period of the fundamental. Period T_1 of wave C in Figure 4-4 thus is equal to 5 msec. The frequency of wave C is twice that of the fundamental frequency, because f_1, the frequency of wave C, must equal

$$f_1 = \frac{1}{T_1} = \frac{1}{T_0/2} = \frac{2}{T_0} = 2f_0$$

These two sinusoidal components, if they are added together, approximate the complex waveform. To achieve a better approximation of the complex waveform, it would be necessary to add other components that had still higher frequencies to the sum of the first two sinusoids. The frequencies of these higher sinusoidal components would all be harmonically related to the fundamental frequency. The frequency of the third sinusoidal component, for example, would be equal to $3f_0$, the frequency of the fourth component would be $4f_0$, and so on. The frequency of the nth component would be equal to nf_0.

The fundamental frequency of the complex wave of Figure 4-4 thus is 100 Hz. The frequency of the second sinusoidal component is 200 Hz, that of the third component, which is not plotted, would be 300 Hz, and so on. The components are said to be *harmonically related*, because they are integral multiples of the fundamental frequency. Sinusoids, when heard in isolation, are perceived as "pure tones." The sounds produced by tuning forks or certain bird calls (Grenewalt, 1967) are simple sinusoids. The higher the fundamental frequency, the higher the perceived tone is. Adult humans generally can perceive sounds between 20 and about 15,000 Hz. That means that human listeners can hear the sinusoidal components of complex sounds for frequencies between 20 and 15,000 Hz. A sudden "sharp" sound, like a door slamming, may have higher sinusoidal components, but we can't hear them. Children and many adults can hear frequencies higher than 15,000 Hz. The upper limit is about 20,000 Hz, but it falls with age. The meaningful sinusoidal components that constitute human speech are, for the most part, below 7,000 Hz and telephone systems that transmit frequencies no higher than 5,000 Hz are adequate for most purposes (Flanagan, 1972).

Figure 4-5 Graph of a spectrum.

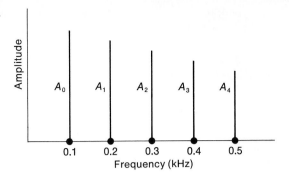

Spectrum

In the Fourier analysis of a complex waveform the amplitude of each sinusoidal component depends on the shape of the particular complex wave. It therefore is necessary to keep track of the amplitude of each component if we want to specify a complex wave in terms of its sinusoidal components. We can conveniently keep track of the frequencies and amplitudes of the sinusoidal components that go together to make up a complex wave by means of graphs like that in Figure 4-5. The horizontal axis is the frequency scale, the vertical axis is the amplitude scale. The amplitude of each component is represented by a line at the frequency of each sinusoidal component. The units plotted on the vertical axis would most likely be units of sound pressure when sound waves are analyzed. This type of graph is known as a graph of the *spectrum*. We have plotted the amplitudes of the first two sinusoidal components shown in Figure 4-4 as well as the next three higher components. Note that the graph consists of vertical lines at each sinusoidal frequency. This signifies that there is sound energy present *only* at these discrete frequencies. This type of spectrum is sometimes called a *line spectrum*. It differs from spectra that have energy distributed over a broad, continuous range of frequencies. We have not kept track of the parameter *phase* that we would need if we were to actually add up a number of sinusoidal components to make a particular complex waveform. However, as already mentioned, phase is not particularly important in the perception or the production of speech. The conceptual value of representing a complex waveform as a spectrum will be apparent in Chapter 5.

FILTERS

In the next chapter we will discuss speech production in terms of the source-filter theory. Before we discuss this theory, which involves an understanding of some of the specific properties of

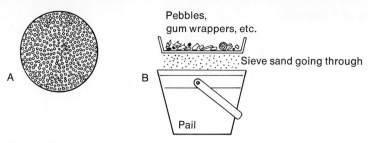

Figure 4-6 Sieve. *A:* Top view of sieve of average hole diameter d_h.
B: Side view of sieve in action.

acoustic filters, we'll briefly introduce some of the general properties of filters. Perhaps the simplest example of a filter is a sieve
or strainer, so we'll return to our demonstration site at the beach
where we looked at ocean waves. This time we'll stay on the sand
for our examples and examine some of the general properties of
filters as they are exemplified in the properties of beach sieves.

Figure 4-6A shows what we would see if we looked down at
the top of a child's sieve. We would see a pattern of holes that
each had approximately the same diameter. Let's call this diameter
d_h, the "average hole diameter." Obviously the holes will not all
have exactly the same diameter, because children's beach sieves
are not precision-machined. Figure 4-6B shows the sieve in action.
Sand particles whose diameter is less than that of the holes in the
sieve flow through the sieve into the child's pail below. Larger
objects such as pebbles, candy wrappers, and sand particles of large
diameter are left in the sieve. The sieve is acting as a mechanical
filter that affects the transfer of particles into the pail. If the sieve
were not placed above the beach pail all of the large-diameter
particles, pebbles, and candy wrappers would have entered the pail.

We can quantitatively describe the filtering properties of the
sieve placed above the pail by means of the graph in Figure 4-7,
which plots the *transfer function* of the sieve. The vertical scale

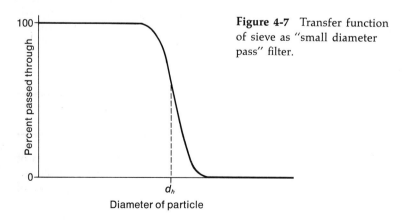

Figure 4-7 Transfer function
of sieve as "small diameter
pass" filter.

denotes the per cent of material that will pass through, i.e., transfer through, the filter. The horizontal scale denotes the size of the particle. The graph thus shows that 100 per cent, i.e., all, particles that are very much smaller than the average hole diameter, d_h, will pass through the sieve. Zero per cent of the very large objects will pass through. Particles that have diameters close to the average hole diameter, d_h, may or may not pass through. It will depend on whether a particular particle is above one of the smaller or one of the bigger holes. Some particles that are larger than the average hole diameter will get through if they happen to be positioned above a hole whose diameter is also larger than the average diameter. Some particles that have smaller diameters won't get through if they are positioned above smaller holes. The filter thus does not abruptly "cut off" the flow of sand at some exact particle diameter; its transfer function instead exhibits a gradual cutoff.

The mechanical filtering system exemplified by the sieve and pail constitutes what we could term a "small diameter pass through" filter. Small particles will go through; bigger particles will be trapped above. We could, using the same pail and filter, collect the material that was trapped in the filter. If we periodically collected the material trapped in the top of the sieve and put that material in the pail, discarding the small particles that flowed through the sieve, we would have the "large diameter pass through" filter whose transfer function is sketched in Figure 4-8. The same sieve and pail permit us to filter for either large- or small-diameter particles depending on how we arrange them.

We obviously could filter out a small range of particle sizes by sequentially using two sieves that had different average hole diameters. If we first placed the sieve with the larger average hole diameter above the pail, collected the material that accumulated in the pail, and then poured this material through the sieve with the smaller diameter, we would be left with particles that were restricted to a small range or "band" of diameters. The transfer function plotted in Figure 4-9 quantitatively represents the result of this sequential process for a case where the average hole diame-

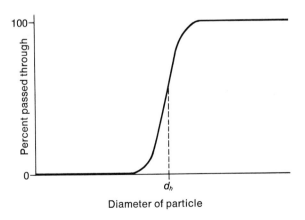

Figure 4-8 Transfer function of sieve as "large diameter pass through" filter.

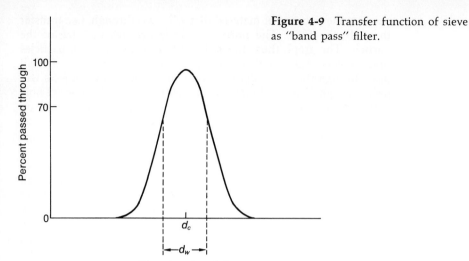

Figure 4-9 Transfer function of sieve as "band pass" filter.

ters of the two sieves are close, though not identical, in size. Note that maximum transfer through the complete filter system occurs about particle diameter d_c and that there exists a range of particle sizes d_w for which most, e.g., 70 per cent, will get through the filter system to be collected.

We have presented this discussion of the filtering properties of beach sieves and pails because the supralaryngeal vocal tract—the air passages of the mouth, pharynx, and nose—acts as an adjustable acoustic filter that allows certain bands of wavelengths of sound to pass through. Wavelength-sensitive filters are analogous to the particle diameter "band pass" filter whose transfer function is sketched in Figure 4-9.

We can describe the properties of the acoustic filters formed by the supralaryngeal vocal tract by noting the wavelengths at which maximum sound energy will pass through as well as the range of wavelengths that will mostly get through (the acoustic analogues of d_c and d_w). The product of the wavelength and frequency of a wave is equal to the propagation velocity (the algebraic relationship $\lambda f = c$), and the velocity of sound is constant for normal atmospheric conditions. It therefore is appropriate to describe the transfer function of the supralaryngeal vocal tract filter in terms of frequency. The center frequencies at which maximum sound energy will pass through the filter system are called *formant frequencies*. We will discuss the supralaryngeal vocal tract filter in the following chapters because the controlled variation of formant frequencies is perhaps the single most important factor that differentiates the speech of *Homo sapiens* from that of other primates.

Source-Filter Theory of Speech Production

5

In Chapter 3 we began our discussion of the evolution of the vocal apparatus. The sound-making system functionally consists of the lungs, the larynx, and the supralaryngeal air passages. The larynx is a complex anatomical structure that has two rather different functions. It serves as an air valve that can close to protect the lungs. This is perhaps the basic "primitive" function of the larynx as it evolved in animals like the lungfish which first moved out of the seas to live on dry land. The larynx also serves as a sound-making device. During the production of voiced sounds, as, for example, in the word "ma," the vocal cords[1] rapidly open and shut at a rate that can vary from about 80 to 300 Hz. This results in a quasiperiodic air flow into the supralaryngeal airways. As we noted in Chapter 3, comparative studies such as those of Victor

---

[1] The vocal cords are often called vocal folds. Neither term really fits the anatomical situation, but we shall use the former, which was used by Ferrein (1741) in the first attempt at a functional theory of speech production.

E. Negus show that the larynges of many animals, including *Homo sapiens,* have evolved to facilitate this sound-making function at the expense of respiratory efficiency. The larynx serves as one of the sources of sound excitation for communication in many animals. However, the characteristics of sound communication, and particularly the phonetic quality of human speech, cannot be fully specified solely in terms of the activity of the larynx. The larynx in human speech merely serves as a source of sound energy that is filtered by the supralaryngeal air passages. Although many descriptions of speech production imply that the larynx (sometimes called the "voicebox") is the sole crucial element in human speech, it is only one of the possible sources of sound energy. For example, when we whisper the vocal cords do not generate a periodic wave. The source of sound energy in whisper is the noise generated through air turbulence. Laryngectomized speakers, who lack larynges, can communicate by whispering. If we want to understand how speech is produced, we must consider the properties of the supralaryngeal air passages.

SOURCE-FILTER THEORY

The laryngeal source

Let's consider the production of human speech for a voiced sound, i.e., a sound in which the vocal cords interrupt the airflow from the lungs, producing *phonation.* The diagram of Figure 5-1 blocks out the independent elements. The lungs during the production of speech maintain an airflow that is relatively steady over a short sentence. Sentences, in fact, tend to be delimited by means of what have been termed *breath-groups,* relatively steady patterns of airflow that are the result of coordinated respiratory maneuvers (Lieberman, 1967).

To initiate phonation the vocal cords move inward from the relatively open position that they have during quiet respiration. The tension of the various laryngeal muscles is adjusted to a value that allows the vocal cords to be pushed open by the airflow from the lungs that impinges on them. In turn, the airflow moving through

Figure 5-1 Block diagram of major elements involved in speech production.

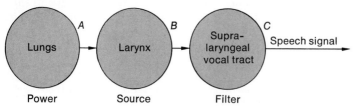

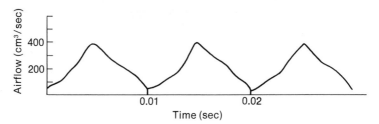

Figure 5-2 Three cycles of a waveform typical of the airflow through the glottis during phonation.

the opening between the vocal cords generates a force that tends to suck the vocal cords together. This aerodynamically generated force, which is a consequence of the Bernoulli effect, is one of the main factors governing phonation.[2] The vocal cords close through the action of the Bernoulli force and the elastic properties of the laryngeal muscles. When the vocal cords are closed or nearly closed, the airflow through the larynx momentarily stops or is reduced. The Bernoulli force, which is generated by moving air, thus stops. The static air pressure generated by the air impinging on the vocal cords pushes them open and the process then repeats itself.

In Figure 5-2 are plotted three cycles of a possible pattern of periodic airflow from the larynx. This would correspond to an observation of the airflow at point *B* in the block diagram of Figure 5-1. Note that the period of the complex waveform is 0.01 sec, i.e., 10 msec. The fundamental frequency of this periodic glottal airflow therefore is 100 Hz. (The term *glottal* refers to the airflow through the opening between the two vocal cords, which is called the glottis.) The spectrum of this glottal airflow is plotted in Figure 5-3. Note that the glottal spectrum shows that the waveform of Figure 5-2 has energy at the fundamental frequency (100 Hz) and at higher harmonics. Note that the amplitude of the harmonics gradually falls. We have not drawn the complete spectrum, but there is perceptible acoustic energy to at least 3.0 kHz present in the typical glottal airflow of a male speaker phonating at a fundamental frequency of 100 Hz (0.1 kHz). The vertical amplitude scale is in a unit called the *decibel* (db). It is a logarithmic unit that is convenient for plotting the extreme ranges of amplitude that are typical for speech signals.[3]

The rate at which the vocal cords open and close during phonation determines the period and hence the fundamental frequency of the glottal airflow. Within broad limits a speaker can vary this

[2] The Bernoulli effect can be observed whenever air flows through a constricted air passage. Newspapers and scraps of paper, for example, are often sucked into narrow alleyways between buildings.

[3] A decibel is, by definition, equal to 20 log to the base 10 of the sound pressure relative to a fixed reference. A decibel scale allows a large amplitude range to be plotted.

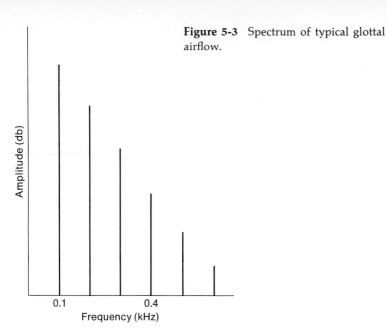

Figure 5-3 Spectrum of typical glottal airflow.

rate, which is determined by the shape and mass of the moving vocal cords, the tension of the laryngeal muscles, and the air pressure generated by the lungs. Adult male speakers can phonate at fundamental frequencies that range between 80 and 300 Hz. Adult females and children normally phonate at fundamental frequencies that range up to about 500 Hz. The longer vocal cords of adult males, which are a consequence of secondary sexual dimorphism in *Homo sapiens,* yield a lower range of fundamental frequencies. (The thyroid cartilage grows differentially during puberty in males; cf. Kirchner, 1970, pp. 15–17.)

The perceptual interpretation of fundamental frequency is *pitch.* When a human speaker sings a sustained vowel sound and changes the fundamental frequency of phonation, we perceive the difference as a change in pitch. Musical performances consist, in part, of singing at controlled, specified fundamental frequencies. If the singer sings at the wrong fundamental frequency, the performance is marred because we will perceive it as being off-pitch. Controlled changes in fundamental frequency also can be used for linguistic purposes. In many languages, e.g., Chinese, the same vowels and consonants signify different words when different fundamental frequency patterns are employed. In most human languages controlled changes in fundamental frequency at the end of a breath-group also can signify differences in the sentence's meaning, e.g., whether the sentence is a question or a statement (Lieberman, 1967; Atkinson, 1973). The vocalizations of many other animals, as we noted in Chapter 3, also appear to involve modulations of fundamental frequency. The controlled variation of fundamental frequency is therefore one of the phonetic parameters that may be employed in speech communication.

The supralaryngeal filter

We all know that a trained singer can sing an entire sequence of vowel sounds at the same pitch or alternately sing through a wide range of pitches on the same vowel. The activity of the larynx is responsible for changes of fundamental frequency, which are perceived as pitch changes. However, differences in vowel quality are independent of the activity of the larynx, being the consequence of changes in the shape of the supralaryngeal airway. During the production of human speech the shape of the supralaryngeal airway continually changes. The supralaryngeal airway always acts as an acoustic filter, suppressing the transfer of sound energy at certain frequencies, letting maximum energy through at other frequencies. The frequencies at which local energy maxima may pass through the supralaryngeal air passages are called *formant frequencies.* The formant frequencies are determined by the damped resonances of the supralaryngeal vocal tract, which acts as an acoustic filter. These resonances are, in turn, a consequence of the shape and size, more concisely the cross-sectional area function, of the air passages of the supralaryngeal vocal tract.[4] Vowels like [a], [i], [u], [ɪ], and [ʌ] owe their phonetic quality to their different formant frequencies. Human speakers generate these different formant frequency patterns by changing the shape of their supralaryngeal airways using the muscles of the lips, tongue, pharynx, jaw, and velum as well as the laryngeal hanger muscles, which can raise or lower the larynx slightly.

This aspect of speech production is analogous to the operation of a pipe organ. In a pipe organ the source of excitation for all of the pipes is identical. The musical quality of different notes played on a pipe organ is determined by the length and shape (whether the pipe is open or closed at one end) of the different pipes. The resonances of the pipes determine the note. In the production of sounds like [a] and [i] a human speaker, of course, does not connect his larynx to different pipes. But the anatomy of the supralaryngeal vocal tract in *Homo sapiens* is such that it allows the speaker to change the shape of the air passages so that they are the functional equivalent of a whole complex array of organ pipes.

In Figure 5-4 is plotted the transfer function of the supralaryngeal vocal tract for the vowel [ʌ] (the first vowel in the word *about*). This is the idealized supralaryngeal filter function for a speaker having a supralaryngeal vocal tract of approximately 17 cm. (The length of the supralaryngeal vocal tract for this vowel would be measured along the centerline of the air passage from the lips of the glottal opening of the larynx, excluding the nasal cavity; cf. Fant, 1960.)

The formant frequencies for this vowel are 0.5, 1.5, and 2.5 kHz. The symbols F_1, F_2, and F_3 are generally used to denote the formant frequencies of speech sounds. F_1 is the lowest formant frequency,

---

[4]We will discuss the properties of the supralaryngeal vocal tract and the relationship between shape and formant frequencies in Chapters 6 and 7.

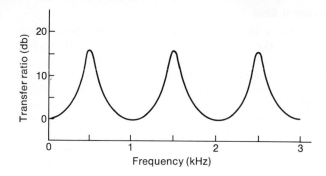

Figure 5-4 Transfer function of supralaryngeal vocal tract for the vowel [Λ]. For our purposes, the term *transfer function* is equivalent to *filter function.* Note the locations of the formant frequencies at 0.5, 1.5, and 2.5 kHz.

which is 0.5 kHz in this example; F_2 is the second formant, 1.5 kHz in this example. The formant frequencies are essentially the center frequencies of the supralaryngeal vocal tract acting as a complex filter that lets maximum sound energy through in several bands of frequency. The frequency bands of each formant have an appreciable bandwidth, from 60 to 100 Hz. Other vowels would have different formant frequencies. The formant frequencies of the vowel [i], for example, would be about 0.24 kHz for F_1, 2.2 kHz for F_2, and 3.2 kHz for F_3. The first three formants of vowels play the major role in specifying these sounds. Higher formants exist, but they are not necessary for the perception of vowel differences. The bandwidths of the formants of different vowels also do not markedly distinguish different vowels.

In Figure 5-5 is plotted the spectrum that would result if the laryngeal source whose spectrum we plotted in Figure 5-3 were filtered by the transfer function plotted in Figure 5-4. The resulting spectrum would describe the speech signal at the output of the supralaryngeal vocal tract at point C in Figure 5-1.

Note that sound energy would be present at each of the harmonics of the glottal source, but the amplitude of each harmonic would be a function of both the filter function and the amplitude of the particular harmonic of the glottal source. A human listener

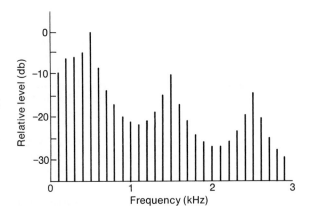

Figure 5-5 Spectrum of the output of supralaryngeal vocal tract if the transfer function of Figure 5-4 were "excited" by the glottal source whose spectrum is plotted in Figure 5-3.

hearing a speech signal having the spectrum plotted in Figure 5-5 would recognize the signal as a token of the vowel that had a fundamental frequency of 100 Hz.

In Figure 5-6 is plotted the speech waveform that corresponds to the spectrum in Figure 5-5. Note that this waveform resembles the glottal waveform plotted in Figure 5-2 only insofar as it has the same period, 10 msec. The interposition of the supralaryngeal vocal tract has otherwise modified the waveform between points B and C of Figure 5-1.

The source-filter theory of speech production that we have briefly sketched was first proposed by Johannes Müller (1848). It has been developed on a quantitative basis in recent years. Studies such as those of Chiba and Kajiyama (1958), Fant (1960), and Stevens and House (1955) make possible a quantitative prediction of the filtering effects of particular configurations of the supralaryngeal air passages.

In Chapter 7 we will discuss the perception of speech, which appears to involve specialized neural mechanisms. The perception of fundamental frequency in humans appears to be made primarily through waveform measurements that derive the period (Flanagan, 1972). The procedures used in making these measurements are fairly complex, and they can be simulated only through the use of elaborate computer programs (Gold, 1962). The procedures that human listeners make use of in deriving the formant frequencies of speech from the acoustic signal appear to be even more complex. These perceptual "recognition procedures" must involve the analysis of the speech signal in terms of its spectrum, but they go far beyond the simple examination of a spectrum for local energy maxima. The formant frequencies plotted in Figure 5-5, for example, are manifested as local energy maxima at 0.5, 1.5, and 2.5 kHz in Figure 5-5. However, this is fortuitous, because the fundamental frequency of the glottal source was 100 Hz, which placed harmonics at each of the formant frequencies. A human listener who heard a speech signal that had the spectrum plotted in Figure 5-7 would also say that it was a token of the vowel [Λ].

Figure 5-6 Speech waveform as measured by a microphone sensitive to air pressure. The human ear is itself sensitive to air pressure.

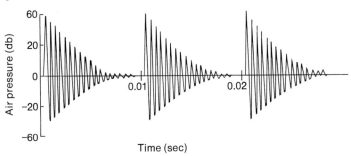

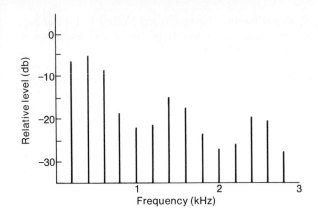

Figure 5-7 Spectrum of the sound [Λ] produced with a different fundamental frequency. The speech signal still has the phonetic quality of the vowel [Λ] although it has a different fundamental frequency than the [Λ] whose spectrum is plotted in Figure 5-5.

Note that the listener would have to deduce the location of the formant frequencies from a spectrum that actually lacked peaks at the formants. Electronic instruments such as the sound spectrograph will not show a formant frequency unless acoustic energy is present at or near the center frequency of the formant (Koenig et al., 1946). Conventional sound spectrographs will best resolve formant frequencies when the fundamental frequency of phonation is less than 120 Hz. Children's and women's voices are very difficult to analyze on a conventional sound spectrograph, though human listeners have no difficulty whatsoever in perceiving their formant frequencies. A number of studies (e.g., Andrew, 1963) implicitly assume that speech perception is the auditory analogue of the visual interpretation of a sound spectrograph. These studies erroneously conclude that low fundamental frequencies are necessary for the perception of formant frequencies and that various nonhuman primates lack speech because their voices are too high pitched.[5]

Human listeners appear to derive formant frequencies through a procedure that makes use of their internalized knowledge of the mechanisms and physics of speech production. It is possible to program digital computers to "recognize" vowels using this sort of procedure (Bell et al., 1961). The computer program has access to a memory in which the acoustic consequences of various possible vocal tract shapes are stored. The computer systematically generates internal spectra using this memory, which are then matched against the spectrum of the incoming speech signal. The process does not select the individual formant frequencies on the basis of local energy maxima but rather on the match between the total spectrum of the incoming speech signal and the internally generated signal specified by all three formant frequencies. The computer program is relatively complex, because it must model the performance of human listeners who appear to have neural mechanisms that are specially adapted to the perception of speech.

---

[5] If this were true, most of the world's human population (women, children, and some adult men) would be unintelligible.

Phonetic Features 6

In Chapter 5 we introduced the notion of a phonetic feature, i.e., a sound contrast that may be used in speech communication to transmit information. We can readily devise a simple communications system that makes use of pitch distinctions to transmit meaningful information. A high-pitched cry, for example, can readily be differentiated from a low-pitched cry. If we represent a high-pitched cry by means of the letter "H" and a low-pitched cry by the letter "L," we can transcribe a number of "words" that may be formed from H and L combinations. A "word" in this communication system would be the same linguistic construct that occurs in natural human languages; it would be the smallest meaningful unit that could be spoken (Postal, 1968). The "word" HL in our communications system could have the same semantic referents as the English word *mother*, the word HLL could have the same semantic referents as the English word *father*, LH could be the phonetic equivalent of *goes*, and so on.

Note that we are making use of a particular sound contrast that can be readily effected by the speech-producing anatomy to transmit linguistic distinctions. The sound contrasts used as phonetic features obviously must be ones that the speaker can produce if they are to serve as signals. The constraints of the speech-producing mechanism thus inherently structure the total inventory of possible sound contrasts. Sound contrasts that cannot be produced are not possible signaling units. Sound contrasts that are difficult to produce are not as "useful" as ones that are readily produced. If we were devising a communications system we would not be as likely to make use of a sound contrast that was difficult to produce, all other things being equal.

One of the other things that we would, of course, have to consider if we were devising a communications system is whether the sound contrasts that we wanted to use were perceptible, whether it was possible to readily differentiate and identify them. We obviously could not make use of sound distinctions that were not audible to members of the same species. For example, humans can make sounds that are audible to dogs but are inaudible to "normal" human listeners. These sounds would not be suitable signaling units even if they were easy to make. Humans can make other sound distinctions that are audible, but very difficult to identify. The human larynx can phonate over a wide range of fundamental frequencies, and a trained singer could repeatedly phonate at ten distinct fundamental frequencies holding vowel quality constant. Most normal listeners would be able to differentiate the pitches of these ten different signals if they were sung in sequence. But these musical tones, which we could denote as $T_1, T_2, T_3, \ldots, T_{10}$, could not serve as phonetic features because it would be almost impossible for normal human listeners to reliably identify the individual signals when they occurred in random contexts. We know that this is the case because psychoacoustic studies of the identification of auditory signals by human listeners show that it is impossible to keep track of and identify ten signals that differ only in their perceived pitch (Miller, 1956). It would be impossible to communicate a message that consisted of the words $T_1 \, T_6 \, T_9$ $T_7 \, T_8 \, T_3 \quad T_2 \, T_4 \, T_5 \, T_{10}$ because listeners would not be able to identify each tone as it occurred in a mixed sequence. The constraints of the human auditory system would preclude the use of this system even though the tones could be readily produced.

It should be obvious that the constraints of both the producing and the perceiving system would be crucial factors in structuring the inventory of phonetic features. This would be no less true for a system of gestural communication. Movements of the little finger might be easy to make, but they would not be very visible over a distance of 10 meters. Little-finger gestures thus could not serve as "phonetic" features for a hypothetical australopithecine gestural language useful in hunting.

The relationship between articulatory and perceptual constraints and the possible set of phonetic features can perhaps be best explicated by considering some of the possibilities available to modern *Homo sapiens*. We can consider only some of the possibilities because we simply do not as yet know enough about either the production or the perception of human speech to provide a complete listing of its phonetic features.

SOURCE FEATURES

Let's start by considering some of the possible phonetic features that involve the control of the source of sound energy. The laryngeal source, as we noted in Chapter 5, generates a quasiperiodic wave flow of air that is filtered by the supralaryngeal vocal tract during the production of voiced sounds. It is possible to instead pass a nonperiodic turbulent flow of air through the supralaryngeal vocal tract. The sound [h] in the word *happy* is an example of a sound produced by means of an unvoiced source, turbulent airflow through the larynx.

Voicing

The phonetic feature *voicing* therefore can serve as a sound contrast to convey information. Two words could be differentiated in a possible language solely by means of this feature. In English, for example, the sounds [z] and [s] differ in that [z] is produced using a periodic source whereas [s] is produced solely by means of the noiselike energy developed by the turbulent air flowing through the dental constriction. The term *dental* specifies the region of the supralaryngeal vocal tract where the tongue forms a constriction in the production of this sound.

Note that there is a two-way distinction inherent in the feature *voicing*. A sound can be produced using a periodic laryngeal source, or it can be produced without using a periodic source. The binary nature of this feature can be formally recognized by the notation + *voiced,* indicating sounds produced using a periodic laryngeal source. Sounds made using other sources can be denoted by − *voiced.* The binary nature of this feature was recognized in the early nineteenth century by Müller (1848), and recent phonetic theories, for the most part, also recognize it. Some phonetic theories (Jakobson et al., 1952) claim that all phonetic features are binary, although this is not necessarily the case. Binary, all-or-nothing signals have undoubted advantages in communications systems whether they are electronic (Siebert, 1973) or biological (Halle, 1957). The on-off signals that constitute Morse Code, for example, are easier to detect than graded signals scaled along a continuum of relative energy.

The aspects of the human speech-producing apparatus that make the feature *voicing* possible involve the general morphology of the human larynx, which has relatively long arytenoid cartilages and a system of muscles that can approximate, i.e., close, these cartilages precisely and rapidly (Negus, 1949). As the arytenoid cartilages approximate, an entire set of muscles, including the lateral cricoarytenoid, the internal and external thyroarytenoids, and the interarytenoids, is tensioned so that phonation can begin about 100 msec after the start of the initial closing motion (Farnsworth, 1940; Lieberman, 1967; Lisker and Abramson, 1971). A human speaker can likewise rapidly abduct, i.e., open, the arytenoid cartilages by means of the posterior cricoarytenoid muscle so that phonation ceases.

Phonation onset

Human listeners also appear to have some neural "devices" that respond to the presence of a periodic source. Slight differences in the timing of the larynx, which will advance or delay the presence of periodic energy in the speech signal relative to some other acoustic marker, are used in all human languages to differentiate words. In English, the sounds [b] and [p] in the words *bat* and *pat* differ only with respect to when phonation starts relative to the acoustic signal that begins these words.

If we were to examine an X-ray movie of a human speaker producing the two words *bat* and *pat*, we would see that the speaker in both cases first closes and then opens his lips. In both cases he moves his tongue toward the shape necessary for producing the vowel [æ] and the final consonant [t]. The motion of the speaker's tongue is continuous; there is no point at which we can say that the tongue is in the position for a "pure" [æ] or a "pure" [t]. The presence of the [t] after the [æ] influences the tongue's movements for the [æ], and the presence of the [æ] influences the tongue's movements for the [t]. The speech gestures are "encoded," i.e., structured into units that are at least syllable sized. We will discuss the concept of encoding in more detail in Chapter 7. For the moment, the point that we wish to stress is that the articulatory activity of the supralaryngeal vocal tract is identical for the words *bat* and *pat*. What's different is the activity of the laryngeal muscles with respect to the abrupt lip opening that marks the start of the initial sound in both of these words.

For both words the audible acoustic signal commences at the instant that the speaker's lips open. In the case of the word *bat* the speaker's larynx is already in its closed, phonatory position at this moment. The vocal cords have already moved into their closed, or nearly closed, position and phonation is a consequence of the airflow through the vocal tract. High-speed movies of the larynx show that phonation starts up about 10 to 20 msec after the start of airflow if the vocal cords are already in their "phonation neutral" position (Lieberman, 1967). When the lips open in the word *bat*, air can flow through the vocal tract and phonation starts shortly thereafter.

For the word *pat* the situation is different. The vocal cords are still open at the instant that the speaker's lips open. The sound that initially occurs is not voiced, because phonation cannot occur when the vocal cords are open. The open position of the vocal cords instead allows a relatively large airflow, and the initial sound is generated by the air turbulence that occurs as the lips are abruptly opened. An initial "burst" of air, therefore, can occur when a [p] is produced, particularly when it occurs in initial position. The speaker producing the word *pat* starts to close his vocal cords after the release of the [p], but it takes about 100 msec for the vocal cords to reach the configuration necessary for phonation (Lieberman, 1967). The distinction between [b] and [p] thus rests on the delay in the start of phonation relative to the opening of the speaker's lips. The sound [p] involves the feature +*voicing delay.*

A series of comprehensive acoustic and physiological studies have shown that the timing between phonation and the opening of the supralaryngeal vocal tract is a phonetic feature in a number of related and unrelated languages. Three timing distinctions occur (Lisker and Abramson, 1964, 1971). Voicing may be coincident or slightly delayed, with respect to the opening of the vocal tract, e.g., in English [b], [d], and [g]. Voicing may be delayed about 100 msec, e.g., in English [p], [t], and [k]. Voicing may also be advanced 100 msec before the opening of the vocal tract, e.g., in Spanish [b].

The various articulatory maneuvers a speaker must employ to generate these timing distinctions are quite complex. Available data (Perkell, 1969; Rothenberg, 1968) show that different articulatory maneuvers are employed in various phonetic contexts to effect similar acoustic results. One speaker may start phonation before the release of the primary occlusion by opening his nose slightly. In a different context, the volume of the sealed supralaryngeal vocal tract may be expanded by moving the anterior wall of the pharynx forward. The expansion of the volume of the supralaryngeal vocal tract generates an airflow through the larynx that in turn starts phonation.

The factor that is maintained in the production of these different stops is the timing between the start of phonation and the release of the stop. The three cross-language categories are 100-msec advance voicing, coincident (actually coincident or slightly delayed) voicing,[1] and 100-msec delayed voicing. The responses of human listeners to stop consonants bears closer inspection, for it reveals a fundamental characteristic of the perception of phonetic features. If a large number of examples of the English stops [p] and [b] are measured, it becomes evident that there is a good deal of variation in the timing between the onset of phonation and the release of

[1]The placement of the "categorical" boundary between the "0 delay" (coincident voicing) and "delayed" phonation onset distinctions about 20 msec *after* the opening of the supralaryngeal vocal tract itself reflects a physiological constraint. This delay is a consequence of the interaction of the mechanical properties of the vocal cords and the aerodynamic forces that provide the power source for phonation. Data from high-speed motion pictures of the larynx (Lieberman, 1967) show that it takes about 20 sec for the vocal cords to build up to their full vibratory pattern at the onset of phonation. There thus is a short delay in the onset of phonation even when the vocal cords are already in their "phonation neutral" position at the moment that the occlusion is released.

the stop. Some [b]'s have a phonation delay of 10 msec, others 20 msec, and so on. Some [p]'s have phonation delays of 50 msec, others 60 msec, others 40 msec. The responses of listeners to these stimuli show that there is a sharp "categorical" distinction. Stops that have phonation delays less than 25 msec are perceived as [b]. Stops that have phonation delays greater than 25 msec are perceived as [p]. The situation is seemingly odd because these same listeners cannot perceive any difference between versions of [p] that differ as much as 20 msec in their phonation delay. For example, listeners are not able to hear any difference between two sounds that have phonation delays of 30 and 50 msec, respectively. But if the phonation delays of two sounds are 10 and 30 msec, one sound will be heard identified as [b], the other as [p]. In other words, listeners cannot differentiate sounds within each phonetic category though they sharply differentiate stimuli across the phonetic boundary on the basis of the same physical parameter, the 20-msec timing distinction. These distinctions occur across many related and unrelated languages (Lisker and Abramson, 1964). The basis of the 20-msec timing distinction appears to rest in a basic constraint of the auditory system. Hirsch (1959) and Hirsch and Sherrick (1961) carried out a series of experiments to determine the difference in time that is required for a listener to judge which of two stimuli with diverse characteristics came first. A time difference of 20 msec was found to be necessary for a variety of stimulus conditions.

The phonetic feature *phonation onset* thus appears to be inherently structured in terms of this perceptual constraint as well as the articulatory constraints of the speech-producing apparatus. The control of the source of excitation for speech is independent of the configuration of the supralaryngeal vocal tract. Speakers thus can change the timing between the laryngeal source and the opening of the supralaryngeal vocal tract. The three simplest categories for timing rest in three simple distinctions—advanced, coincident, and delayed. The magnitude of the time interval that differentiates the categories is a consequence of the minimum temporal resolution of the auditory system.

The 20-msec timing distinction has been shown to mark the perception of stop sounds by 4-week-old infants (Eimas et al., 1971; Eimas and Corbit, 1973). Experiments monitoring their behavior while they listen to artifically synthesized stimuli have shown that they partition the temporal variations that can occur between phonation and the release of the primary occlusion of the supralaryngeal vocal tract at precisely the same 20-msec intervals used by normal adults and older children. There seems to be no way in which month-old infants could "learn" to respond to speech stimuli in this manner. The 20-msec voicing onset interval appears to reflect an innately determined constraint of the auditory system in *Homo sapiens*. Electrophysiological studies in cats (Kiang and Peake, 1960) indeed suggest that this 20-msec interval may reflect a basic temporal constraint characteristic of the auditory systems of other species as well.

The breath-group

In Chapter 5 we noted that controlled variations of fundamental frequency may convey linguistic information. In many languages, e.g., Chinese, two words may differ phonetically solely with respect to the pattern of fundamental frequency. The pattern of fundamental frequency plays a role in signaling the end of a sentence in most if not all human languages (Lieberman, 1967). Both traditional and generative grammars (Chomsky, 1957, 1968) regard a sentence as the minimal unit from which a complete semantic interpretation can be made. The traditional functional description of a sentence, that it expresses a complete thought, has real validity. It is easy to perform a small experiment that tests this statement. All that one has to do is read a short passage after moving the sentence-final "period" punctuation one word over. The resulting sequences of words will for the most part be unintelligible. The primary function of orthographic punctuation is to indicate the ends of sentences, and the sentence-final "period" symbol is essential. Question marks can be optionally replaced by special words in most languages. (English is a special case insofar as some of the options have fallen out of use in comparatively recent times; cf. Lieberman, 1967.) Commas are usually optional insofar as the reader would be able to derive the sentence's meaning if they were omitted.

During normal speech the prosodic content of the message, which is largely determined by the perceived pitch as a function of time, signals the ends of sentences. The phonetic feature that speakers make use of to segment the train of words is the *breath-group*, which enables listeners to group words into meaningful sentences. It probably is one of the most central, basic aspects of language, and it, or some equivalent phonetic feature, must have been present in the earliest forms of hominid language. It is not a question of language being more difficult without signaling the boundaries of sentences. Language would be impossible without this information, for we would be reduced to one-word utterances each with a fixed, immutable meaning. Language is not a code in which particular signals have fixed meanings. It is impossible to transmit a message in a code if the message is not already in the code book. Language has the potential of transmitting new, unanticipated information. Syntax and the sentence are necessary factors for the presence of language, and the *breath-group* is one of the basic, primitive phonetic features that must be present in all languages.

This view of the basic, primitive status of the breath-group is consistent with the physiological mechanisms that structure and constrain its form. In the production of normal speech the acoustic cues that characterize the normal breath-group are a consequence of minimal deviation from the respiratory activity that is necessary to sustain life. The primary function of the human respiratory system is *not* to provide air for speech production. Oxygen transfer to the bloodstream is the primary vegatative function of the respiratory system. Speech production is a secondary function. Constant respiratory activity is necessary to sustain life, and in the absence of speech there is an ongoing cyclic pattern in which inspiration is followed by expiration as the lungs alternately expand and deflate, forcing air in and out through the nose, mouth, pharynx, and trachea. In Figure 6-1A a graph of the volume of the lungs during quiet respiration is plotted. The graph represents a quiet passive state when the subject is at rest. Note that the durations of the inspiratory and expiratory phases are almost equal. If the subject were running or performing some more strenuous physical activity, the quantity of air that went in and out of the lungs would increase. The basic pattern in which almost equal time was allotted to the inspiratory and the expiratory phases would remain unchanged (Mead and Agostoni, 1964). If we were to measure the pressure of the air in the human subject's lungs during quiet respiratory activity, we would find that the alveolar air pressure (the term *alveolar* refers to the lungs) was higher than the atmospheric air pressure outside of the subject's nose and lips during the expiratory phases when air was being pushed out of the lungs (Figure 6-1B). The alveolar air pressure would have to be lower than the atmospheric air pressure in the inspiratory phases in order to get air to flow into the lungs.

The anatomical mechanism that has evolved to carry out the constant pattern of alveolar activity is both complex and efficient. The major amount of work involved in respiration occurs when the lungs expand during inspiration. The lungs are rather like rubber balloons insofar as they are elastic. The inspiratory muscles

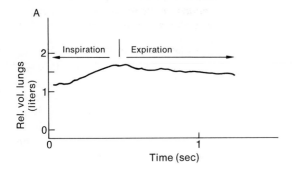

Figure 6-1 Relative volume of air in lungs (*A*) and alveolar air pressure (*B*) during quiet respiratory activity. (After Lieberman, 1967.)

expand the rib cage and effectively store energy as the lungs expand. During expiration much of the force that pushes air out from the lungs comes from the elastic recoil. Human speech almost always takes place during expiration because the speaker is able to control the rate at which the lungs deflate by working against the elastic recoil force. During the production of speech the speaker can vary the duration of an expiration over broad limits. Whereas the duration of an expiration is about 2 sec during quiet respiration, it can vary between 300 msec and 40 sec during the production of speech.

In Figure 6-2A a graph that shows respiratory activity during speech is plotted. One thing is certain from it: the air pressure during the expiratory phase must be greater than the atmospheric air pressure. During the inspiratory phase it must, in contrast, be lower than the atmospheric air pressure. Therefore, at the end of the expiratory phase of the breath-group plotted in Figure 6-2 there must be a fairly abrupt transition in the alveolar air pressure from the greater (positive) air pressure necessary for expiration to the lower (negative) air pressure necessary for inspiration. If a speaker moves his larynx into the phonation position during an expiration and does nothing to change the tensions of the various laryngeal muscles, then the fundamental frequency of phonation will be

Figure 6-2 Relative volume of air in lungs (*A*) and alveolar air pressure (*B*) during the production of speech. (After Lieberman, 1967.)

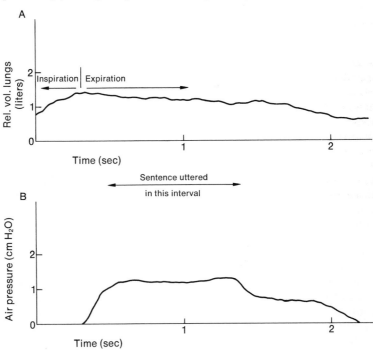

determined by the transglottal air pressure drop (Lieberman, 1967; Atkinson, 1973). Müller (1848) first noted that the rate at which the vocal cords open and close, which determines the fundamental frequency of phonation, is a function of the air pressure differential across the vocal cords. If a speaker maintains a relatively unobstructed supralaryngeal vocal tract and keeps his larynx in a fixed phonation position, then the fundamental frequency will be determined by the alveolar air pressure. These conditions are met in the cries of newborn humans (Truby et al., 1965) where the supralaryngeal vocal tract's configuration is maintained throughout the cry and where phonation occurs until the very end of the breath-group. The fundamental frequency at the end of the breath-group in these cries always falls because, in the absence of increased activity of the laryngeal muscles, the alveolar air pressure goes from a positive to a negative value at the end of the breath-group. The transition in alveolar air pressure is a consequence of the act of breathing. The falling fundamental frequency contour at the end of the breath-group is a consequence of a state of minimal departure from the vegetative state of the organism. In other words, the easiest way of producing sound over the course of an expiration will necessarily produce a fundamental frequency contour that falls at the end of the breath-group.

The normal breath-groups used by adult speakers are modeled on the state of minimal control insofar as the fundamental frequency contour always falls at the end of the breath-group. In Figure 6-2B alveolar air pressure and fundamental frequency are plotted. Note that the alveolar air pressure is maintained at a relatively steady level for the nonterminal portions of expiration. This is typical for unemphasized sentences in American English (Lieberman, 1967; Atkinson, 1973). The steady alveolar air pressure in a sense is the simplest way of maintaining phonation at, or about, the same fundamental frequency. At the end of the expiration the alveolar air pressure abruptly falls. The fundamental frequency follows the air pressure function because the speaker does not tension laryngeal muscles that could offset the falling air pressure. The feature of the normal breath-group that appears to be language universal is the terminal falling fundamental frequency contour that follows from this condition of minimal departure from the vegetative aspects of respiration. Human speakers have the ability to produce virtually any sort of terminal fundamental frequency contour, but they usually don't. The falling fundamental frequency contour universally signals the end of an "ordinary" sentence.

Many sentences, such as English yes-no questions, end with a terminal rising fundamental frequency contour. These sentences are produced by means of a *marked* breath-group (Lieberman, 1967). The notation +*breath-group* can be used for the marked, and −*breath-group* for the normal. The rising fundamental frequency contour of the marked breath-group is the consequence of maneuvers of laryngeal muscles such as the thyroarytenoids, lateral cricoarytenoid, and cricothyroid. These muscles are tensioned at the end of the breath-group where they counteract the falling air pressure. However, the configuration of the larynx throughout the entire $+breath$-$group$ is different from its state in a $-breath$-$group$. The shape and tension of the vocal cords are adjusted from the very start of a $+breath$-$group$ in a manner that makes their motion less dependent on air pressure. The internal muscles of the larynx as well as muscles such as the sternohyoid, which affects the position of the larynx relative to the rest of the body, change the "mode" of phonation (Atkinson, 1973). The larynx thus behaves in a different way throughout the entire $+breath$-$group$. Atkinson's experiments involved monitoring the air pressures below and above a speaker's larynx while the activity of specific laryngeal muscles was measured by means of inserted electrodes. His data demonstrate that a speaker of English at the start of a $+breath$-$group$ adjusts his larynx to a mode of phonation that minimizes the effects of the falling air pressure. The rise in fundamental frequency at the end of a $+breath$-$group$ is in a sense the simplest perceptual contrast with a falling fundamental frequency contour of the $-breath$-$group$. The $-breath$-$group's$ defining characteristic is the terminal fall in fundamental frequency. The simplest and clearest contrast with this acoustic cue is a rising (or not-falling) terminal fundamental frequency contour. $Breath$-$group$ thus can be viewed as a binary phonetic feature that is structured by the physiology of the respiratory system and perceptual simplicity.

SUPRALARYNGEAL FILTER FEATURES

The three phonetic features that we have discussed, *voicing, phonation onset,* and *breath-group,* do not exhaust the set of phonetic features that involve the laryngeal source. We will discuss others that crucially involve laryngeal maneuvers in Chapter 11. It is important, however, to discuss in more detail the role of the supralaryngeal vocal tract, which acts as an acoustic filter.

Stop consonant

The feature *stop consonant,* already discussed with respect to phonation onset, has as its acoustic correlate perhaps the simplest and clearest perceptual contrast that can be made. The acoustic signal is abruptly interrupted or reduced. The acoustic cues that signal a stop consonant necessarily result in a binary feature. The speech signal can either be or not be interrupted, so the feature has the two values $+stop$ $consonant$ and $-stop$ $consonant$. The articulatory maneuvers that speakers use to produce a signal that is $+stop$ $consonant$ have one common attribute, they must abruptly seal and then open the vocal tract.

Human speakers can occlude their vocal tracts at a number of different points. Stop consonants can be articulated by closing the

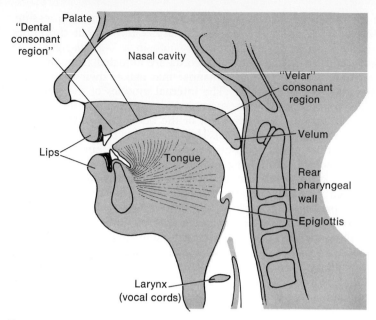

Figure 6-3 The adult human vocal tract.

lips, e.g., [b] and [p], or by sealing the vocal tract by moving the tongue against the hard palate near the teeth, [d] and [t], or further back along the hard palate, [g] and [k]. The schematic diagram of the adult human vocal tract in Figure 6-3 notes these anatomical landmarks. Stop consonants can also be produced by moving the vocal cords together and keeping them closed by the action of the laryngeal muscles. Many languages, e.g., Danish, make use of glottal stops produced by essentially "squeezing" the vocal cords together. Most stop consonants, however, involve occlusions of the supralaryngeal vocal tract. It is obvious that the biological basis for the phonetic feature *stop consonant* does not rest in the ability of a particular muscle to effect a closure of the vocal tract. The binary perceptual contrast inherent in the interruption of the acoustic signal is clearly the basis for this feature.

Nasal

The nose is obviously part of the supralaryngeal vocal tract. Air will flow through the nasal cavity if the velum is lowered to its relaxed position. Figure 6-3 shows the velum in its closed position. Muscles such as the tensor and levator veli-palatini and the superior pharyngeal constrictors when they are tensioned can raise the velum and isolate the nasal cavity from the other airways. When the velum is relaxed and the cavity is fully or nearly fully open to the airflow generated by the acoustic source, the speech signal becomes +*nasal.* Opening the nasal cavity is analogous to connecting another pipe to the source on a pipe organ. The nasal cavity modifies the filter function of the supralaryngeal vocal tract, and human listeners can perceive the modification. For example, the sounds [m] and [n] in the words *map* and *nap* are +*nasal.* The velum is open during the production of the initial consonant in both words.

The biological basis of the feature *nasal* rests both in the particular speech-producing anatomy of modern *Homo sapiens,* which allows a speaker to either open or close the nose during the production of speech, and in the perceptibility of the modifications of the filtering properties of the supralaryngeal vocal tract. A speech sound that involves a small velar opening with an attendent small airflow through the nose will not be perceived as +*nasal* (Flanagan, 1972). The feature appears to be binary, because a fairly substantial airflow is necessary for a sound to be perceived as +*nasal.* The feature *nasal* thus appears to be a signaling unit in *Homo sapiens* because two conditions are met. Humans have a speech-producing mechanism that allows the nasal cavity to be either connected to or disconnected from the other supralaryngeal air passages. Humans also have neural mechanisms that are sensitive to the presence of a certain level of filter function modification.

Formant frequency and vocal tract variation

The changes in the formant frequency pattern that occur when a speech sound is +*nasal* have a clear physical basis, and they can be calculated if a suitable mathematical model of the vocal tract is employed (Fant, 1960). However, the physical basis of the relationship between the formant frequencies and the shape and size of the supralaryngeal vocal tract is easier to see for unnasalized vowel sounds, in particular [Λ].

The vowel [Λ] (the first vowel in the word *about*) is perhaps the "simplest" and most basic vowel sound. The sketch in Figure 6-4 shows a stylized midsagittal view of the supralaryngeal vocal tract as derived from X-ray movies of speech for this vowel. The speaker's velum is raised, closing the nose off from the rest of the

Figure 6-4 Lateral (side) view of the supralaryngeal vocal tract for vowel [Λ].

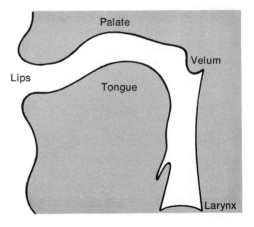

supralaryngeal airways. The speaker's lips are neither advanced nor retracted. The speaker's tongue is in a fairly unperturbed position with respect to the shape that it assumes during quiet respiration (Perkell, 1969). The area function for this vowel is acoustically equivalent to a uniform tube open at one end. The area function is plotted in terms of the cross-sectional area as a function of distance from the glottis. The vocal tract is thus open at the speaker's lips. The glottis is equivalent to a complete closure because the average glottal opening is quite small during normal phonation. The speaker's nose would be sealed by the velum during the production of a —nasal vowel, so we have only one tube in the supralaryngeal airway for the vowel [Λ].

We can calculate the formant frequencies of the supralaryngeal filter function for this vowel fairly simply. We can also get some "feel" for the physical basis of this formant frequency pattern. The supralaryngeal vocal tract for this vowel behaves rather like an organ pipe, and we can see how the formant frequencies are related to the shape and length, i.e., the area function, of the pipe.

In Figure 6-5 is sketched a uniform pipe open at one end, with a superimposed dashed line representing the pressure waveform of the lowest-frequency sinusoidal sound wave that could be sustained in this tube. Sound waves are air pressure waves. At a given instant of time, a sinusoidal air pressure wave will be distributed in space. It will have a peak pressure at one point, a zero pressure at a distance of $\frac{1}{4}$ wavelength from the maximum, a peak pressure at 1 wavelength from the first peak, and so on. A pressure wave with these points marked is shown in Figure 6-6. How does the pressure waveform sketched in Figure 6-5 relate to that in Figure 6-6?

Let's imagine that we are trying to "match" the physical constraints of the pipe sketched in Figure 6-5 with the power required to sustain a sinusoidal air pressure wave. In other words, we're trying to take advantage of the physical dimensions of the pipe to minimize the amount of power (or energy) that we would need to generate an air pressure wave. The pressure in an air pressure wave comes from the constant collision of the air molecules. It is obvious that maximum air pressure could most easily be sustained at the closed end of the tube, where air molecules would bounce from the rigid wall of the tube to hit other molecules. H therefore represents the position of the highest air pressure in Figure 6-5. Zero air pressure is, by definition, the atmospheric air pressure. It is obvious that, in the absence of any sound, the air pressure outside of the tube would be atmospheric pressure. It logically

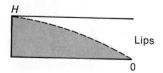

Figure 6-5 A uniform pipe open at one end showing pressure waveform of lowest-frequency sinusoidal sound wave that can be sustained in it (first formant frequency).

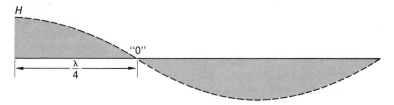

Figure 6-6 Air pressure wave.

would be easiest to sustain an air pressure wave that had "zero" (i.e., atmospheric) pressure at the open end of the tube. Therefore, 0 appears in Figure 6-5 at the open end of the tube.

The question is now whether there exists a sinusoidal wave that could have its high pressure at the closed end of the tube and also have zero pressure at the open end of the tube. The answer to this rhetorical question is that there are a number of sinusoidal waves that would satisfy these "boundary" conditions. The dashed line in Figure 6-5 represents just one of them, the sinusoidal wave that has the lowest frequency that could meet these boundary conditions. The distance between points H and 0 is, of course, one fourth of the total wavelength of this wave. In Figure 6-6 it is obvious that one fourth of the total wavelength separates the high point of the wave from the "zero" value.

The tube open at one end thus will lend itself to sustaining a sound wave at a frequency whose wavelength is four times the length of the tube. The physical attributes of the tube, say, that it has a closed end 17 cm away from its open end, make it possible to generate, with minimum energy input, an air pressure wave whose wavelength is equal to four times 17 cm. If the glottal source were exciting the tube at the closed end, then it would generate a pressure wave at the frequency corresponding to this wavelength with minimum input energy. For a given input energy an air pressure wave would be generated at this frequency with maximum amplitude.

The frequency of the pressure wave at which maximum amplitude will be generated is equal to 500 Hz for a 17-cm tube at sea level in a normal atmosphere. This follows from the relationship that we discussed in Chapter 4, $\lambda f = c$. The velocity of sound in air at sea level is approximately 33,500 cm/sec. Because the length of the tube is 17 cm, the wavelength is four times 17 cm, i.e., 68 cm. The frequency of the wave at which a maximum amplitude will be generated is therefore equal to 33,500/68 or about 500 Hz (0.5 kHz). This frequency is the first formant frequency, F_1. It is the lowest frequency at which maximum sound energy would be generated by a source at the closed, glottal end of the tube.

Air pressure waves at higher frequencies also would satisfy the boundary conditions of the tube, maximum pressure at the glottis and zero pressure at the open lip end. In Figure 6-7 is sketched a sinusoidal wave that has three times the frequency of the first

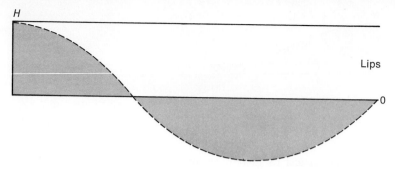

Lips

0

Figure 6-7 The uniform pipe of Figure 6-5 showing sinusoidal sound wave with three times higher frequency (second formant frequency).

formant frequency and also meets these conditions. Its wavelength would be one third that of the first formant. The second formant frequency for this tube, which is an idealized model of the vowel [Λ], would be 1.5 kHz for a supralaryngeal vocal tract 17 cm long. The third formant for this tube would be 2.5 kHz, five times the first formant frequency. The physical dimensions of the 17-cm tube open at one end thus yield the formant frequencies $F_1 = 0.5$ kHz, $F_2 = 1.5$ kHz, $F_3 = 2.5$ kHz. The transfer function of this vowel is plotted in Figure 5-5.

Formant frequencies are always determined by the size, length, and shape and ends of the supralaryngeal vocal tract, i.e., the cross-sectional area function. It is harder to calculate and visualize the physical situation in speech sounds that involve more complex shapes than the vowel [Λ]. The formant frequencies are also usually not integral multiples of each other. However, the formant frequencies always are determined by the shape and dimensions of the supralaryngeal vocal tract.

Formant raising and formant lowering

Suppose that instead of having a fixed-length tube we had a tube whose length was adjustable. As the length increased the formant frequencies would all fall; as the length decreased the formant frequencies would all rise. This follows from the fact that the velocity of sound is constant, so frequency is inversely proportional to wavelength. The human supralaryngeal vocal tract can easily change its overall length. A speaker can, for example, raise or lower the larynx 1 cm by means of the complex system of muscles and ligaments that connect it to the skeletal structure. A speaker can also purse the lips to lengthen the supralaryngeal vocal tract. The supralaryngeal vocal tract can likewise be effectively shortened by flaring the lips. Closing the lips also has the same effect as lengthening the supralaryngeal vocal tract. A speaker can make use of these different articulatory maneuvers to produce acoustic signals in which the formant frequencies move upward or downward in frequency.

Formant frequency transitions play a dominant role in structuring human speech. The two simplest patterns are the ones that we have discussed, uniform transitions to higher or lower frequencies for all three formant frequencies of the vowel. We can formally represent these two possibilities by means of the two binary features *formant raising* and *formant lowering*. These features play a part in human language (Chomsky and Halle, 1968), and they may also play a role in the communications of other species, living (Andrew, 1963) and extinct.

7 Physiology of Speech

One of the traditional concerns of linguistics is the distribution and nature of the sounds that different human languages use to convey meaningful distinctions. No two languages make use of exactly the same set of sounds. Closely related languages such as French and Spanish may have more sounds in common than English and French, or Finnish and French. The extent of variation is seemingly infinite. Superficially, it appears as though just about any arbitrary set of different sounds would suffice for conveying the words of a human language. For example, in reviewing attempts to trace the evolution of language, Simpson notes that

> Audible signals capable of expressing language do not require any particular phonetic apparatus, but only the ability to produce sound, any sound at all. (1966, p. 473)

Simpson appears to believe that the phonetic aspects of human language are trivial and that they play no role in defining the essential nature of human language. Any set of arbitrary sounds would do if Simpson's views were true.

There is an element in Simpson's statement that makes it appear true at first reading. Humans can communicate using arbitrary sounds. Our folklore contains many tales that relate the adventures of prisoners incarcerated in adjacent cells who "talked" by tapping their spoons against the wall, thwarted lovers who communicated by imitating bird calls, and so on. In many cultures hunters communicate during the chase by means of cries or whistles that imitate animal sounds. Human language therefore can be maintained by the use of arbitrary sounds. In theory, and in practice, only one binary sound contrast is really necessary. The dot-dash distinction that is the basis of the Morse Code is an arbitrary, invented sound distinction that served as the primary means of high-speed long-distance communication for over 50 years.

In Morse Code the sequence of long and short sounds that are the acoustic consequences of the electrical signals transmitted through a wire represent the letters of the alphabet. The letter *a*, for example, is transmitted by the code [·–], where the dot represents a short sound and the dash a long sound. The letter *s* is transmitted by the sequence [···], the letter *o* by the sequence [–––], and so on. As everyone who has learned Morse Code knows, it is possible to transmit a message; however, it's quite different from listening to human speech. Errors are frequent, the Morse Code operator must listen to the signal with extreme concentration, the process is tiring, and it's extremely slow compared to human speech. Morse Code in fact turns out to be virtually useless as a medium for normal human communication.

The basis for this assertion rests on the vast amount of data resulting from over 50 years of research on the construction of machines that would read aloud to blind people. As we noted in Chapter 2, it is not particularly difficult to construct machines that "recognize" the printed letters of the alphabet. In fact, it's not really necessary to recognize printed letters at all, because at some time in the process of printing a book a linotype machine or typewriter is used. It's a trivial problem to connect a device to the keys of a typewriter that will make a different sound for each key. If any set of arbitrary sounds actually were functionally equivalent to the sounds of human speech there would be no particular problem in, for example, producing magnetic tape recordings that "talked out" books to blind readers.

Unfortunately, this is not the case. Although listeners can be taught to recognize and associate arbitrary sounds with letters, the process always has the same limitations as conventional Morse Code. It's slow, tiring, full of errors, and demands the utmost attention from the listener. The listener has to spend so much effort on deciphering the signal that it becomes difficult or impossible to follow the message. The maximum rate of transmission is about one tenth that of normal human speech (Liberman, 1970), so slow that listeners tend to forget what a sentence was about before they come to its end.

The sounds of human speech turn out to have some rather special properties that make rapid acoustic communication possible, given the temporal limitations of the human auditory system. No other sounds will do for humans if they wish to communicate at the rates typical of normal speech. We will discuss these aspects of human speech in this chapter, because they can be related to some of the species-specific properties of the human supralaryngeal vocal tract. Because we can, in turn, relate these properties of the supralaryngeal vocal tract both to the properties of the neural mechanisms that are involved in the perception of human speech and to certain aspects of skeletal morphology, we can gain some insights on the nature of human linguistic ability and its evolution.

It is important to note at this point that we are focusing on *acoustic* communication. Most of these remarks don't pertain to the transfer of linguistic information by means of visual symbols or manual gestures. We also must stress that we are discussing the speech communications of present-day *Homo sapiens*. We will generalize to other closely related animals, the living primates and the various extinct hominids who are represented by fossil evidence. Other animals such as birds may not be subject to the same restrictions, and their communications may make use of rather different phonetic signals that reflect their divergent evolution.

THE HIERARCHY OF PHONETIC FEATURES

One indication that the sounds of speech are not arbitrary rests in the fact that the distribution of sounds in the different languages of present-day humans is not without a hierarchical structure. Certain sounds tend to occur more frequently in different languages, whereas other sounds are comparatively rare. We would not expect this to be the case if the choice of sounds were truly arbitrary. If, as Simpson claims, any set of sounds would suffice, we should not expect to find certain sounds occurring again and again in unrelated languages such as Japanese and English.

When we use the term *unrelated* it is in a narrow historical sense. Japanese and English are not historically related as, for example, English and French are. One of the triumphs of nineteenth-century linguistic research was the discovery that many languages that were spoken by people who had different cultural heritages had common "ancestral" sources. Everyone knew that Spanish and French were closely related. The historical record clearly showed that both were Romance languages historically derived from Latin. However, it was surprising to discover that Latin, Greek, and Sanskrit were related and were derived from a common "ancestral" language, Proto-Indo-European.

It does not seem unusual to find that certain sounds are shared to a greater or lesser degree by historically related languages. It is surprising to discover that certain sounds are more common in historically unrelated languages. For example, Troubetzkoy (1969), in his monumental work *The Principles of Phonology* (the untranslated title published in 1939 is *Grundzüge der Phonologie*), noted that vowels like [a], [i], and [u] occurred in practically all of the languages that he studied. Other vowels like [e] and [æ] occurred far less frequently. Bilabial stops like [p] and [b] again occurred far more frequently than velar stops like [g] and [k]. Troubetzkoy concluded that there is a universal set of sounds that characterizes all languages. No particular language makes use of all the possibilities but some sounds are more basic than others. The more basic sounds are the ones that occur more frequently in different languages.[1]

Other linguistic evidence supports Troubetzkoy's views. Jakobson (1968), for example, studied the process of word acquisition by children and found that they did not initially use all the sounds of their native language when they pronounced meaningful words. They tended to begin with sounds like [m], [b], and [a]. Jakobson further noted that these sounds were among the most common sounds in all human languages and that the sequence in which children acquired the sounds of their native language mirrored the frequency of occurrence of these sounds throughout the languages of the world. In other words, the sounds that most frequently occurred in different languages were the ones that children would first use as they acquired their particular native language.

Linguistic evidence like that cited is, of course, suggestive insofar as it can be interpreted as the consequence of some general biological principles that make certain sounds more highly valued, or more "useful" for conveying language. However, it does not explain these biological principles. If we want to find out *why* certain sounds occur more frequently, we must form and test biologically functional, i.e., physiological, hypotheses. We have to recognize that a linguistic theory must *explain* why some sounds occur more often. Johannes Müller noted that

> a great number of other sounds can be formed in the vocal tube between the glottis and the external apertures of the air-passages, the combination of which into different groups to designate objects, properties, actions, etc., constitutes language. . . . Each language contains a certain number of sounds, but in no one are all brought together. On the contrary, different languages are characterized by the prevalence in them of certain classes of sounds, while others are less frequent or altogether absent. It comes within the province of physiology to investigate the natural classification of the sounds of language. (1848, p. 1044)

Müller's comments are still germane. Physiology is the science dealing with the function of living organisms or their parts. Lin-

---

[1]Like many other aspects of science, the same things seem to be "rediscovered." Müller (1848) cites similar observations that were made by Purkinje (1836).

guistic theories that rely solely on observations of the frequency of occurrence, the sequence of acquisition, or the interrelations of phonetic features have not explained, and cannot explain, *why* human languages make use of certain sounds, *why* some sounds occur rarely, and *why* certain sounds that normal human speakers can make are never used.

ACOUSTIC STABILITY

A sound, if it is to be useful as a signal in a communications system, must obviously be one that a speaker can produce and a hearer can identify. Let's suppose that we have been asked to evaluate the utility of two hypothetical communications systems. The waiters in an expensive and unusual restaurant have to somehow transmit acoustic, nonvocal signals to the cook to order steaks, lobsters, and so on. They are forbidden to talk. Two alternate systems are suggested by the interior decorator who is responsible for the decor of this unusual eatery. In one system the waiters have a set of ten handbells. Each handbell produces a distinct sound whenever it is shaken. The meaningful phonetic sounds in this communications system are the sounds produced by the bells. The alternate communications system makes use of waiters who play violins. The meaningful phonetic sounds in this communications system are the different notes that the violins can produce. Which system should we choose? We want to have a communications system that will be reliable. We furthermore have no information that identifies a pool of unemployed violinists who want to become waiters.

It's obvious that the restaurant should feature bell-ringing waiters, because the bells each produce "stable," i.e., relatively invariant, acoustic signals. The waiters simply have to shake a particular bell to produce a desired signal. Violins obviously can also be played so that they produce desired signals, but it isn't very easy. Almost anyone can learn to ring a bell. The interior decorator could even jazz up the decor by using trained seals or dogs to ring the bells.

It is probable that our hypothetical restaurant would not prove to be successful and the owner might switch to violinists as the receipts fell. However, the reason for choosing the bell-ringers is clear. A communications system will be more reliable if the phonetic signals that are its basic elements are both invariant and distinct *and* simple to produce. The listener's task is minimized if the acoustic signals are distinct and unchanging. The sender's task is likewise minimized if it is easy to produce the required signals. We will make use of the term *acoustic stability* as a descriptor that unites all of these desirable properties. Speech sounds that are acoustically stable are ones that are distinct and can be produced by means of relatively imprecise articulatory maneuvers. Acoustic stability is a functional, physiological attribute of certain speech sounds. The examples that follow should make the value of this concept clearer.

In Figure 7-1A is sketched a stylized model of the cross-sectional area of the supralaryngeal vocal tract for the vowel [a]. The discussion that follows is essentially a paraphrase of K. N. Stevens' analysis (1972). Stevens' insights on acoustic stability have provided a new way of looking at the nature of speech sounds. Note that the shape of the supralaryngeal vocal tract for this vowel approximates a two-tube resonator. The posterior portion of the supralaryngeal vocal tract, which corresponds to the pharynx, is constricted and has the cross-sectional area A_1. The anterior, oral cavity is relatively large. The cross-sectional area of the oral cavity, A_2, is about ten times as large as A_1 (Fant, 1960). To a first approximation, the first two formant frequencies can be calculated as simple $\frac{1}{4}$-wavelength resonances of these two tubes. The discussion in Chapter 6 regarding the first resonance of a uniform tube applies to each tube because the coupling between the oral and pharyngeal tubes will be small as long as the cross-sectional areas A_1 and A_2 are substantially different.

The physical reasoning behind this approximation is not difficult to follow. At the closed end of the back tube the air pressure that best "matches" the obstruction of the closed end is obviously a pressure maximum. The air pressure that best matches the end of the constricted tube at point X is zero pressure. This follows from the fact that the cross-sectional area A_2 is ten times greater than A_1. The size of the unconstricted tube is so much greater than that of the constricted tube that it is equivalent to directly connecting

Figure 7-1 *A:* Two-tube model of supralaryngeal vocal tract for the vowel [a]. *B:* Area function.

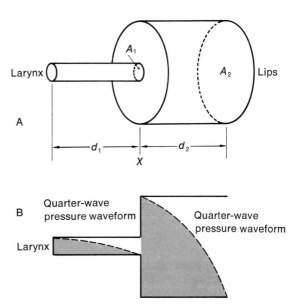

the constricted tube to the outside atmosphere. A ten-to-one difference in cross-sectional area is enormous. The effect on air pressure
can be visualized by imagining what would happen to the members
of a crowd as they exited from a passageway that was 3 feet wide
to one 30 feet wide. The people in the crowd might be pushing
against one another in the 3-ft-wide passage. However, they could
spread out in the 30-ft-wide passage and never touch each other.
The collision of the gas molecules that generated the air pressure
waveform in the constricted tube is thus minimized at point X
where the cross-sectional area abruptly changes. The air pressure
waveform in the unconstricted tube is also a quarter-wave pattern,
because the oral tube is nine-tenths "closed" at point X. The two
pressure waveforms are sketched in Figure 7-1B.

The quarter-wave resonance model is only a first approximation
to the behavior of the vocal tract for the vowel [a], e.g., the vowel
of the word *hod*. It does, however, make evident the salient properties of this sound. The change in cross-sectional area, point X,
occurs at the midpoint of the supralaryngeal vocal tract (Fant, 1960).
F_1 and F_2, the first and second formant frequencies, therefore are
equal. If we perturbed the position of point X from this midpoint,
we would not expect these two formant frequencies to change very
abruptly. For example, if we moved point X 1 cm forward or backward we would generate the same first and second formant frequencies. The front tube would be longer and would generate the
lower resonance F_1 if point X were moved 1 cm backward. If point
X were instead moved 1 cm forward the back cavity would generate
the lower first formant. The first formant frequency would be
identical for these two situations. It is immaterial whether the front
or the back cavity generates the first formant frequency; all that
matters is that the same frequency is generated. The second formant frequency would also have the same value for these two cases.
It would be generated by the shorter tube. The first and second
formant frequencies for the vowel [a] thus won't change too much
so long as point X is perturbed about the midpoint of the supralaryngeal vocal tract. An increase in the length of the front, oral
cavity necessarily results in a decrease in the length of the back,
pharyngeal cavity, and the two cavities "trade off" in generating
the first and second formant frequencies.

The quarter-wave model for the vowel [a] is, as we have noted,
a first approximation because there is actually some coupling between the front and back tubes. In Figure 7-2 calculated values
for F_1 and F_2 are plotted for various positions of point X about
the midpoint of a 17-cm-long supralaryngeal vocal tract. These
calculations were made using a computer-implemented model of
the supralaryngeal vocal tract (Henke, 1966). The computer program calculates the formant frequencies of the supralaryngeal vocal
tract for specified area functions. Note that the first and second
formant frequencies converge for $X = 8.5$ cm, the midpoint of the
supralaryngeal vocal tract. The quarter-wave approximation of [a]
yields the same frequency for F_1 and F_2, but the coupling between

Figure 7-2 The first formant frequency, F_1, and the second formant frequency, F_2, for a stylized model of the supralaryngeal vocal tract having the shape of the two-tube model sketched in Figure 7-1A. The formant frequencies vary as the position of the area function discontinuity, point X, is shifted forward and backward. (After Stevens, 1972.)

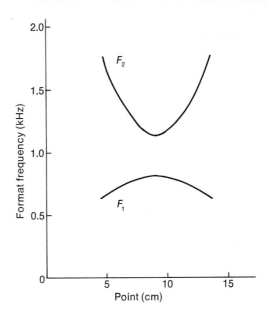

the two tubes results in slightly different formant frequencies. Note that there is a range of about 2 cm in the middle of the curve of Figure 7-2 within which the second formant varies over only 50 Hz and the first formant changes even less. Within this region the two formants are close together. The transfer function for [a] in Figure 7-2 thus has a major spectral peak. In contrast, for the 2-cm range from $X = 11$ to 13 cm, the second formant frequency changes by about 0.4 kHz and the centered spectral peaks would be absent.

In Figure 7-3 illustrations of approximate midsagittal sections, cross-sectional area functions, and acoustic transfer functions of the vocal tract for the vowels [i], [a], and [u] are presented. Articulatory and acoustic analyses have shown that these vowels are the limiting articulations of a vowel triangle that is language universal (Troubetzkoy, 1939; Liljencrants and Lindblom, 1972). The body of the tongue is high and fronted to form a constricted oral cavity in [i], whereas it is low to form a large oral cavity in [a] and [u]. The pharynx is expanded in [i] and [u] and constricted in [a]. The oral and pharyngeal tubes are maximally expanded and maximally constricted in the production of these vowels. Further constriction would result in the generation of turbulent noise excitation and the loss of vowel quality (Fant, 1960; Stevens, 1972).

Note that all three vowels have well-defined spectral properties. A central spectral peak occurs at about 1 kHz for [a]. A high-frequency spectral peak occurs for [i] and a low-frequency spectral peak occurs for [u]. All three vowels are acoustically stable. They have well-defined acoustic properties that don't change for small errors in articulation (Stevens, 1972). The small changes in formant frequencies that do occur when the articulatory configuration is perturbed, e.g., the 1-cm perturbations that we discussed for the

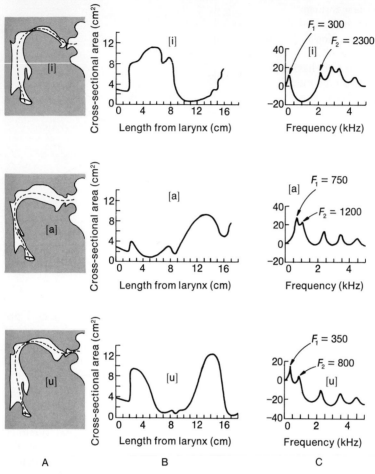

Figure 7-3 Approximate midsagittal sections (*A*), cross-sectional area functions (*B*), and acoustic transfer functions (*C*) of the vocal tract for the vowels [i], [a], and [u]. We will discuss the articulatory maneuvers that are necessary to produce these vowels in Chapter 9 (cf. Figure 9-8 and the discussion relating to these data). (After Lieberman et al., 1972b.)

vowel [a], are not perceptually significant because human listeners cannot differentiate between formant frequencies that differ by less than 60 Hz (Flanagan, 1955).

Note that all three of these vowels are produced by means of area functions that involve discontinuities at or near the midpoint of the supralaryngeal vocal tract. We will return to discuss the significance of the midpoint area function discontinuity when we compare the supralaryngeal vocal tract of *Homo sapiens* with that of other living primates and extinct hominids. The midpoint area function discontinuity has an important functional value. It allows human speakers to produce vowel signals that are acoustically distinct with relatively sloppy articulatory maneuvers.

Figure 7-4 is the acoustic vowel triangle that was derived by Peterson and Barney (1952) from 1,520 words spoken by 76 speakers (33 men, 28 women, and 15 children). The speakers represented a sampling of American English dialects, though most were from the Middle Atlantic speech area. A few of the speakers were not native speakers of English. They each recorded two lists of ten words twice. The words all had the form [h]-vowel-[d], i.e., *heed* [i], *hid* [ɪ], *head* [ɛ], *had* [æ], *hod* [a], *hawed* [ɔ], *hood* [ʊ], *who'd* [u], *hud* [ʌ], *heard* [ɝ]. The formant frequencies for the vowels of these words were measured and plotted. The phonetic context of the word-initial [h] resulted in a reasonably steady formant frequency pattern for these vowels, which simplified the measurements.

The individual symbols of Figure 7-4 represent the first and second formant frequencies of one of the ten-word lists for all the speakers. The graph, for example, includes an [i] that had a first formant frequency of 0.21 kHz and a second formant frequency of 2.1 kHz. The data points are all labeled with the phonetic sym-

Figure 7-4 Formant frequencies F_1 and F_2 for various vowels spoken by a set of 76 different speakers. (After Peterson and Barney, 1952.)

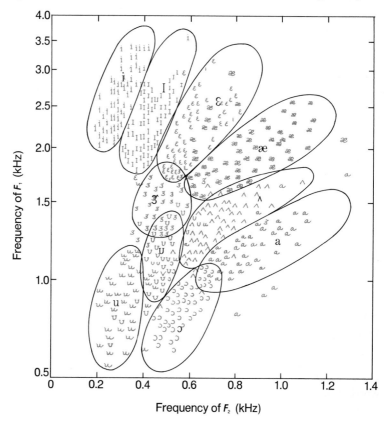

bols of the vowels that the speakers intended to convey. The labeled "loops" in Figure 7-4 encompass about 90 per cent of the data points for each phonetic category. Some of the data points for each vowel spill out into other vowel loops. Note that some of the vowel loops overlap.

The Peterson and Barney data are puzzling. Experiments using speech synthesizers show that with the possible exception of the [ɝ] vowel, that in *heard,* only the first and second formant frequencies are necessary to identify a vowel (Cooper et al., 1952). But the data in Figure 7-4 show that the F_1 versus F_2 vowel space, in itself, is not sufficient to identify all vowel stimuli. Data points in the overlap regions of the loops cannot be assigned to a particular phonetic category in the absence of other information.

Peterson and Barney also explored the responses of human listeners to the words that their speakers recorded. The results were again puzzling. The speakers in this study did not all speak a uniform dialect of American English. To insure against their listeners' "learning" a particular dialect, the words recorded by subgroups that each consisted of four men, four women, and two children were randomized and presented to a panel of 70 listeners who had to identify each word. The panel of listeners might, for example, hear the word *hid* spoken by a man, followed by the word *had* spoken by a child, followed by the word *head* spoken by a woman. Some of the vowels were classified in a consistent manner. On all the 152 sounds intended as [i] by the speaker there were 10,267 votes by the listeners that they were [i], four votes for [ɪ], six votes for [ɛ], and three votes for [ɔ]. The vowel [u] also was identified with great consistency. On the other hand, vowels like [ɪ], [ɛ], and [æ] were confounded. The vowel [ɛ], for example, was identified as [ɪ] 694 times, [ɛ] 9,014 times, and [æ] 300 times. The human listeners were not able to reliably identify some of the vowels under these listening conditions. Peterson and Barney ascribed most of the listeners' difficulties to dialect variations.

Dialect variations are indeed probably the cause of some of the vowel confusions (particularly the [a] versus [ɔ] confusion). However, a more systematic effect appears to be the main source of the listeners' confusions: they probably were confused because they were uncertain about the size of the supralaryngeal vocal tracts of the individual speakers. This leads directly into the general question of how human speech is perceived. We will return to the Peterson and Barney data and vowel perception within the general context of the perception of speech.

SPEECH ENCODING AND DECODING

We opened this chapter with a general discussion of the rate at which human speech transmits information—about 20 to 30 segments per second. That is, phonetic distinctions that differentiate meaningful words, say, the sounds symbolized by the notation [b], [æ], and [t] in the word *bat*, are transmitted and identified at a rate of 20 to 30 segments per second. As we noted in Chapter 2, it is obvious that human listeners cannot simply transmit and identify these sound distinctions as separate entities. The fastest rate at which sounds can be identified is about 7 to 9 segments per second. The "individual" sounds [b], [æ], and [t] are encoded, i.e., "squashed together," into the syllable-sized unit [bæt] (Liberman et al., 1967). A human speaker in producing this syllable starts with his supralaryngeal vocal tract in the shape characteristic of [b]. He does not maintain this articulatory configuration but instead moves his tongue, lips, and so on, toward the positions that would be attained if he were instructed to produce an isolated, sustained [æ]. He never reaches these positions because he starts toward the articulatory configuration characteristic of [t] before he reaches the "steady-state" (isolated and sustained) [æ] vowel. The articulatory gestures that would be characteristic of each isolated sound are never attained. Instead they are melded together into a composite, characteristic of the syllable. The sound pattern that results from this encoding process is itself an indivisible composite. Just as there is no way of separating with absolute certainty the [b] articulatory gestures from the [æ] gestures (you can't tell when the [b] ends and the [æ] begins), there is no way of separating the acoustic cues that are generated by these articulatory maneuvers.

If the syllable [bæt] were recorded on a magnetic tape, it would be impossible to isolate either the [b] or the [t]. You'd always hear the [æ] vowel. The acoustic cues that, in fact, transmit the initial and final consonants are the modulations of the formant frequency pattern of the [æ] vowel. The process is in effect a time-compressing system. The acoustic cues that characterize the initial and final consonants are transmitted in the time slot that would have been necessary to transmit a single isolated [æ] vowel.

In Figure 7-5 are reproduced two simplified spectrographic patterns that will, when converted to sound, produce approximations to the syllables [di] and [du] (Liberman, 1970). The dark bands on these patterns represent the first and second formant frequencies

Figure 7-5 Simplified spectrographic patterns that produce "synthetic" sounds [di] and [du]. (After Liberman, 1970.)

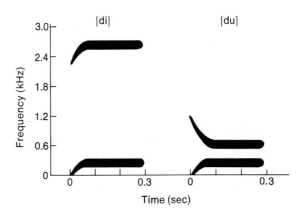

as functions of time. Note that the formants rapidly move through a range of frequencies at the left of each pattern. These rapid movements, which occur in about 0.05 sec, are called *formant transitions*. The transition in the second formant conveys the acoustic information that human listeners interpret as a token of a [d] in the syllables [di] and [du]. It is again impossible to isolate the acoustic pattern of [d] in these syllables. If tape recordings of these two syllables are "sliced" with the electronic equivalent of a pair of scissors (Lieberman, 1963b), it is impossible to find a segment that contains only [d]. There is no way to cut the tape so as to obtain a piece that will produce [d] without also producing the next vowel or some reduced approximation to it.

Note that the second formant transitions are different for the two syllables. If these transitions are isolated, listeners report that they hear either an upgoing or a falling frequency modulation. In context, with the acoustic correlates of the entire syllable, these transitions cause listeners to hear an "identical" [d] in both syllables. How does a human listener effect this perceptual response?

We have noted the formant frequency patterns of speech reflect the resonances of the supralaryngeal vocal tract. The formant patterns that define the syllable [di] in Figure 7-5 thus reflect the changing resonant pattern of the supralaryngeal vocal tract as the speaker moves his articulators from the occlusion of the tongue tip against the palate that is involved in the production of [d] to the vocal tract configuration of the [i]. A different acoustic pattern defines the [d] in the syllable [du]. The resonances of the vocal tract are similar as the speaker forms the initial occlusion of the [d] in both syllables; however, they are quite different for the final configurations of the vocal tract for [i] and [u]. The formant patterns that convey the [d] in both syllables are thus quite different because they involve transitions from the same starting point to different end points. Human listeners "hear" an identical initial [d] segment in both of these signals because they "decode" the acoustic pattern in terms of the articulatory gestures and the anatomical apparatus that is involved in the production of speech. The listener operates in terms of the acoustic pattern of the entire syllable. The acoustic cues for the individual "phonetic segments" are fused into a syllabic pattern. The high rate of information transfer of human speech is thus due to the transmission of acoustic information in syllable-sized units. The phonetic elements of each syllable are "encoded" into a single acoustic pattern, which is then "decoded" by the listener to yield the phonetic representation.

In order for the speech "decoding" process to work, the listener must be able to determine the absolute size of the speaker's vocal tract. Similar articulatory gestures will have different acoustic correlates in different-sized vocal tracts. The frequency of the first formant of [a], for example, varies from 730 Hz to 1.03 kHz in the data of Peterson and Barney (1952) for adult men and children. The frequencies of the resonances that occur for various consonants likewise are a function of the size of the speakers' vocal tracts.

The resonant pattern that is the correlate of the consonant [g] for a speaker with a large vocal tract may overlap with the resonant pattern of the consonant [d] for a speaker with a small vocal tract (Rand, 1971). The listener therefore must be able to deduce the size of the speaker's vocal tract before he can assign an acoustic signal to the correct consonantal or vocalic class.

There are a number of ways by which a human listener can infer the size of a speaker's supralaryngeal vocal tract. He can, for example, note the fundamental frequency of phonation. Children, who have smaller vocal tracts, usually have higher fundamental frequencies than adult men or adult women. Adult men, however, have disproportionately lower fundamental frequencies than adult women (Peterson and Barney, 1952), so fundamental frequency is not an infallible cue to vocal tract size. Perceptual experiments (Ladefoged and Broadbent, 1957) have shown that human listeners can make use of the formant frequency range of a short passage of speech to arrive at an estimate of the size of the speaker's vocal tract.[2] Recent experiments, however, show that human listeners do not have to defer their speech decoding until they hear a 2- or 3-sec interval. Instead, they use the vocalic information encoded in a syllable to decode the syllable (Darwin, 1971; Rand, 1971). This may appear to be paradoxical, but it is not. The listener makes use of the formant frequencies and fundamental frequency of the syllable's vowel to assess the size of the vocal tract that produced the syllable.

This brings us back to our discussion of the uncertainty of the listeners in the Peterson and Barney (1952) vowel identification experiment. Sounds like the vowels [i] and [u] are *determinate* in the sense that a particular formant frequency pattern could have been generated by means of only one vocal tract using a particular articulatory maneuver (Stevens and House, 1955; Lindblom and Sundberg, 1969). A listener can use these vowels to instantly identify the size of the supralaryngeal vocal tract that he (or she) is listening to. These vowels can indeed serve the same function in the recognition of human vowels by computer. Gerstman (1967) devised a computer program that assigned *all* of the vowel sounds in the Peterson and Barney study to the phonetic class intended by the speaker. The computer program uses the formant frequencies of the [i] or [u] vowel of each speaker to derive an individual acoustic vowel space. The computer program is then able to assign all the other vowel signals of each speaker into the correct vowel category by partitioning the speaker's acoustic vowel space.

The determinate vowels [i] and [u] and the acoustically stable vowel [a] essentially delimit the individual speaker's vowel space. The other vowels that occur in the speaker's language appear to

---

[2]The listener, of course, has no conscious knowledge of the exact length of the speaker's vocal tract. A listener, for example, could not report that a particular speaker's vocal tract was 17 cm long. This is not surprising since we don't have any conscious knowledge of the entire speech decoding process or for that matter of the detailed mechanics of other processes such as breathing or walking.

be spaced out to perceptually segment the available acoustic range. This appears to be a general principle. A language that had only three vowels would have [i], [u], and [a]. A five-vowel language would partition the vowel space by inserting a vowel equidistant between [i] and [a] and one between [u] and [a]. A language that had seven vowels would insert two vowels between [i] and [a] and two between [u] and [a] (Liljencrants and Lindblom, 1972). It is necessary to know what a particular speaker's vowel space is because a speaker who has a large, long supralaryngeal vocal tract may produce an [ɪ] vowel that has the same formant frequencies as the [æ] vowel of a speaker who has a smaller, shorter supralaryngeal vocal tract.

Vowels like [ɛ], [ɪ], and [ʌ] are indeterminate. A particular speaker can use alternate articulatory maneuvers to generate the acoustic signal that specifies one of the vowels (Stevens and House, 1955). Different speakers who have supralaryngeal vocal tracts that differ in size and length can generate the same acoustic signal by means of different articulatory maneuvers. A speaker whose vocal tract is longer than another's can, for example, produce an acoustically identical [ʌ] vowel by flaring his lips and raising his larynx. The classic articulatory descriptors of traditional phonetics, e.g., "high vowel," "low vowel," "front," and "back" simply are not relevant to these vowels, which are defined by their acoustic relation to the determinate [i], [u], and [a] vowels. Ladefoged et al. (1972), by means of cineradiographic data, for example, have shown that the positions of the tongue body and jaw have no classificatory value in specifying the "front" vowels [ɪ], [ɛ], and [æ]. The indeterminate vowels of a particular speaker essentially "float" with respect to the acoustic space specified by the determinate vowels.

A listener who hears an indeterminate vowel has to guess what the size of the speaker's supralaryngeal vocal tract is; a sound like the fricative [s] will provide a listener with more information. However, vowels like [i] and [u] are optimal "vocal tract calibrating" signals; [i] is perhaps best and [u] next best (Gerstman, 1967). The listeners in the Peterson and Barney experiment therefore had very little difficulty with the [i] or [u] sounds. Their judgments of the [a] vowels, which were nearest to the [a] vowel, were confused with the [ɔ] vowels because of the variability of these vowels across different dialects of American English. They could not classify the indeterminate vowels such as [ɛ] and [ɪ] with certainty because they were uncertain about the size of the speakers' vocal tracts when the sounds appeared in a random sequence. In a recent replication of the Peterson and Barney experiments (Shankweiler et al., 1974) the performance of listeners on these central vowels was five times better when they heard the "precursor" [Hi] before each vowel sound.[3] The determinate vowel lets the listener know the size of the vocal tract he's listening to.

[3] The occurrence of stereotyped, introductory words like *Hi* and *Hey* may indeed have a functional value in letting a listener know the size of the speaker's vocal tract. It's probably significant that telephone conversations almost always open with these words or *Hello* (H. Sarles, personal communication).

Vowels like [i] and [u] thus are really more useful sounds than vowels like [ɪ], [ɛ], and [ʊ]. The former are acoustically stable and they serve as efficient vocal tract calibrating signals. The process of speech decoding that makes human speech a rapid means of communication crucially depends on a listener's knowing the size of the speaker's supralaryngeal vocal tract. It therefore is not surprising to find that these sounds are highly valued and that they occur in all human languages.[4]

THE PHYSIOLOGY OF SPEECH

We have discussed three physiological, i.e., functional, aspects of human speech in this chapter. Two of these factors, speech encoding and determinateness, are closely linked. We shall, in the chapters that follow, show that these factors are in a sense "unique" to *Homo sapiens*. No other living animal appears to have a language that makes use of encoded acoustic signals. Neural mechanisms appear to exist in *Homo sapiens* that are involved in the decoding of speech signals. These neural mechanisms would appear to be the result of a long process of mutation and selective adaptive pressures. *Homo sapiens* also appears to have a "unique" supralaryngeal vocal tract that has adapted to the particular requirements of encoded speech. The supralaryngeal vocal tract of *Homo sapiens* is essentially "matched" to the neural mechanisms that decode speech.

However, we should not dwell on the "uniqueness" of *Homo sapiens*. As Darwin noted, "Evolution proceeds in small steps," and we will attempt to trace the evolution of the human supralaryngeal vocal tract by means of the fossil record. Unfortunately, the fossil record does not permit a direct assessment of the evolution of the neural mechanisms that underlie speech and language, but we will be able to make a number of reasonable inferences from the behavior of living animals and the artifacts of early hominid culture.

Many of the physiological factors that are operant in human speech are also operant in structuring the possible acoustic communications of living nonhuman primates. Although we concentrated on the vowel sounds of human speech in our discussion of *acoustic stability*, it is apparent that this factor also must play a role in determining the "utility" of other speech sounds. Bilabial stops

[4]It is important to note that we are discussing the phonetic rather than the "phonemic" level of language. Statements that a particular language, e.g., Kabardian (Kuipers, 1960), has only one centralized vowel concern the phonemic level: the claim is that a particular language does not minimally differentiate between words at the phonemic level by means of vowel contrasts. At the phonetic level these languages make use of vowels like [i], [u], and [a] as well as glides like [y] and [w], which have similar determinate properties. The presence of these sounds is conditioned by the occurrence of other consonants in the word, so they are not phonemic. However, they do occur in the acoustic signal and guide the listener's speech-perceiving process.

like [b] and [p], for example, occur more frequently than other stops like [d] and [g] in different human languages. Bilabial stops are obviously more stable than other stops because they are produced simply by closing and opening the lips. The position of the lips is, of course, fixed with respect to the rest of the vocal tract. In contrast to the production of [d] and [g], the speaker does not have to even consider the problem of precisely positioning the tongue against some specific location on the palate. The acoustic cue that defines a bilabial stop is also distinct. The formant frequencies all rapidly fall as the lips seal the vocal tract and rise when the lips open (Delattre et al., 1955). Bilabial stops are therefore acoustically stable sounds. Chimpanzees and other nonhuman primates have the physical mechanism that is necessary to produce bilabial stops. The physiological factor of acoustic stability derived from the study of human speech is thus a useful concept in the study of the possible vocal communications of nonhuman primates. We will attempt to keep the gradual nature of evolution and the common elements of human language in view as we look at other aspects of hominid behavior and the phonetic abilities of nonhuman primates.

Comparative Studies of Speech Production in Primates

8

Comparative studies of the speech-producing abilities of nonhuman primates and humans are not new. They date back to at least the end of the seventeenth century, when Perrault (1676) and Tyson (1699) used the methods of comparative anatomy to demonstrate similarities between the larynges of the chimpanzee and *Homo sapiens.* The role of the supralaryngeal vocal tract was not understood, and the larynx was mistakenly identified as the primary anatomical structure necessary for the production of human speech. Chimpanzees appeared to have a larynx similar to the human larynx, so these early studies concluded that the chimpanzee had speech-producing anatomy necessary for the production of "articulate" human speech. Its speech deficiencies were supposed to be solely due to a lack of mental ability or of neural control of the speech-producing apparatus, e.g., tongue, lips, and larynx.

These views regarding the mental limitations of nonhuman primates were in keeping with the philosophical discourse and debate of the seventeenth and eighteenth centuries. In the first half of the seventeenth century Descartes (1892, 1955) had developed his concept of the *bête machine;* i.e., animals are machines or mechanisms. In contrast to all animals, only humans were supposed to possess abstract thought and language. Animals supposedly had the anatomical mechanisms that would allow them to talk to people, but no animals in fact were able to converse or argue with humans; it was demonstrable that they lacked human language. A vital human quality necessary for language, the brain to "rationalists," the brain and "soul" to Descartes, thus was lacking in animals. La Mettrie (1747), in *de l'Homme Machine,* for example argued that humans were also machines and that the "soul" was an irrelevant factor. La Mettrie accepted the "fact" that apes had the necessary vocal apparatus for speech. He said that apes were, in effect, retarded people who had slightly deficient brains. La Mettrie believed that with a little effort it should be possible to teach an ape to talk, say, if it were carefully tutored as though it were a deaf child. The ape would then, in La Mettrie's words, "be a perfect little gentleman." This supposedly would demonstrate the nonexistence of the "soul."

The belief that apes have a sound-producing apparatus adequate for speech production has persisted to the present time. Osgood (1953), for example, states that the "chimpanzee is capable of vocalizations almost as elaborate as man's." Yerkes and Learned (1925) identified more than 32 human speech sounds for the chimpanzee. Attempts to teach chimpanzees to talk continued until quite recently. A study by Hayes (1952) applied without success the method suggested by La Mettrie: a chimpanzee was raised as though it were a retarded child. However, no one has ever been able to teach a chimpanzee to talk (Kellogg, 1968).

A number of attempts have been made to demonstrate that the chimpanzee lacks the necessary vocal apparatus by examining the detailed anatomy of its larynx. However, though it is evident that the chimpanzee larynx is not identical to the human larynx (Kelemen, 1948, 1958, 1961), the most one can demonstrate is that the speech of a chimpanzee wouldn't be as pleasing to humans as human speech. The fundamental frequency would be higher and phonation might have a breathy quality, but these factors would limit a potential chimpanzee language no more than they limit human language. The laryngeal source, as we have seen, is not the important factor in the production of human speech. The role of the supralaryngeal vocal tract as an acoustic filter was not generally appreciated until the past few years. Although the primary research on the source-filter theory of human speech production dates back to the end of the eighteenth century and is discussed in Müller's comprehensive handbook of physiology (1848), modern quantitative studies really began to develop in the years before World War II. The general availability of digital computers in the 1950s resulted in rapid progress, but the results of work such as that of Fant (1960) and Chiba and Kajiyama (1958) did not become widely known until the 1960s. There still is a certain degree of confusion on this matter outside of the specialized literature on acoustic phonetics. The functional, physiological aspects of human speech are still not generally appreciated by most anthropologists and linguists. Meaningful comparative analyses of the vocalizations of various primates can be made; however, the physiological factors that make some vocal signals more useful than others (discussed in Chapters 6 and 7) must be taken into account.

DIRECT ACOUSTIC ANALYSIS

The most obvious way to compare the vocal abilities of primates is to record and analyze the signals that various primates produce, although there are some inherent limitations to the conclusions that can be drawn from the acoustic analysis of any particular sample of animal sounds. One can never be certain that *all* of the possible vocalizations of a particular species have been recorded. It is also difficult to say anything about the relative frequencies of occurrence of particular sounds. These limitations would apply to the analysis of the vocalizations of human speakers. The particular sounds recorded would depend on the particular language or dialect of the speaker. The sample of utterances might also depend on the particular social or situational context. Despite these limitations, it obviously is better to have an analysis of some of the sounds than no analysis at all.

The simplest way of obtaining recordings of the vocalizations of nonhuman primates is to record captive animals. This obviously raises serious questions about how representative the recorded sample will be of the animals' communications in their natural environments. We can, however, determine what aspects of their recorded vocalizations are similar to human speech and what aspects are different. If our acoustic analysis is structured in terms of the anatomical basis of speech production, we can begin to determine the articulatory and anatomical bases of these differences so that we can tell with greater certainty the direction in which human speech-producing ability has evolved from these related animals. The acoustic analysis, of course, has to be directed. It has to look for the presence or absence of the phonetic features that convey meaningful information in human speech as well as potential features that may not occur in human speech. We can perhaps best illustrate both the utility and the limits of direct acoustic analysis by reviewing the results of some recent studies. We will also discuss the use of the sound spectrograph and other instruments in this context. The results of an acoustic analysis are significant only insofar as the reader understands the limits and artifacts that may be introduced by the particular instrumentation and signal processing.

We will begin with a relatively simple example. In Figure 8-1 a spectrogram of one of the vocalizations of a 3-year-old female gorilla (*Gorilla gorilla*) is presented. The vertical axis in Figure 8-1

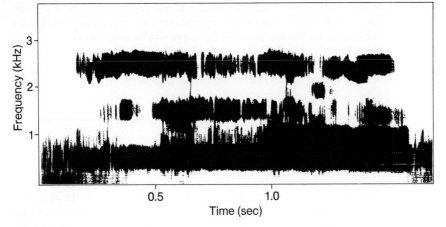

Figure 8-1 Spectrogram of cry produced at moderate intensity by 3-year-old gorilla. The bandwidth of the analyzing filter was 300 Hz. The fundamental frequency of phonation ranged from 100 to 120 Hz. The configuration of the gorilla's supralaryngeal vocal tract apparently approximated a uniform tube open at one end, the "schwa" vowel, because the formant frequencies of the cry occurred at 0.5, 1.5, and 2.4 kHz. (From Lieberman, 1968.)

is a frequency scale. Time is plotted on the horizontal axis. The dark areas in the spectrogram show the presence of relative energy concentrations in the acoustic signal after the complex processing of the spectrograph's electronic circuitry. The dark patch that lines up with 2.4 kHz on the frequency scale indicates that a relative energy maximum occurred at this frequency after approximately 0.25 sec. We see that this energy concentration started at about 0.25 sec by referring to the time scale on the horizontal axis. The dark area at 2.4 kHz forms a sort of "bar" that extends through the entire vocalization. Two other "bars" also occur, at approximately 0.5 and 1.5 kHz. Note the presence of vertical striations in the spectrogram; these striations actually occur throughout the dark "bars" but don't show up well when reproduced. The dark "bars," in other words, are not solid.

What is the interpretation of this spectrogram? In order to interpret it we have to know that it has been produced by means of the 300-Hz bandwidth filter of the sound spectrograph. (The machine is called the *spectrograph*; its output is the *spectrogram*.) In Chapter 5 we noted that the acoustic speech signal of a voiced sound is the result of the supralaryngeal vocal tract filtering the laryngeal source. The 300-Hz bandwidth filter of the sound spectrograph allows energy to build up for each fundamental period of the acoustic signal.[1] These periodic energy peaks are manifested

[1] As the bandwidth of an analyzing filter increases, its ability to respond to temporal variations also increases (Flanagan, 1972, pp. 144–155).

in the vertical striations in the spectrogram. The sound spectrograph, in effect, transforms the periodic variations that can be seen in the waveform of a voiced sound such as that shown in Figure 5-6 into vertical striations.

The vertical striations in the spectrogram made with the 300 Hz bandwidth filter thus provide us with information about the activity of the gorilla's larynx. The periodicity of the glottal signal shows up in the spectrogram—the shorter the periodicity, the closer the striations will appear. We therefore can readily calculate the fundamental frequency of phonation because the number of periods that occur in a given interval of time can be seen on the spectrogram. The bandwidth of the sound spectrograph's analyzing filter must, however, be set to its "wide-band," 300 Hz setting to resolve the individual glottal cycles. In Figure 8-1, ten to twelve of these striations occur in 0.1 sec in various parts of this spectrogram. We thus can tell that the fundamental frequency of phonation of the gorilla cry varied from 100 to 120 Hz in this cry.

The horizontally oriented "bars" at 0.5, 1.5, and 2.4 kHz in this spectrogram signal the presence of formant frequencies. As we noted in Chapter 5, the formant frequencies are the frequencies at which maximum energy will pass through the supralaryngeal vocal tract. The sound spectrograph makes use of electronic processing that produces dark bars at, or near, the formant frequencies *so long as the filter bandwidth of the machine is at least twice the fundamental frequency* (cf. Flanagan, 1972). This relates back to the point we noted in Chapter 5, that conventional sound spectrographs having "wide-band" filters of 300 Hz work best for speakers whose fundamental frequencies are less than 120 Hz. The electronic processing of the sound spectrograph is also sensitive to the recorded level of the acoustic signal. The techniques and knowledge necessary for the actual production and interpretation of spectrograms are beyond the scope of this discussion. The reader can usefully refer to Koenig et al. (1946) and Flanagan (1972) as well as to the manuals that accompany particular sound spectrographs. The point that we want to emphasize here is that the output of the sound spectrograph, the spectrogram, can be interpreted. However, artifacts that may be introduced through either the process of tape recording or the electronic processing of the sound spectrograph must be identified.

Our detailed interpretation of the spectrogram of Figure 8-1 really is based in part on our knowledge of the physiology of speech production, the acoustics of speech, and the characteristics of the sound spectrograph. We can see that the fundamental frequency of phonation was unstable and ranged from 100 to 120 Hz. Large pitch perturbations, i.e., rapid fluctuations in the glottal periodicity, occurred from one period to the next. These variations in periodicity are not typical of normal human speech (Lieberman, 1960) but do tend to occur in certain abnormal larynges (Lieberman, 1963a). Human speakers who have these abnormal larynges produce "hoarse"-sounding speech. The overall spectrum also indicates that the fundamental glottal spectrum has more energy in its higher harmonics than is usually the case for human vocalizations. This inference follows from the fact that the spectrogram was made without using the high-frequency compensation that is necessary for analyzing human speech.[2] The increased high-frequency content of the glottal spectrum also occurs in "breathy" or "hoarse" human phonation. Kelemen's (1958, 1961, 1969) anatomical studies of the larynges of nonhuman primates thus are correct insofar as the laryngeal source in the gorilla would yield a hoarse and unpleasant sound *to human ears*. Other vocalizations of the gorilla demonstrate similar variations in periodicity.

However, the activity of the larynx is not the primary factor in determining the properties of human speech. The supralaryngeal vocal tract's filtering properties are the crucial element. What can we say about the supralaryngeal vocal tract's activity in the vocalization pictured in Figure 8-1? Note that energy concentrations can be seen in Figure 8-1 at 0.5, 1.5, and 2.4 kHz. Measurements of the skull and mandible of an adult gorilla yield an estimated supralaryngeal vocal tract length of about 18 cm. If a gorilla uttered the "schwa" vowel [Λ] (the first vowel in the word *about*), i.e., a vowel having a supralaryngeal vocal tract shape that approximates a uniform tube open at one end, we would expect to find formant frequencies at 0.46, 1.4, and 2.3 kHz. The situation is that we discussed on pp. 62–64 for an idealized [Λ] vowel. The formant frequencies of a uniform tube open at one end will occur at intervals of

$$\frac{(2k + 1)C}{4L} \tag{1}$$

where C is the velocity of sound, L is the length of the tube, and k is an integer ≥ 0 (i.e., $k = 0, 1, 2, 3, \ldots$). It is, moreover, not important that the tube be exactly uniform. A tube shaped like a trumpet, i.e., slightly flared, would have similar, slightly higher, formant frequencies (Fant, 1960). We can therefore infer that the energy concentrations in the spectrogram of Figure 8-1 reflect the filter function of the gorilla's supralaryngeal vocal tract in a "schwa" position.

Note that the formant frequencies are not spaced at harmonic multiples of the fundamental frequency. The characteristic of this vocalization that we want to stress is that the output of the gorilla's larynx is being filtered by the supralaryngeal vocal tract, as is the

[2] The spectrogram was made using the "FLAT" position of the spectrograph. As we noted in Chapter 5, the human glottal source has a spectrum in which the amplitude falls at about 6 db per octave (cf. Figure 5-3). The sound spectrograph won't produce satisfactory results unless the amplitude of the signal falls into a particular, specified range. For example, if the spectrograph is overloaded, the entire spectrogram will be darkened. Human speech must be processed using a high-frequency compensating circuit. The vocalizations of nonhuman primates generally contain more energy at higher frequencies, so the spectrograph must be operated without this high-frequency circuit, in its "FLAT" position (cf. Koenig et al., 1946).

case for human speech. The gorilla vocalization, like human speech, must be analyzed in terms of the activity of the laryngeal source and the area function of the supralaryngeal vocal tract.

We can see this crucial aspect of speech production in the vocalizations of other nonhuman primates. In Figure 8-2 a spectrogram of a cry produced at a low degree of vocal effort by a 2-year-old chimpanzee (*Pan troglodytes*) is presented. The bandwidth of the spectrograph's analyzing filter was 300 Hz. The cry consisted of two "bursts" of phonation at 150 and 210 Hz separated by an interval of about 0.3 sec. The fundamental frequency again is apparent in the vertical striations of the original spectrogram. The spectrogram shows formant frequencies at 0.65, 1.65, and 3.1 kHz. The chimpanzee's lips were observed to be protruded and rounded when it made this cry. If its vocal tract had approximated a 13-cm uniform tube open at one end, we would expect formant frequencies at 0.62, 1.86, and 3.1 kHz. The first formant, F_1, is actually somewhat higher, whereas the second formant, F_2, is somewhat lower. This shows that the chimpanzee is capable of modifying the cross-sectional area function to produce signals that in a human would deviate from the [Λ] vowel toward [a]. The chimpanzee supralaryngeal vocal tract thus can change its filtering properties to produce formant frequency variations.

This is more apparent in the spectrogram of Figure 8-3, which is a cry produced at a high degree of vocal effort by the same 2-year-old chimpanzee. The bandwidth of the spectrograph's analyzing filter was 300 Hz. The vertical striations that reflect the fundamental frequency of phonation can easily be seen in this spectrogram. The fundamental frequency of phonation during the

Figure 8-2 Spectrogram of cry produced at low degree of vocal effort by 2-year-old chimpanzee. The bandwidth of the analyzing filter was 300 Hz. The fundamental frequency was 150 and 210 Hz, respectively, for the two "bursts." The formant frequencies occurred at 0.65, 1.65, and 3.1 kHz. The chimpanzee's supralaryngeal vocal tract thus approximated a slightly flared [a]—like uniform tube open at one end. (From Lieberman, 1968.)

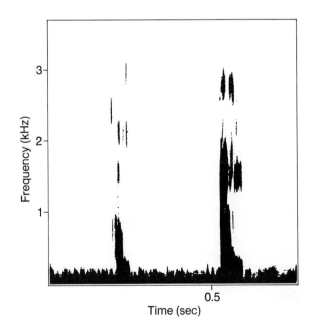

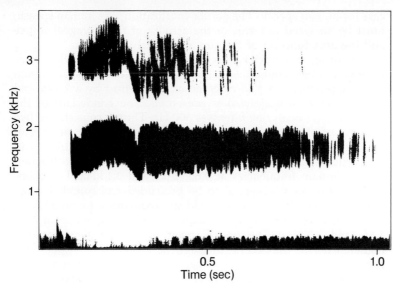

Figure 8-3 Spectrogram of cry produced at high level of intensity by 2-year-old chimpanzee. The bandwidth of the analyzing filter was 300 Hz. Note the presence of voicing "striations" during the transitions in the initial part of the cry. The fundamental frequency of phonation was 140 Hz. The transitions thus must reflect changes in the length of the supralaryngeal vocal tract. (From Lieberman, 1968.)

initial part of the cry was relatively steady at about 240 Hz. The two energy concentrations at 1.5 and 2.8 kHz occurred after the initial part of the vocalization, where there were transitions from 1.3 to 1.7 to 1.3 kHz and from 2.8 to 3.2 to 2.5 kHz. These energy concentrations must reflect the filter function of the chimpanzee's supralaryngeal vocal tract. The overall length of the supralaryngeal vocal tract must have been initially decreasing and then increasing, because F_1 and F_2 rise and fall together.

The chimpanzee's lips appeared to be retracted and immobile when it uttered this cry. It probably moved its larynx forward and backward to change the length of its supralaryngeal vocal tract during the early part of the utterance in Figure 8-3. Similar motions of the larynx can be observed in adult human speech (Perkell, 1969; Ladefoged et al., 1972) and in the vocalizations of newborn humans (Truby et al., 1965). Many human languages appear to differentiate speech sounds by means of formant frequency transitions that are the consequence of laryngeal movements that change the overall length of the supralaryngeal vocal tract (Chomsky and Halle, 1968). Chimpanzees appear to have the same mechanism available. The anatomical basis for the two binary phonetic features *formant raising* and *formant lowering* (cf. p. 64) is therefore present in the chimpanzee.

Energy concentrations that reflect the presence of formant frequencies at 1.5, 2.8, and 4.5 kHz occurred during the steady-state portion of this cry. Because the chimpanzee's lips were retracted when it produced this cry, in contrast to the cry of Figure 8-2 where its lips were protruded and rounded, the overall length of its supra-laryngeal vocal tract was closer to 12 cm than to 13 cm. The formant frequencies of a uniform 12-cm tube open at both ends are 1.4, 2.8, and 4.2 kHz. If the chimpanzee's vocal tract approximated a uniform tube, open at both ends, we would expect to find the energy concentrations that are apparent in Figure 8-3. The chimpanzee's glottal opening would have to be large during the cry for this to be true. This may be what happened. Kelemen (1948), in his anatomical study of the chimpanzee larynx, notes the presence of the "hiatus intervocalis," i.e., an opening of the glottis that is always present. The cry in Figure 8-3 was produced at a high degree of vocal effort, where the chimpanzee was probably using a high subglottal air pressure (Lieberman, 1967). In the absence of a con-current increase in the tension of the muscles that keep the vocal cords together (the medial compressors; Van den Berg, 1960) the vocal cords will be blown apart. The net effect of the hiatus inter-vocalis and the high degree of vocal effort thus would be an open glottis and the formant frequencies indicated by Figure 8-3.

In Figure 8-4 a spectrogram of a cry produced by a newborn human 7 min after birth is presented. This spectrogram is of inter-

Figure 8-4 Spectrogram of human cry produced 7 min after birth. The cry started with periodic excitation and shifted to aperiodic excitation. Note initial formants at 1.25, 3.0, and 5.0 kHz. Energy concentrations then shifted to 2.25 and 4.8 kHz with aperiodic excitation. The supralaryngeal vocal tract configuration apparently approximated a tube with uniform boundary conditions when the glottal opening was large during the aperiodic breathy excitation. (From Lieberman et al., 1972a.)

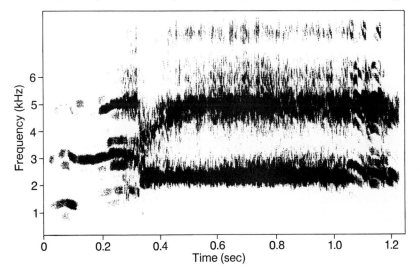

est because it shows some of the same phenomena as the two chimpanzee cries that have been discussed. The cry started with a well-defined periodic structure. The harmonics of the fundamental frequency each show up as a separate band because the fundamental frequency was about 500 Hz. However, careful adjustment of the recording level on the sound spectrograph permits a reasonable estimate of the formant frequencies. Energy concentrations were present during the initial, voiced part of the cry at 1.25, 3.0, and 5.0 kHz. Note that the cry lost its harmonic structure after 0.3 sec, where the spectrogram shows that it became noisy. We can tell that the cry was noisy after 0.3 sec because the harmonics of the fundamental that appear as parallel "wavy" lines on the initial part of the spectrogram disappear.[3]

Note the abrupt discontinuity in the first energy concentration in Figure 8-4, which shifted to about 2.25 kHz. The second energy concentration also shifted to about 4.8 kHz during the noisy part of this cry. The formant frequencies abruptly shifted when the glottal excitation became noisy. The supralaryngeal vocal tract was apparently approximating a uniform tube open at both ends during the noisy part of this cry, which therefore has a formant pattern like the chimpanzee cry in Figure 8-3. In contrast, during the initial part of the cry the infant's supralaryngeal vocal tract was apparently approximating a uniform tube closed at one end, as in the chimpanzee cry in Figure 8-2. The formant frequencies of a uniform tube open at both ends will occur at intervals of

$$\frac{(k)(C)}{2L} \tag{2}$$

where C is the velocity of sound, L is the length of the tube, and k is an integer ≥ 1 (i.e., $k = 1, 2, \ldots$). The first formant frequency of a supralaryngeal vocal tract that resembles a uniform tube will double in frequency when the "boundary condition" at the larynx changes from a closed to an open state. This is what we notice happening in Figure 8-4. The formant frequencies were initially consistent with the expected formants of a supralaryngeal vocal tract that approximates a uniform tube closed at one end. The second and third formants were 3.0 and 5.0 kHz. Equation (1) predicts that the second and third formants of a uniform tube closed at one end will be 3.0 and 5.0 kHz if $F_1 = 1.0$ kHz. F_1 as measured from Figure 8-4 appears to be about 1.25 kHz, but it may have been somewhat lower. The harmonics of the glottal source are too far apart (approximately 500 Hz) to make a precise determination possible from the spectrogram. After 0.3 sec the first formant abruptly shifted to 2.25 kHz, approximately twice its previous

---

[3] There are no vertical striations in the spectrogram at the fundamental period. The spectrogram was made using the "narrow-band" 50 Hz bandwidth analyzing filter of the spectrograph, which has a "sluggish" temporal response. The individual harmonic components of the glottal excitation instead appear as discrete horizontal wavy lines in the spectrogram. The horizontal lines are wavy because the infant's fundamental frequency was not steady and went up and down. If the fundamental frequency were steady, the horizontal lines would be straight.

value. The "new" second formant also abruptly shifted to approximately twice the value of the "new" first formant, as equation (2) predicts. The "old" formant at 3.0 kHz disappeared.

The infant did not abruptly change the overall length of his vocal tract to change the formant patterns. His larynx instead appears to have changed from a closed to an open state. This could occur if the infant increased his subglottal air pressure and failed to increase the muscular forces that act to move the vocal cords closed during the phonatory cycle. He would blow his vocal cords apart, producing noiselike aperiodic excitation, and he would also terminate his supralaryngeal vocal tract with an open glottis.

Truby et al. (1965), in their study of neonatal vocalizations, present a number of spectrograms that show effects similar to those in Figure 8-4. They also present simultaneous plots of air pressure for some of these cries showing that these effects (noiselike excitation and formant patterns consistent with a supralaryngeal vocal tract terminated by an open glottis) occur when the subglottal air pressure exceeds a critical value (about 6 cm H_2O over the mean subglottal air pressure[4]). The infant's vocal cords are then thrown into an open position because he apparently does not increase the tension of the muscles that apply "medial compression" (Van den Berg, 1960) to his vocal cords.

Close examination of the spectrograms of the cries of 20 newborn infants (Lieberman et al., 1972a) revealed no formant patterns inconsistent with a supralaryngeal vocal tract that substantially remained a uniform or slightly flared tube. In some instances the formants all moved higher or lower in frequency during the course of the cry, as in the chimpanzee cry in Figure 8-3. About 80 per cent of the cries appeared to have been made with the glottis closed, phonation occurred throughout the cries, and the formant frequency pattern was close to that predicted by equation (1). About 20 per cent of the cries appeared to be made with an open glottis. The excitation was noisy and the formant pattern approximated that predicted by equation (2). Similar results are evident in Lynip's (1951) spectrographic analysis of the utterances produced by one girl from birth to 60 weeks of age. The subjective transcriptions of Irwin (1948) also are consistent with this finding as are the sound-synchronized cineradiographic studies of Truby et al. (1965). The range of formant frequency variation of the newborn is quite restricted compared to that of an adult human speaker.

The range of formant variation of the newborn human is moreover very similar to that observable in nonhuman primates (Lieberman, 1968). The spectrogram in Figure 8-5 of a cry produced by a human infant in the first 5 min of life is quite similar to the gorilla cry in Figure 8-1 if the differing vocal tract lengths are taken into account. The formant frequencies occurred at approximately 1.1, 3.3, and 5.8 kHz. They therefore conform to equation (1).

In Figure 8-6 the spectrogram of an aggressive "bark" of a rhesus

---

[4]Air pressure can be measured in terms of the equivalent pressure exerted by a column of water (H_2O).

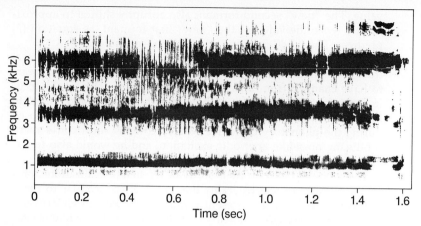

Figure 8-5 Spectrogram of human cry produced during first 5 min of life. The fundamental frequency was about 0.4 kHz. Note the formant frequencies at 1.1, 3.3, and 5.8 kHz. (From Lieberman et al., 1972a.)

monkey is presented. Formant frequencies occurred at approximately 1, 3, and 6–8 kHz. The bandwidth of the spectrograph's analyzing filter was increased to 1.2 kHz by playing the tape recording into the spectrograph at one-fourth normal speed. An oscillogram of the signal is presented in Figure 8-7, which shows the actual waveform of the acoustic signal. The amplitude of the acoustic signal is plotted with respect to the vertical axis. The fundamental frequency of phonation was about 400 Hz and was determined from the oscillogram. (The periodicity of the waveform

Figure 8-6 Spectrogram of aggressive "bark" of rhesus monkey. The bandwidth of the anlyzing filter was 1.2 kHz. Formant frequencies occurred at 1, 3, and 6–8 kHz. (From Lieberman, 1968.)

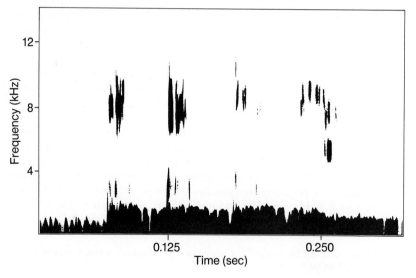

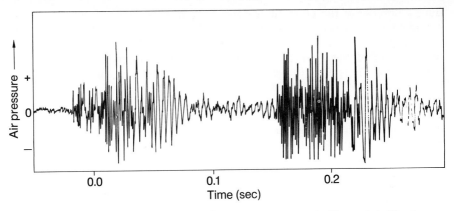

Figure 8-7 Oscillogram of same utterance as in Figure 8-6. The tape recording was played at one-quarter speed. The fundamental frequency of phonation was about 400 Hz. The waveform resembles that characteristic of extremely hoarse human vocalization. (From Lieberman, 1968.)

is apparent on the oscillogram.) Note that the cry is quite similar to the chimpanzee vocalization pictured in Figure 8-2. The formant frequencies of the rhesus monkey cry were scaled up in frequency because the supralaryngeal vocal tract of the rhesus monkey is much smaller than that of an adult chimpanzee. Both vocalizations had formant frequencies in accord with equation (1). The rhesus monkey's was higher in frequency simply because its supralaryngeal vocal tract is smaller. The rhesus monkey "bark" also had a faster temporal pattern than the chimpanzee vocalization. Both appear to involve the same sort of supralaryngeal vocal tract shape. The range of phonetic variation of the cries of nonhuman primates appears to be fairly limited. For example, sounds like the human vowels [i] and [u] never seem to occur (Lieberman, 1968; Bastian, 1965).

THE PHONETIC REPERTOIRE OF NONHUMAN PRIMATES

The acoustic analysis of the comparatively small sample of vocalizations that we have illustrated in this chapter would not in itself be sufficient to let us come to any positive conclusions regarding the possible phonetic repertoires of nonhuman primates. However, we can draw on other acoustic analyses (Andrew, 1963; Lieberman, 1972) as well as our knowledge of the anatomy of these animals (Negus, 1949) and the source-filter theory of speech production that we reviewed in Chapter 5. If we bring this information to bear on the analyzed data sample, it is clear that nonhuman primates have the speech-producing anatomy that *would* allow them to produce a number of the phonetic features of human speech, i.e., the sound contrasts that convey meaningful information. Note that we are not claiming that nonhuman primates in fact make use of all of these possibilities. Indeed, no individual human language makes use of *all* of the phonetic features that human speakers can inherently produce. We will instead note some of the phonetic features that nonhuman primates could produce with their speech-producing anatomy. The value of this analysis is that it may lend some new directions to the future analysis of the vocal communications of nonhuman primates. It would be interesting to see whether animals such as chimpanzees in fact make use of a subset of the phonetic features that typify human language. It would be equally important to discover that chimpanzees did not make use of the phonetic possibilities inherent in their speech-producing mechanisms. In one case, we would gain crucial insights into the nature of communication in chimpanzees; i.e., we would begin to understand how chimpanzees communicate.

If we found that chimpanzees did not make use of the full range of phonetic sound contrasts that their speech-producing mechanism could make, we would have to concentrate on their gestural communication and perhaps look for the presence of neural distinctions between *Homo sapiens* and the chimpanzee that make sound signals more useful for humans. We will discuss some aspects of the perception of speech in humans and sound communication in other animals in Chapter 11. Various psychoacoustic and neuroelectric techniques are available that can yield answers to these questions. For the moment let's return to the question of the possible phonetic repertoire of a "typical" nonhuman primate. We'll first discuss phonetic features that would be common to humans and nonhuman primates and then some phonetic possibilities that might be exclusive to certain nonhumans.

We'll start by discussing phonetic features that involve the laryngeal source. As Negus (1949) observes, there is a continual elaboration of the larynx as we ascend the phylogenetic scale in terrestrial animals. Negus demonstrates (cf. Chapter 3) that the elaboration of the larynx does not confer any selective advantages with respect to either respiratory efficiency or the protection of the lungs from the intrusion of foreign bodies. The larynges of animals such as wolves are capable of producing a number of distinct calls that could serve as vehicles of vocal communication. The same is true for the larynges of nonhuman primates; theirs appear to have adapted, in part, for phonation. It is perhaps not as obvious as the case of wolf cries, because primates typically do not produce long continuing cries where modulations of fundamental frequency become very apparent. Neither do humans typically produce long sustained episodes of phonation. Studies such as Kelemen's (1948) that have attempted to show that chimpanzees cannot talk because of laryngeal deficiencies are not correct. Kelemen shows that the chimpanzee's larynx is different from the larynx of a normal adult human male and will not produce the same range of fundamental frequencies. Moreover, the spectrum (cf. Chapters 4 and 5) of the chimpanzee's glottal source will be different from that of a normal adult human male. The spectrograms discussed in this chapter show that there is much more energy at higher harmonics of the fundamental frequency than is the case for a typical human speaker. The chimpanzee's voice thus would sound "harsh"—to a human listener! However, human listeners don't really count with regard to chimpanzees. Female chimpanzees also don't look very pretty to adult human males, but it doesn't really matter. Kelemen does show that chimpanzees could not sign with the Metropolitan Opera Company. However, chimpanzees and other pongids and New and Old World monkeys probably could produce the following phonetic features by making use of laryngeal and subglottal articulatory maneuvers.

Voiced versus unvoiced

The supralaryngeal vocal tract could be excited either by the quasiperiodic excitation of the larynx or by means of noise generated by air turbulence. Air turbulence will occur whenever the flow of air exceeds a critical value. During phonation the vocal cords are adducted, i.e., moved together and closed or nearly closed, and the flow of air through the larynx is relatively low. In humans turbulent noise generally does not occur during the production of *voiced* vowels, i.e., vowels produced with normal phonation. In the production of a sound like [h], the first sound in *Harry*, the vocal cords are in a more open position. The resulting air flow is much higher (Klatt et al., 1968), and noise is generated at the glottal orifice. The noise is filtered by the supralaryngeal vocal tract to produce the sound [h]. The sound spectrograms in Figures 8-1 and 8-3 show noiselike sounds. It is perfectly clear that nonhuman primates can produce sounds that are either *voiced*, e.g., the sound in the spectrogram of Figure 8-2, or *unvoiced*.

High fundamental versus
normal fundamental frequency

Several studies (Van den Berg, 1960; Atkinson, 1973) have shown that the human larynx can be adjusted so that phonation occurs in what is known as the falsetto register. The fundamental frequency of phonation in this register is higher than it is in the normal register. The mode of operation of the larynx is actually somewhat different in these two registers (Van den Berg, 1960; Lieberman, 1967). The spectrum of the glottal source also changes in falsetto, and comparatively little energy occurs at higher-frequency harmonics of the fundamental. The larynges of nonhuman primates inherently should be capable of producing this distinction (Negus, 1949; Wind, 1970).

Low fundamental frequency versus
normal fundamental frequency

The larynx likewise may be adjusted to phonate at a low fundamental frequency. This lower register, termed "fry," produces very low fundamental frequencies (Hollien et al., 1966) that are quite irregular (Lieberman, 1963a). Human speakers often sound hoarse when they phonate in their "fry" register. Recent electromyographic data from monitoring of the electrical activity of various laryngeal muscles show that distinct muscular adjustments initiate phonation in this low fundamental frequency register (Atkinson, 1973).

Dynamic fundamental frequency variations

Virtually all human languages make use of dynamic variations in the temporal pattern of fundamental frequency (Lieberman, 1967). In languages like Chinese dynamic tone patterns, i.e., rapid changes in fundamental frequency, differentiate words. The syllables [má] and [mà] in Chinese transmit two different words. (The symbol [´] indicates a rising fundamental frequency contour and the symbol [`] a falling one.) The spectrograms of chimpanzee and gorilla vocalizations typically show fundamental frequency variations that could serve as phonetic features based on dynamic fundamental frequency variations. Vocalizations could be differentiated by means of either rising or falling patterns or combinations of rising and falling contours with high or low fundamental frequencies. The sounds might again be "harsh"-sounding to a human ear (Kelemen, 1948) but they could serve as meaningful phonetic features.

Strident laryngeal output

The high fundamental frequency cries mixed with breathy, i.e., noisy, excitation that can be observed in the spectrograms and oscillograms of Figures 8-3 and 8-4 for nonhuman primates and newborn humans constitute a phonetic feature. Speakers of American English sometimes make use of this phonetic feature to convey emotional qualities. The phonetic feature does not have a strictly "linguistic" role in American English because it is not used to convey different words. This is not a crucial objection to our noting the possible use of this sound contrast as a phonetic feature. Many sound contrasts that serve as phonetic features in other languages are not used in English, e.g., the dynamic fundamental frequency variations that are used in Chinese. English is not the "universal" language, and the native speaker's intuitions regarding what is "natural" and what is "unnatural" are not particularly useful. Our intuitions are likely to be tainted by what Francis Bacon (1620) termed "The Idols of the Theatre" and "The Idols of the Tribe."[5]

The breath-group

The *breath-group*, which we discussed in Chapter 6, could likewise function as a phonetic feature for nonhuman primates.

[5]Bacon was discussing the limitations of unaided human perception and the influence of tradition with regard to the findings of the "new" physics. Heavy and light stones fall at the same rate though human "intuition" had held that heavy ones surely must fall faster. Telescopes likewise revealed a new picture of the solar system and stars that differed from that of the unaided eye. Intuition was useless in resolving the differing claims of sun-centered versus earth-centered astronomical theories. We likewise cannot rely on intuition with respect to language.

Phonation onset

The anatomical basis of the phonetic feature *phonation onset*, which we also discussed in Chapter 6, rests in the independent nature of the laryngeal source and the supralaryngeal vocal tract. All primates thus can, in principle, make use of this sound contrast as a phonetic feature.

Stop

The feature *phonation onset* obviously involves articulatory maneuvers in the supralaryngeal vocal tract. The supralaryngeal vocal tract must be occluded to produce sounds like the English "stops" [p] and [b]. All primates inherently can occlude their supralaryngeal vocal tracts to produce the phonetic feature *stop*.

Consonantal "place of articulation"

The point at which the supralaryngeal vocal tract can be occluded can vary. All primates can close their vocal tracts by moving their lips together. A *bilabial* point of articulation thus is a possibility for all primates. A *dental* point of occlusion or constriction, which is effected in adult *Homo sapiens* by moving the tongue up toward the hard palate, also could be a phonetic possibility for all primates, as cineradiographic studies of the swallowing movements of newborn *Homo sapiens* (Truby et al., 1965) indicate. The supralaryngeal vocal tract can be occluded at the level of the glottis, i.e., at the level of the vocal cords, in all primates. This follows from one of the surviving, basic, vegetative functions of the larynx, which can close to protect the lungs from the intrusion of foreign material. A *glottal* point of articulation is thus a possibility for all primates. A chimpanzee has the speech-producing anatomy that would, *with the proper muscular controls,* be sufficient to allow it to produce the English sounds [b], [p], [t], [d] and the glottal stop [?] as well as prevoiced dental and bilabial stops like those that occur, for example, in Spanish. Glottal stops normally are not used to differentiate words in English, though they occur in many dialects of English. They are used more extensively in many other languages, e.g., Danish. It is important to note that the phonetic feature *consonantal point of articulation* is a multivalued feature and that we are simply discussing the *upper* bounds set by the gross anatomy of primates. An animal would have to possess the neural and muscular control that is necessary to position the tongue against the palate during speech at a precise moment if the *dental* point of articulation were to be realized.

Adult *Homo sapiens* differs from all other primates insofar as additional points of articulation are present. We will return to this important aspect of human speech production in the following chapters.

Continuant versus interrupted

Sounds may be differentiated either by being prolonged without interruptions or by being interrupted. The spectrograms of Figures 8-2 and 8-6 illustrate this phonetic feature, which can be effected either by direct control of the laryngeal muscles to start and stop phonation or by occlusion of the supralaryngeal vocal tract.

Formant frequency raising

All primates can shorten the length of their supralaryngeal vocal tracts at the "front" end by flaring and/or pulling their lips back. In adult *Homo sapiens* the supralaryngeal vocal tract can also be shortened at its "back" end by pulling the larynx upward as much as 20 mm during the course of a single word (Perkell, 1969). The mobility of the larynx is comparatively restricted in newborn *Homo sapiens* (Truby et al., 1965; Negus, 1949) and in nonhuman primates (Negus, 1949). The reduction in laryngeal mobility follows both from the position of the larynx with respect to the supralaryngeal vocal tract and from the fact that the hyoid bone is very close to the thyroid cartilage (Negus, 1949). The reduction in laryngeal mobility in forms other than adult humans can be observed in radiographic pictures of both speech and swallowing (Negus, 1949; Truby et al., 1965). For example, the larynx moves upward and forward during swallowing in adult humans, whereas it only moves forward during swallowing in newborn humans.

The acoustic consequence of shortening the length of the supralaryngeal vocal tract—irrespective of the articulatory maneuvers that effect the shortening—is a rising formant frequency pattern. This can, for example, be seen in the spectrogram in Figure 8-3.

Formant frequency lowering

All primates can also lengthen their supralaryngeal vocal tracts by protruding their lips or by moving their larynges downward or backward. Adult humans again have more freedom in this regard because the human larynx has greater mobility. Closing the lips to produce a smaller orifice at the mouth has the same acoustic effect as increasing the length of the supralaryngeal vocal tract (Stevens and House, 1955; Fant, 1960). All of these articulatory maneuvers generate a falling formant frequency pattern. The acoustic phenomenon can be seen in the spectrogram of Figure 8-3, where both rising and falling formant frequency transitions occurred. In human speech formant transitions are the normal case. They appear to be rarer in the acoustic signals of nonhuman primates.

Nonhuman phonetic features

We have not included many of the phonetic features that occur in human speech because nonhuman primates lack the anatomical apparatus necessary to produce the acoustic contrasts that typify these features. The study of these anatomical differences will be our primary concern in the chapters that follow. However, the anatomical differences that differentiate *Homo sapiens* and other primates allow nonhumans to produce some phonetic distinctions that are not possible for humans.

Oral versus nonoral

Nonhuman primates can produce cries in which their oral cavities are closed by the epiglottis while the nose remains open. The gorilla vocalization in Figure 8-1 probably was produced in this manner.

Air sac variations

Some nonhuman primates, e.g., the howler monkey, have large air sacs above their vocal cords. These air sacs can act as variable acoustic filters as their volume changes. The vocalizations of primates with air sacs have not yet been subjected to quantitative acoustic analysis. It is possible that their calls are differentiated by modulations introduced by the air sacs.

Acoustic analyses of the calls of nonhuman primates are still in their infancy. This is not surprising inasmuch as the acoustic analysis of human speech has only been feasible in the last 10 years, with the advent of digital computers and a quantitative source-filter theory of speech production. The supralaryngeal vocal tracts and larynges of most nonhuman primates produce acoustic signals that fall outside of the range of formant frequencies and fundamental frequencies that occur in human speech, and it is difficult, if not impossible, to rely on the unaided perception of human listeners. We simply are not equipped to "decode" the signals of nonhuman primates; we lack perceptual mechanisms "tuned" to the frequency

Figure 8-8 Spectrogram of loud chimpanzee cry that sounded like diphthong [aw]. The bandwidth of the analyzing filter was 600 Hz. Note the decrease in the high-frequency energy of the glottal excitation apparent in the change in density in the second, third, and fourth "bars" towards the end of the cry. Note that there were *no* transitions involving the first and second formants. The ape's tongue thus did not change the shape of his supralaryngeal vocal tract. (From Lieberman, 1968.)

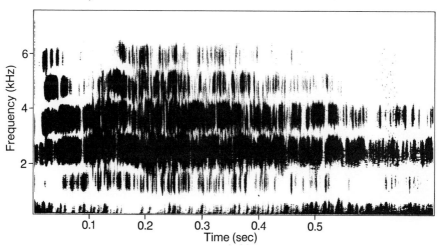

ranges in question. Many of the subjectively based transcriptions of the vocalizations of chimpanzees are very misleading. A chimpanzee vocalization might be transcribed as [aw], though its acoustic signal in no way resembled the signal characteristic of the human sound [aw]. The spectrogram in Figure 8-8 is an example of such a sound. A human listener who attempts to "force" this signal into the framework provided by the sounds of human speech might transcribe it as an [aw] because the high-frequency content of the glottal excitation decreased markedly toward the end of the vocalization. However, the formant transitions that typify the human sound [aw] do not occur in the spectrogram of Figure 8-8. If the perceptual transcription were accepted without question, we might assume that chimpanzees had the ability to produce the supralaryngeal vocal tract maneuvers that are necessary to produce the human sound [aw], but in fact they do not.

Perceptually based phonetic transcriptions are an extremely useful "tool" in the analysis of language, if their limitations are kept in mind. Some of the factors that call for caution rather than unreflecting acceptance of perceptually based phonetic transcriptions of nonhuman vocalizations follow from the species-specific neural mechanisms that appear to underlie the perception of human speech. We have special mechanisms that result in what seem to be "simple" decisions. These "simple" decisions on close inspection turn out to involve neural processes that classify acoustic signals into phonetic categories according to fairly complex criteria. We have briefly discussed the encoding and decoding of speech in Chapters 2 and 7. We will return in Chapter 11 to the perception of speech and the neural mechanisms that may be involved.

Supralaryngeal Vocal Tract Modeling of Living Primates

9

The acoustic analyses discussed in Chapter 8 indicated that non-human primates and newborn humans never produce sounds like the vowels [i] and [u]. If true, this is significant, because we have shown (cf. Chapter 7) that these sounds have functional roles in the perception of human speech. However, the acoustic analyses are subject to the limits of the data sample. It is reasonably certain that newborn humans do not make sounds that are fundamentally different from those discussed in Chapter 8; the references therein reflect independent observations of hundreds of infants.

The situation is not as clear for the analysis of nonhuman primate cries. The acoustic analyses of primate cries that we have discussed are consistent with the results of a number of independent studies (Andrew, 1963; Rowell and Hinde, 1962; Reynolds and Reynolds, 1965; Goodall, 1965) that involved spectrographic analysis or the observers' auditory impressions of the cries of various nonhuman primates in field conditions. The results are also consistent with exhaustive spectrographic analyses of chimpanzees (Marler, personal communication) and other primates (Green, 1973). But there always is a possibility that some animals *might* make some different cries under some behavioral conditions that have so far eluded human observation. In other words, the nonhuman primates might be able to make some more sounds that have not yet been recorded.

Negative conclusions based solely on observations of actual behavior are always difficult to establish. For many years chimpanzees were thought to be incapable of using tools. Closer observations (Beck, in press) showed that chimpanzees and many other primates do in fact use tools. The previous negative conclusions were the result of imperfect or, rather, incomplete observations of chimpanzee behavior.

There are two possible interpretations of the negative results of our acoustic analyses:

1. The animals could have made more sounds, but didn't. Other sounds might possibly have occurred in different behavioral contexts, but the experimenters were not fortunate. The monkeys and apes, in other words, didn't care to talk to the experimenters!
2. The monkeys and apes didn't talk because they couldn't. They either lack the anatomical mechanisms necessary for speech or lack the ability to control their speech-producing anatomy.

We can extend the acoustic analyses and resolve these questions by making use of a computer-implemented model of the supralaryngeal vocal tract. The modeling shows that the limitations on the phonetic abilities of nonhuman primates and newborn humans appear to primarily involve the supralaryngeal vocal tract.

The supralaryngeal vocal tract's filtering properties, as we noted in Chapter 5, are completely specified by its shape and size, i.e., its cross-sectional area function. If we could determine the range of shape variations of a supralaryngeal vocal tract, we could determine range of formant frequency variations.

We could, for example, examine the vocal tracts of newborn humans to determine the possible range of supralaryngeal vocal tract shapes. We then could make brass models of the possible shapes by pounding and forming brass tubes. We could record the actual formant frequencies that corresponded to particular shapes by exciting the tubes with an artificial larynx or a reed. We thus could determine the constraints that the supralaryngeal vocal tract imposed on the phonetic repertoire, independent of the possible further limitations imposed by the infants' control, or lack of control. We also would not be affected by the possible lack of cooperation on the part of the infants. We would be able to explore all of the sounds that they could make without having to wait for the particular behavioral situation in which a particular vocal tract shape was generated. The only difficulty would be in making sure that we had explored the full range of vocal tract shapes. The acoustic properties of the brass models would closely approximate the filtering properties of the vocal tract shapes that they modeled.[1]

The modeling technique that we have described actually was once the principal means of phonetic analysis. The technology of the late eighteenth and early nineteenth centuries was adequate for the fabrication of brass tubes that had complex shapes, and many early studies made use of them. The mechanical speech synthesizers devised at the end of the eighteenth century by Kratzenstein (1780) and von Kempelen (1791) generated acoustic signals by exciting tubes with mechanical reeds. Willis (1828) also used metal tubes and reeds to synthesize vowel sounds.

We could, if we wished, continue to use mechanical models to assess the constraints that the supralaryngeal vocal tract of an animal imposes on its phonetic repertoire. We could determine the range of possible supralaryngeal vocal tract shapes by dissecting animals, making casts of the air passages, and taking note of, among other things, the musculature, the soft tissue, and the effects of the contraction of particular muscles. We could enhance our knowledge by making cineradiographs of the animal during episodes of phonation, respiration, and swallowing. It would then be possible, though somewhat tedious, to make models of possible supralaryngeal vocal tract configurations. The models could even be made of plastic materials that approximate the acoustic properties of flesh. If these models, made of plastic or metal, were excited by means of a rapid, quasiperiodic series of puffs of air (i.e., an artificial larynx), we would be able to hear the actual sounds that a particular vocal tract configuration produced. If we systematically made models that covered the range of possible vocal tract configurations, we could determine the constraints that the supralaryngeal vocal tract morphology imposed, independent of the further possible constraints imposed by, for instance, the animals' motor control. We would, of course, be restricted to *continuant* sounds, i.e., sounds that were not transient or interrupted, because we could not rapidly change the shape of our vocal tract model. We could, however, generalize our results to consonant–vowel syllables like the sounds [bɪ] and [dæ], because we could model the articulatory configurations that occur at specified intervals of time when these sounds are produced.

Note that these modeling techniques would allow us to assess the limits on the phonetic repertoire that follow from the anatomy of the supralaryngeal vocal tract, independent of muscular or neural control and independent of the dialect, habits, and so on, of the animal whose vocal tract we would be modeling. The technology for making these mechanical models, as we noted, existed at the end of the eighteenth century. Von Kempelen's (1791) famous talking machine, which was one of the wonders of the time, modeled the human vocal tract by mechanical means. The method that

---

[1] The bandwidths of the formant frequencies would be somewhat different for the hard-walled brass model and the actual supralaryngeal vocal tract (Fant, 1960).

we have employed simply makes use of the technology of the third quarter of the twentieth century.

COMPARATIVE ANATOMY OF SUPRALARYNGEAL VOCAL TRACT

We will start our discussion of modeling by comparing the anatomy of the supralaryngeal vocal tract of an "advanced" nonhuman primate, the chimpanzee, with those of newborn and adult *Homo sapiens*. Figure 9-1 shows the head and neck of a young adult male chimpanzee sectioned in the midsagittal plane. Note the high position of the epiglottis and the larynx. A similar view of a human fetus at 7 months is presented in Figure 9-2. The adult human vocal tract was sketched in Figure 6-3. The air passages of the supralaryngeal vocal tract for chimpanzee and newborn and adult *Homo sapiens* can be more readily visualized in Figures 9-3 and 9-4. In Figure 9-3 silicone-rubber casts of the air passages, including the nasal cavity, are shown for newborn human, adult chimpanzee, and

Figure 9-1 Head and neck of a young adult male chimpanzee sectioned in the midsagittal plane.

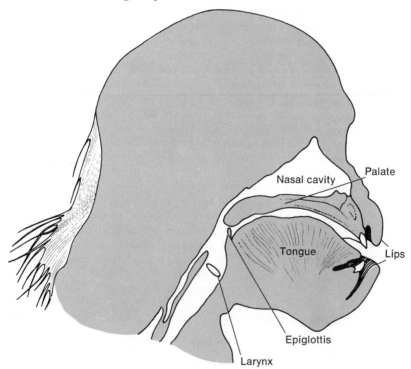

Figure 9-2 Head and neck of a human fetus at 7 months sectioned in the midsagittal plane. (After Negus, 1949.)

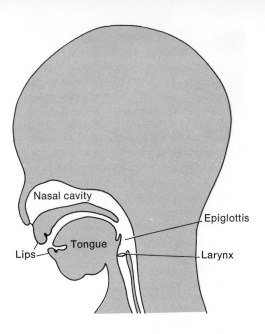

Nasal cavity

Epiglottis

Lips

Tongue

Larynx

adult human. This was done by filling each side of the split air passages separately in the sectioned heads and necks to insure filling the cavities. The casts from each side of a head and neck were then fused together to make a complete cast of the air passages (Lieberman et al., 1972b).

Even though the cast of the newborn air passages is much smaller than those of chimpanzee and adult man, it is apparent that the

Figure 9-3 Casts of the nasal, oral, pharyngeal and laryngeal cavities of newborn human (left), adult chimpanzee (center), and adult human (right). (After Lieberman, Crelin, and Klatt, 1972b.)

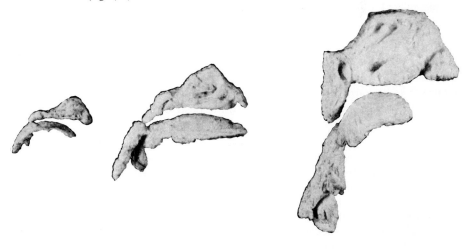

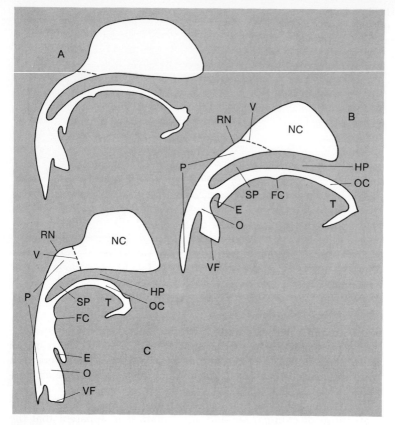

Figure 9-4 Diagrams of the air passages of newborn human (A), adult chimpanzee (B), and adult human (C). The anatomical details that are keyed on the chimpanzee and adult human are as follows: P, pharynx; RN, roof of nasopharynx; V, vomer bone; NC, nasal cavity; HP, hard palate; OC, oral cavity, T, tongue, FC, foramen cecum; SP, soft palate; E, epiglottis; O, opening of larynx into pharynx; VF, level of vocal folds.

newborn and chimpanzee casts are quite similar and that they are quite different from the cast of the air passages of adult man. In Figure 9-4 diagrams of the air passages are drawn nearly equal in size (Lieberman et al., 1972b) to reveal the basic differences and similarities:

1. Newborn human and the chimpanzee both have their tongue completely at rest within the oral cavity, whereas in adult man the posterior (back) third of the tongue is in a vertical position, forming the anterior (front) wall of the suprapharyngeal cavity. The foramen cecum of the tongue (which is a small pit on the center of the tongue and is a convenient anatomical landmark) is thus located far more anteriorly in the oral cavity in chimpanzee and newborn.

2. In the newborn and chimpanzee the soft palate and epiglottis can be approximated (moved together), whereas they are widely separated in adult man and cannot be approximated. In other words, the epiglottis can't close the oral cavity off from the airway leading to the lungs.
3. There is practically no supralaryngeal portion of the pharynx present in the direct airway leading out of the larynx in chimpanzee and newborn. This difference from the direct airway of the adult man is a consequence of the opening of the larynx into the pharynx, which is immediately behind the oral cavity in chimpanzee and newborn. In adult man this opening occurs farther down in the pharynx. Note that the supralaryngeal pharynx in adult man serves as a common pathway for the ingestion of food and liquids and as an airway to the larynx.
4. In the chimpanzee the level of the vocal cords at rest is at the upper border of the fourth cervical vertebra of the vertebral column, whereas in adult man it is between the fifth and sixth in a relatively longer neck. The vertebral column encloses the spinal cord.

These relationships can be perhaps visualized more readily in the semidiagrammatic representations in Figure 9-5 from Negus

Figure 9-5 Sketches of the vocal tracts of adult human (*A*), orangutan (*B*), and capuchin monkey (*C*). (After Negus, 1949.)

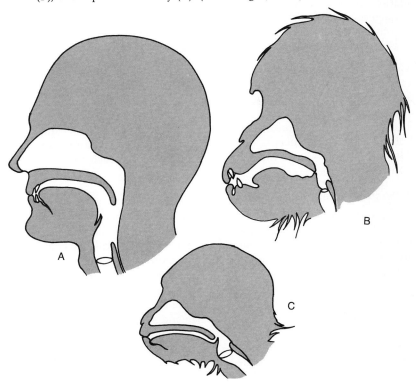

(1949) of the nose, palate, tongue, pharynx, and larynx in adult human, an orangutan, and a capuchin monkey. The vocal cords are represented in these sketches by the short line in the larynx. Negus was illustrating the comparative anatomy of the pharynx with these sketches, for he realized that it is quite different in adult man and in other primates. Negus correctly noted that:

> The pharyngeal resonator of Man is of great importance, but is not a characteristic shared by other Mammals. The descent of the larynx in the neck and the separation of the epiglottis from the soft palate, have given to Man a large pharyngeal cavity, and one capable of considerable alteration in size and shape during phonation. In the Higher Apes the pharynx is slightly more capacious, but it is only in Man that a fully functional size is reached. (1949, p. 146)

Because Negus lacked the computer modeling technique and the quantitative source-filter theory that has been developed in recent years, and was not aware of the crucial role of the supralaryngeal vocal tract in human speech, he overlooked the significance of the pharyngeal cavity in human speech when he confounded the modulation of fundamental frequency in the vocalizations of cats and cows with the formant frequency variations of human speech:

> When one considers the quality of voice of the Cow or the Cat, it becomes obvious that too much importance must not be placed on the pharynx as a factor in phonation; a wide range of pitches and an effective vocabulary of vowels and consonants could be available even with a small or absent pharyngeal resonator. . . . (1949, p. 146)

That is, he confounded the acoustic variations that follow from variations in the activity of the laryngeal source during *phonation* and the filtering properties of the supralaryngeal vocal tract, which are the primary determinants of phonetic quality in human speech. The error is a common one and is the reason for our reviewing both the acoustic concepts that are necessary to describe human speech (Chapter 4) and the source-filter theory of speech production (Chapter 5).

Radiographic data

Negus was one of the first to make use of radiographic data. His comments on the "alteration in size and shape" of the pharynx followed from still radiographs taken at University College, London, during the 1920s. Radiographic data and in particular cineradiographic data have established the range of supralaryngeal vocal tract variation that occurs in human speech. This information is, of course, necessary if we want to model the filtering properties of the vocal tract. Once we know the size and shape of a particular supralaryngeal vocal tract configuration, we know its filtering properties. The formant frequencies of a supralaryngeal vocal tract configuration are fully specified by its shape and size, i.e., its cross-sectional area function. The simplest way of determining the cross-sectional area function is to measure the midsagittal outlines of the air passages of the supralaryngeal vocal tract as they are revealed on lateral X-rays. The cross-sectional area can be determined with reasonable accuracy once the lateral dimensions of the vocal tract are determined (Heinz, 1962).

In Figure 9-6 a tracing from a frame of a cineradiograph (X-ray movie) is reproduced. The tracing is part of a quantitative study (Perkell, 1969) in which measurements of the displacements of various parts of the vocal tract were made for every frame of a slow-motion, sound-synchronized cineradiograph of a single speaker (Professor Kenneth N. Stevens of the Massachusetts Institute of Technology) carefully pronouncing a list of short syllables. The cineradiographic film was specially processed to enhance its quality. The subject's head was stabilized while he spoke, and lead pellets were glued to his tongue to serve as reference points. The film's frames were individually numbered and measured and compared with sound spectrograms. In short, great effort was expended toward insuring accuracy. This study and other equally careful

Figure 9-6   Diagram of a frame from an x-ray motion picture of an adult human during the production of speech. Anatomical features are labeled. (Reprinted from *Physiology of Speech Production* by Joseph Perkell by permission of The M.I.T. Press, Cambridge, Massachusetts. Copyright 1969.)

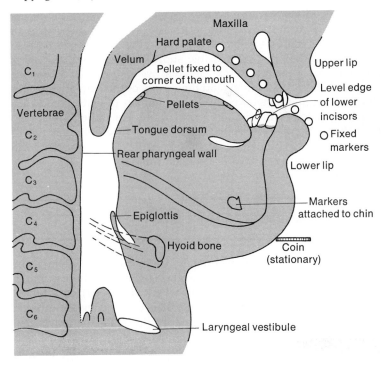

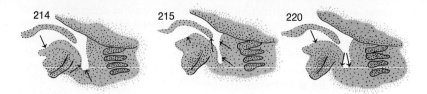

Figure 9-7 Sketches of frames from an x-ray motion picture of newborn human during cry and swallowing. The arrows show the direction of movement. (From Truby et al., 1965.)

studies (e.g., Ladefoged et al., 1972) have provided invaluable information on the vocal tract area functions that occur during the production of human speech. They also tell us what sorts of changes in the area function can be expected in various parts of the supralaryngeal vocal tract. We can see both the movements of particular parts of the tongue in the course of time and the shape of the tongue at a particular instant of time. This last aspect—the shape of the tongue—is particularly important for the vocal tract modeling studies that we will discuss, because we now know the range of deformations that can occur during speech for various parts of the tongue.

We fortunately have been able to gather similar information for both the vocalizations and the swallowing gestures of newborn human infants. In Figure 9-7 sketches of cineradiographic frames from a sound-synchronized X-ray movie of a newborn infant are presented from a study of the cries and swallowing gestures of 30 newborn infants (Truby et al., 1965). We thus don't have to speculate on the range of possible supralaryngeal vocal tract area functions for newborn human infants: we know what variations are possible. We also can extend the results of the cineradiographic studies of human newborns to the nonhuman primate vocal tract, which is anatomically similar. Furthermore, cineradiographic data for baboons have been collected (Zhinkin, 1963); though not as exhaustive or as completely documented, they are consistent with the data obtained for newborn human infants.

COMPUTER-IMPLEMENTED MODELING

One point that may be appropriately discussed at this point is the movements of the larynx that occur during speech. Whereas movements of 20 mm can be observed in Perkell's (1969) data for an adult man, movements of less than 5 mm occur in a newborn infant. This difference appears to be primarily the result of differences in anatomy. In adult *Homo sapiens* the hyoid and cricoid cartilages are separated and the larynx lies well below the mandible (Negus,

1949).[2] In newborn *Homo sapiens* the hyoid and larynx are approximated (Negus, 1949; Truby et al., 1965; Crelin, 1969), and, as we have noted, the larynx is positioned closer to the mandible. The differences in laryngeal anatomy are reflected not only in the activity of the larynx during speech but also in swallowing. Whereas the larynx moves somewhat anteriorly, but mostly upward, during swallowing in adult *Homo sapiens* (Negus, 1949, p. 176), it moves mostly in an anterior-posterior direction in infants (Truby et al., 1965, p. 68), owing to the different anatomical relationships of the larynx, pharynx, mandible, hyoid, and so on.

The vowels [i], [a], and [u]

Figure 7-3 presented midsagittal sections, cross-sectional area functions, and acoustic transfer functions of the vocal tract for the vowels [i], [a], and [u] derived from measurements on adult humans. *Acoustic transfer function* is another name for the filter function of the supralaryngeal vocal tract. The frequencies of the first and second formants are marked on the transfer function of each of these vowels.

Articulatory and acoustic analyses have shown that these three vowels are the limiting articulations of a vowel triangle that is language universal (Troubetzkoy, 1939). All human languages make use of at least one of these three vowels at the phonetic level. It is important to remember that we are discussing the *phonetic* rather than the *phonemic* aspects of language. Many linguists have made use of the concept of a phonemic level of language, in which they transcribe only the minimal set of sound qualities that would be necessary to code all the words of a language. Sound qualities that occur but can be predicted from other sound segments are not transcribed at the phonemic level (Bloomfield, 1933). Thus particular languages, e.g., Kabardian, can be transcribed using a phonemic notation using only one vowel symbol (Kuipers, 1960), though other vowels occur phonetically.

The body of the tongue is high and fronted to form a maximally constricted oral cavity in the production of [i]. In contrast, the body of the tongue is low to form a large cavity in [a] and [u]. The tongue body forms a large pharyngeal cavity in [i] and [u] and a constricted pharyngeal cavity in [a]. These vowels represent the maximum deviations that are possible from the uniform-tube-like shape that the supralaryngeal vocal tract has during respiration and in the production of sounds like the vowel [Λ]. If the tongue body were to move to form any constrictions greater than those shown in Figure 7-3, turbulent noise would be generated at the constriction and the sound would be a consonant. Other vowels are, for example, produced by means of supralaryngeal vocal tract configurations within the limits set by [i], [a], and [u] (Liljencrants and Lindblom, 1972).

We have discussed the functional value of [i], [a], and [u] in

[2]These anatomical relationships are illustrated in Chapter 10.

Chapter 7. The articulatory factor that gives these vowels their *acoustic stability* (cf. pp. 70–75) is the abrupt discontinuity in the cross-sectional area function at or near the midpoint of the supralaryngeal vocal tract. The stylized supralaryngeal area functions shown in Figure 9-8 make this clear. The *determinate* nature of [i] and [u] also follows in part from the fact that these vowels are produced by means of vocal tract configurations that involve extreme and abrupt discontinuities in the supralaryngeal area function. The vowel space reserved for human language is delimited by the vowels [i], [a], and [u]. Study of the theoretical limitations placed on the vowels produced by a related species can therefore proceed by determining the extent to which its articulatory system can match the human vowel triangle.

Some general observations are in order before detailed consideration of the vowel-producing capabilities of chimpanzees and

Figure 9-8   Stylized supralaryngeal vocal tract area functions that characterize the human vowels [i], [a], and [u].

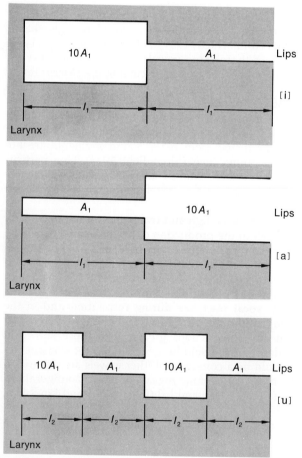

human newborns. The stylized vowels of Figure 9-8 require a relatively large ratio of the areas of the large- and small-diameter sections. In addition, they require rather abrupt boundaries between the sections. These configurations can be approximated in the adult human vocal tract at the junction of the pharyngeal and oral cavities, where a right-angle bend occurs. The geometry of the adult human vocal tract inherently has a discontinuity. The tongue body can be shifted toward the hard palate while it is also shifted anteriorly to produce a constricted oral cavity and an expanded pharyngeal cavity (as in [i]). The tongue body can conversely be shifted backward and downward to form a constricted pharynx and an expanded oral cavity (as in [a]). Muscles such as the genioglossus, styloglossus, and the pharyngeal constrictors can execute these maneuvers (Sobotta and Figge, 1965; Perkell, 1969; MacNeilage and Sholes, 1964; Ladefoged et al., 1972; Bell-Berti, 1973). Midpoint constrictions can be produced by the palatoglossus and styloglossus muscles (in [u]). The supralaryngeal vocal tract of adult man thus can, in effect, function as a "two-tube" system. *The right-angle bend is the crucial anatomical feature.*

The lack of a supralaryngeal pharynx at right angles to the oral cavity prevents chimpanzees and human newborns from employing these maneuvers. The tongue body does *not* form the anterior boundary of the pharynx; therefore, abrupt and extreme area function discontinuities cannot be generated simply by shifting the tongue body around.

The shape of the tongue really doesn't vary much in the production of human vowels. Figure 9-9, from a study by Williams (1965), shows the contours of the tongue derived from cineradiographic

Figure 9-9 Mid-vowel tongue contours aligned and superimposed to form the best visual match. The common point on the contours is the position of the posterior lead pellet marker on the tongue. Cf. Figure 9-6. (After Williams, 1965.)

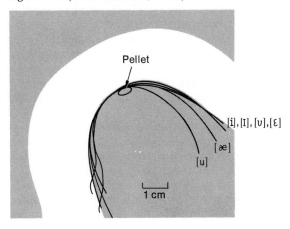

data rotated, aligned, and superimposed to form the best visual match. The lead marker pellet on the tongue of the speaker (the film is the same one that was analyzed by Perkell, 1969) has been used as a reference point. To stress the point that this figure shows, the area functions for human vowels are primarily the result of shifting the mass of the tongue body. The shape of the tongue is never profoundly distorted.

Examination of the range of shape distortions possible in either the oral or the pharyngeal cavity in adult man shows that tongue contours are smooth and gradual *within* either region. This is a necessary consequence of the fact that the tongue is an anatomical structure consisting of continuous and connected tissue. If one part is pushed up, the adjacent parts will be pulled up. If one part is pushed down, the adjacent parts will be pulled down. The inherent properties of the tongue, e.g., its musculature and connective tissue, severely limit the range of deformations that can be generated in the straight single-tube vocal tract characteristic of all living animals except adult *Homo sapiens.*

Chimpanzee and newborn human heads are also both smaller than adult humans'. This imposes a slight, but further, difficulty in the production of vowels like [i], [a], and [u], for which adult humans form large cavities. Comparable cavity area ratios would require smaller constrictions than are used by adult humans, but this would violate the conditions of nonturbulent flow in the constricted part of the vocal tract for vowels.

Chimpanzee vowels

The "best" approximations to the vowels [i], [a], and [u] for a chimpanzee are plotted in Figure 9-10. If the chimpanzee opened its mandible, a flared area function like that plotted for [a] could be obtained, taking into account the constraints just noted. The filled-in squares at intervals of 0.5 cm represent values that were used in a computer program developed by Henke (1966) to calculate the formant frequencies of [a]. The computer program essentially represents the supralaryngeal vocal tract by means of a series of contiguous cylindrical sections, each of fixed area. Each section can be described by a characteristic impedance and a complex propagation constant, both of which are known quantities for cylindrical tubes (Beranek, 1954). Junctions between sections satisfy the constraints of continuity of air pressure and conservation of air flow. In other words, the air pressure must be a continuous function and air particles can neither disappear nor be created at section boundaries.

The computer program calculated the three lowest formant frequencies for any area function specified. The area functions were entered into the computer program by drawing them on an oscilloscope with a light pen. The computer program then printed out the formant frequencies that corresponded to the particular area function. This arrangement made it possible to enter many area functions in a comparatively short time. The area function for the

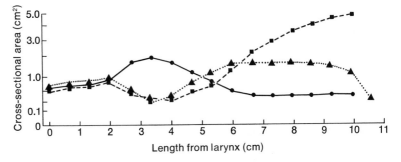

[i] ●——●			[a] ■----■			[u] ▲·······▲		
Formant	Freq.	Freq./1.7	Formant	Freq.	Freq./1.7	Formant	Freq.	Freq./1.7
1	610	360	1	1220	720	1	830	490
2	3400	2000	2	2550	1500	2	1800	1060
3	4420	2600	3	5070	2980	3	4080	2390

Figure 9-10 Chimpanzee supralaryngeal vocal tract area functions modeled on computer. These functions were the "best" approximations that could be produced, given the anatomical limitations of the chimpanzee, to the human vowels [i], [a], and [u]. The formant frequencies calculated by the computer program for each vowel are tabulated and scaled to the average dimensions of the adult human vocal tract (After Lieberman et al., 1972b.)

[a] plotted in Figure 9-10 is really the best [a] approximation of the many configurations that were reasonable possibilities for a chimpanzee vocal tract.

When the two lowest formant frequencies are scaled down in frequency by a factor of 1.7, the ratio of the adult human mean vocal tract length of 17 cm to the chimpanzee vocal tract length of 10 cm, both sets of data can be compared directly. This is done on a plot of first formant frequency versus second formant frequency in Figure 9-11, where the data point for [a] is denoted by the circled number 1. The frequency scales and labeled vowel loops are those of Figure 7-4 from the Peterson and Barney (1952) study. We see that the chimpanzee formant patterns for this vocal tract configuration do not fall within the range of [a] data for humans but rather lie inside the vowel triangle in the [Λ] region.

A chimpanzee could best approximate the vowel [i] by pulling the body of the tongue forward with the mandible lowered slightly. The cross-sectional area of the back cavity would not be large, but might approach the area function estimated in Figure 9-10. We were generous in allowing chimpanzees the benefit of the doubt whenever it would serve to enhance their phonetic ability. The two lowest formant frequencies for the "best" chimpanzee approximation to [i] are plotted as point 2 in Figure 9-11. The formants

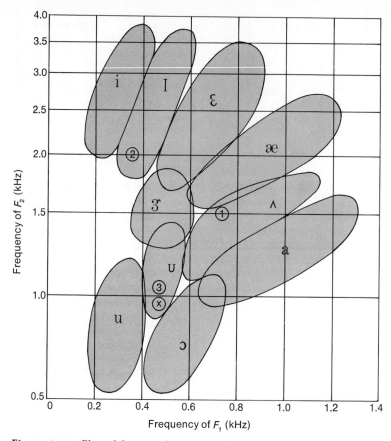

Figure 9-11 Plot of formant frequencies for chimpanzee vowels of Figure 9-10, data points 1, 2, and 3, scaled to correspond to the size of the adult human vocal tract. Data point X represents an additional point for human newborn. The closed loops enclose 90 per cent of the data points derived from a sample of 76 adult men, women, and children producing American-English vowels, cf. Fig. 7.4 (Peterson and Barney, 1952). Note that the chimpanzee and newborn vocal tracts cannot produce the vowels [i], [u], and [a]. (After Lieberman et al., 1972b.)

do not fall within the [i] region for adult humans but rather inside the vowel triangle in the [ɪ] region.

The vowel [u] is virtually impossible for the chimpanzee to articulate. A large front cavity requires the mandible to be lowered because the simian shelf (an internal buttressing of the front of the mandible; cf. Chapter 10) prevents the tongue body movement found in humans, and the lip rounding necessary for a [u] is impossible with a lowered mandible. The formant frequencies of the "best" approximation to [u], given these restrictions, are plotted as point 3 in Figure 9-11. They fall within the range for the vowel [ʊ].

The computer program did not take into account the effects of the chimpanzee pharynx, which acts as a short tube parallel to the direct airway leading out from the larynx through the oral cavity. This aspect of the chimpanzee pharynx can be seen in Figures 9-1, 9-3, and 9-4. The acoustic effects of the chimpanzee pharynx would be similar to those of human hyponasality. When adult humans suffer from respiratory infections that produce congestion of the nasal passages, they sometimes speak while their blocked nasal cavity is open and parallel with their oral cavity.

The chimpanzee pharyngeal section may be essentially closed during the production of an [a] approximation like that plotted in Figure 9-10, but it probably plays an important role in [i] approximations. The presence of the chimpanzee pharynx would have the effect of modifying formant locations, driving F_2 downward, and also the effect of introducing antiresonances into the vocal tract transfer function. Antiresonances, i.e., frequencies at which acoustic energy is in effect "absorbed," are one of the acoustic characteristics of nasality in human speech. Human listeners would thus probably perceive chimpanzee speech as somewhat nasalized. We estimate that the lowest-frequency antiresonance for the [i] approximation plotted in Figure 9-10 would be about 2 kHz for a slightly flared 6-cm pharyngeal section. Data point 2 in Figure 9-11 would be moved downward, closer to the lower bound of the [ɪ] vowel of human speech. It isn't worth worrying about this effect, because the main point is that the chimpanzee, in any event, cannot produce a vowel that has the properties of a human [i], i.e., *acoustic stability* and *determinateness.* This is also true for the chimpanzee with regard to [u] and [a].

Adult human vowels

The supralaryngeal vocal tract configurations typical of the vowels [i], [a], and [u] for adult human *Homo sapiens* were modeled as a control. The results were in accord with the data of Peterson and Barney (1952) and Fant (1960) and are not plotted. These data simply replicated the controls established by Henke (1966) when he developed the computer program.

Newborn human vowels

The supralaryngeal vocal tract of the human newborn does not differ substantially from that of the chimpanzee (Figures 9-2, 9-4, and 9-5). Of course, newborn humans do not have a simian shelf in their mandibles. The simian shelf is an internal structure that fills up the inside of the anterior lower portion of the mandible. Its absence allows the formation of a larger front cavity, and the newborn infant vocal tract therefore can produce a somewhat better approximation to the adult human vowel [u]. The "best" newborn approximation to [u] resembles that of the chimpanzee with a larger front cavity. Its formant frequencies were computed and scaled and are plotted in Figure 9-11 as point X. The resulting vowel sound is still comparable to the English vowel [ʊ] rather than [u], but it is a closer acoustic approximation to [u]. The acoustic output of the newborn vocal tract does not otherwise differ substantially from that of the chimpanzee. The effects of the pharyngeal cavity on speech quality would be similar in newborn human and in chimpanzee.

Perceptual and acoustic studies of the vocalizations of human newborns that we cited in Chapter 8 are consistent with our modeling. The only vowels observed are the vowels that we computed. Human newborns normally develop into adult humans. Spectrographic studies of the vocalizations of children show that they produce the entire range of human vowels between 9 and 15 months after birth (Winitz, 1960). This does not necessarily mean that infants do not produce the range of human vowels before 9 months, because no exhaustive spectrographic studies have yet been completed that survey the interval between birth and 9 months. Anatomical studies of the development of humans show that rapid changes occur during the first year of life (Noback, 1923; Scammon, 1923; Brodie, 1949; Bosma and Fletcher, 1961). Perceptually based investigations of infant speech indicate that phonetic repertoires begin to expand after 3 months of age (Irwin, 1948), consistent with their anatomical development. We really should have used the term *adult-like* rather than *adult* when we differentiated the vocal tract of human newborns from that of "adult" humans. Two-year-old children are obviously not adults, though they already have adult-like supralaryngeal vocal tracts (Negus, 1949).

The chimpanzee's computed phonetic range, like the newborn human's, is consistent with the acoustic analyses noted in Chapter 8 insofar as no sounds were observed that were not computed. Some phonetic possibilities were computed that were not observed. Dental consonants like [d] and [t] should be possible for both chimpanzees and human newborns. The absence of these sounds in the analyzed samples of the vocalizations of chimpanzees may reflect either muscular and/or neural limitations or the effects of chance—we may have missed the occasions when chimpanzees produced these sounds. However, the computer modeling is consistent with the main conclusion of the acoustic analyses. It demonstrates that a human supralaryngeal vocal tract is a *necessary* condition for human phonetic ability.

Reconstruction and Modeling of Fossil Supralaryngeal Vocal Tracts

10

The preceding chapters should have demonstrated how it is possible to gain some insights into the nature of human linguistic ability by considering the functional aspects of human speech. Human phonetic ability does not seem a trivial part of human linguistic ability once its functional attributes are revealed. Chapters 8 and 9 discussed the phonetic repertoires of living nonhuman primates and some of the differences that are apparent when nonhuman primates and newborn human vocalizations are compared with adult-like human speech. In Chapter 9 we made use of a computer modeling technique to establish the constraints that particular supralaryngeal vocal tracts impose on phonetic ability. The modeling technique demonstrated that the anatomy of the normal adult human supralaryngeal vocal tract is necessary to produce some of the sounds that make human speech a rapid medium of vocal communication. These facts, in effect, constitute a "clue" to the solution of a mystery, the mystery of when man began to talk and develop human language.

When fossil hominids were first discovered and identified in the nineteenth century, one of the most frequent questions was whether these creatures could have talked. Darwin's works had set the stage; "primitive" fossil hominids were to be expected if his theories were correct. It was manifest that apes could not talk. The earliest hominids were believed to have been closely related to the living apes (Huxley, 1863). Because evolution proceeded "by small steps" (Darwin, 1859, p. 95), fossil hominids representing intermediate steps in the evolutionary sequence that started with an apelike ancestral form and concluded in modern man must have had more "primitive" speech and language than modern man.

The problem after unearthing and restoring a fossil is how to assess its capacities for speech and language. Nothing remains of the brain, the soft tissue of the vocal tract, or small bones like the hyoid and the cartilages of the larynx. However, many attempts have been made to assess the speech-producing abilities of various fossils. Two approaches are possible—study of the brain case of fossils and reconstruction of the speech-producing anatomy. With respect to the former, certain neural mechanisms must be present in humans for both the perception of speech and the acquisition and use of the lexical, syntactic, and semantic aspects of language. If one assumed that apes could not talk because they lacked the neural prerequisites, one could examine the skull of a fossil and attempt to demonstrate that the hominid either had or lacked certain "essential" areas of the brain. Lenneberg (1967) presents a coherent review of much of the literature and makes a convincing argument for the presence of particular, specialized neural structures that are necessary factors for human language. However, it is difficult to make any substantive inferences about the presence or absence of particular neural mechanisms in the brains of extinct fossils, because we can deduce only the external size and shape of the brain from a fossil skull. This statement must not be taken as an "attack" on studies that reconstruct the external shape and volume of fossil brains. We will discuss these studies in Chapter 11. Studies of the rate and direction of brain development and comparative electrophysiological and psychological studies of living animals can provide valuable insights into the nature and evolution of human language.

However, these studies, in isolation, cannot yield any definitive answers[1] because we simply lack a detailed knowledge of how the human brain functions. The human brain is not a telephone exchange, nor is it a digital computer in the sense attached to any existing man-made computer. Many of the statements that one frequently encounters concerning the "nature" of the human brain are misleading or false. We don't know how the brain works. For example, we could not really assess the linguistic abilities of a

---

[1]Just as the methods that we will discuss in this chapter would not yield any particularly revealing insights if we did not relate human speech production to speech perception and more generally to human language.

modern man simply by examining his brain. Fortunately, we can derive some insights on the nature of speech perception in various fossil hominids by using the second possible approach—study of their speech-producing anatomy in relation to speech encoding and decoding. The relationship between speech anatomy and speech perception is very much like that between bipedalism and the detailed anatomy of the pelvic region. The anatomy is a necessary condition, though neural ability and muscular control are also necessary.

The methodology that has enabled us to reconstruct the speech-producing anatomy of extinct hominids is that proposed by Charles Darwin. Darwin in Chapters 10 and 13 of *On the Origin of Species* (1859) discussed both the "affinities of extinct Species to each other, and to living forms," and "Embryology." We have applied the methods of comparative and functional anatomy to the speech-producing anatomy of present-day apes and monkeys and to that of normal human newborns. We first assessed the speech-producing ability of these living animals in terms of their speech-producing anatomy. We found that their supralaryngeal vocal tracts inherently restricted their speech-producing abilities. The results of these studies were discussed in Chapters 8 and 9. We then noted that certain functional aspects of the morphology of the skulls of these living animals resembled similar features of extinct fossil hominids.[2]

The reconstructions of the supralaryngeal vocal tracts of the La Chapelle-aux-Saints, Es-Skhūl V, Broken Hill, Steinheim, and Sterkfontein 5 fossils were made by my colleague Edmund S. Crelin by means of the homologues that exist between these skulls and those of living forms, the marks of the muscles on the fossil skulls, and the general methods of comparative anatomy. The particular fossils were deliberately chosen because they are each representative of other fossils. The Sterkfontein 5 fossil is generally classified as a specimen of *Australopithecus africanus* (Pilbeam, 1972). The other fossils are generally classified as specimens of various types of *Homo sapiens* (Pilbeam, 1972). The La Chapelle-aux-Saints fossil, for example, is usually classified as a specimen of *Homo sapiens neanderthalensis* but it has been classified as a specimen of a distinct species, *Homo neanderthalensis* (Boule and Vallois, 1957). In Chapter 12 we will draw on the results of other comparative, quantitative studies that provide a statistically valid basis for sorting out various fossil hominid populations and will return to the question of classification.

Crelin's (1969) previous experience with the anatomy of human newborns was especially relevant because we can see in it many of the skeletal features associated with the soft tissue structures that must have occurred in certain of these fossil forms. In most cases we used casts of fossil materials made available by the

---

[2]The use of the plural pronoun *us* is *not* stylistic. The research that will be discussed has been a joint enterprise.

Wenner-Gren Foundation. For the La Chapelle-aux-Saints and Steinheim fossils, casts made available by the University Museum, Philadelphia, Pennsylvania, were employed. The original La Chapelle-aux-Saints fossil and the La Ferrassie fossil and La Quina child's fossil were examined with the cooperation of the Musée de l'Homme in Paris and the Musée des Antiquites Nationales in St. Germain-en-Laye, France. The original Es-Skhūl V fossil was examined with the cooperation of the Peabody Museum at Harvard University, Cambridge, Massachusetts. Photographs provided by the Musée de l'Homme were helpful. It was necessary to check the casts against the photographs and originals to make certain that the anatomical details of the skull bases were accurate. The base of the skull is an aspect of fossil morphology that has been comparatively neglected. We found that, in fact, the casts were quite accurate, but the direct comparisons removed any doubts.

NEANDERTAL MAN AND NEWBORN AND ADULT *HOMO SAPIENS*

Neandertal man (*Homo sapiens neanderthalensis*), represents one of the most interesting and controversial types of fossil hominid. When the first specimen of Neandertal man was found and identified as a fossil in August 1856 in a cave in the Neandertal Valley in Germany, it became a subject of controversy. The anatomist Virchow (1872), for example, claimed that it was either a pathological specimen or the skull of an imbecile. As other, more complete but similar fossil remains were found, the weight of scientific appraisal shifted to support the theory that Neandertal man represented a related but divergent hominid form (Boule, 1911–1913). The controversy continues today. Some anthropologists, e.g., Brace (1964), claim that Neandertal man really doesn't differ in any significant way from modern man. Neandertal man and modern man, in other words, are supposed to be too similar to rule the former out of the latter's ancestry.

In Figure 10-1 is reproduced a lateral view of the Neandertal fossil that was found at La Chapelle-aux-Saints in France in 1908. A similar view of the skull of a male adult modern human is reproduced in Figure 10-2. It is apparent that the two skulls are very different. Adherents of the "lumping" school of thought, however, claim that Neandertal fossils do not differ substantially from modern *Homo sapiens,* that they form a subset of hominids with skeletal characteristics grading imperceptibly into those typical of the modern population of *Homo sapiens.* Quantitative multivariate and univariate statistical analyses (Howells, 1970, in press) do not support this theory. These studies show that a class of fossil hominid skulls exists that includes the La Chapelle-aux-Saints fossil. These fossils differ from the skull of modern man as well

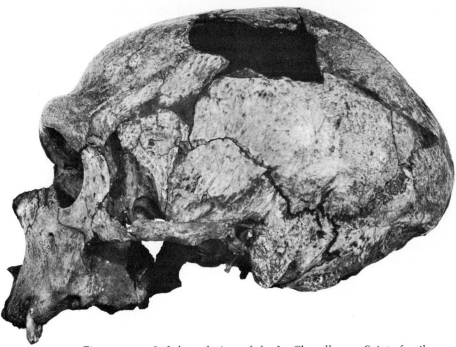

Figure 10-1 Left lateral view of the La Chapelle-aux-Saints fossil. (Courtesy of the Musée de l'Homme.)

Figure 10-2 Left lateral view of skull of adult male *Homo sapiens*.

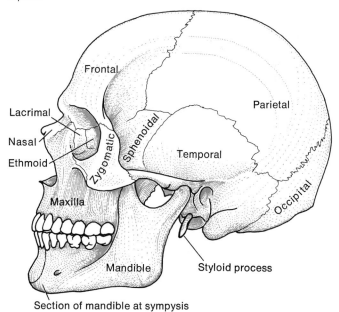

as from other fossil skulls. The term *Neandertal* should be reserved for this class of hominids, which includes the original Neandertal fossil as well as skulls like La Chapelle-aux-Saints. We could perhaps use the term *classic Neandertal* to differentiate these fossils from other ones that have also been labeled "Neandertal," but it could as well be argued that the term should be reserved for the fossils to which it was first applied rather than used for others like the Es-Skhūl V fossil that were found later and appear to be quite different. We will return to this question (the "Neandertal problem") and speciation in Chapter 12. For the moment it will suffice to note that the comments that pertain to the skeletal morphology of the La Chapelle-aux-Saints fossil also are relevant for many other fossil hominids.

The basis for our reconstruction of the supralaryngeal vocal tract of the La-Chapelle-aux-Saints fossil is the similarities that exist between the skulls of the fossil and newborn *Homo sapiens* (i.e., newborn modern man). This at first might seem quite implausible. How can an adult fossil skull that has massive supraorbital brow ridges, a huge, massive mandible, and a generally prognathous[3] aspect be compared with the newborn human skull? The answer is that certain other aspects of the morphology of newborn human and Neandertal skulls are similar, even if these are not. We're not claiming that newborn humans are little Neandertalers, but rather that they share certain skeletal features. Vlček (1970), in his comparative study of the development of skeletal morphology in Neandertal infants and children, independently arrived at similar conclusions.

As we noted, there are a great many Neandertal fossil skulls. These include a number of infants and children whose ages, at time of death, ranged from about 2 years to 14 years. Vlček was therefore able to study the ontogeny of Neandertal skull development in relation to that of modern man. He concludes that

> Certain primitive traits that are present in the skeletons of neandertal forms occur again in different periods of the foetal life of contemporary man with different degrees of intensity. Thus we can observe the development and the presence of many morphological characteristics typical of the neandertal skeleton in the skeleton of contemporary man in the course of his ontogenetic development. (1970, p. 150)

Vlček notes three aspects of the comparative study of development in *Homo sapiens* and Neandertal man:

1. There are morphological features that are constant throughout the age range of Neandertal fossils studied. These features are still noticeable at certain stages of the ontogenetic development of contemporary man.
2. There are morphological features that exist in Neandertal

[3] The jaws project beyond the upper part of the face.

fossils that never appear in modern man at any stage of ontogenetic development.

3. In contrast, there are new morphological features that appear in *Homo sapiens*. These features never are manifested in any Neandertal fossils.

Figure 10-3 shows lateral views of six Neandertal skulls from Vlček's study arranged with the youngest one at the top left and the oldest at the bottom right. The Pech-de-l'Azé skull (keyed P.A. in the figure) is that of a child about 2 years old. It was found in the same region of France as the La Chapelle-aux-Saints fossil.

Figure 10-3 Skulls of Neandertal infants and children. (After Vlček, 1970.)

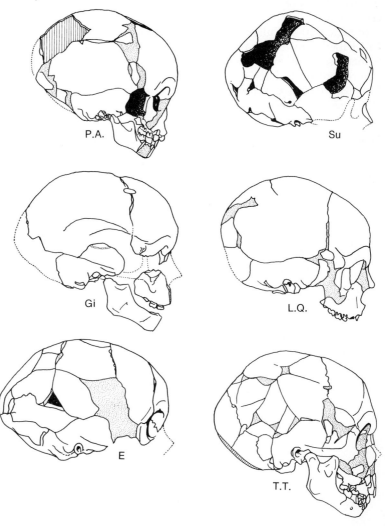

The Subalyuk fossil (keyed Su) is that of a child about 3 years old from Hungary. The Gibralter 2 fossil (keyed Gi) is that of a child who was about 5 years old. The La Quina H 18 fossil (keyed L.Q.) was about 6 years old and was found in France. The Engis 2 fossil (keyed E) from Belgium is that of a child who was about 8 years old. The Teschik-Tasch fossil (keyed T.T.) was about 8 to 10 years old. It was found in the Bajsun-Tau Mountains of southern Uzbekistan (USSR).

The ontogenetic development of specialized features that never occur in modern man can be clearly traced in these views. Note, for example, the gradual development of the supraorbital torus (brow ridge) and of prognathism (facial projection). The underlying similarity of these fossils, despite their wide geographical distribution, is also evident. Vlček (1970) discusses other fossil material and the details of the ontogenetic development of Neandertal specializations.[4]

In Figure 10-4 skulls of adult and newborn *Homo sapiens* and the La Chapelle-aux-Saints fossil are presented. The La Chapelle-aux-Saints fossil, which was found in 1908 in the Dordogne region of France, probably dates to between 100,000 and 45,000 years ago. The exact dating is not important, because Neandertal fossils (e.g., all those discussed in connection with Vlček's study) persisted

---

[4]The *similarities* that exist between Neandertal infant and human skulls are consistent with their deriving from a common ancestral form. The *different* features which develop in the course of the ontogenetic development of modern humans and the Neandertal fossils indicate that modern *Homo sapiens* and the Neandertal fossils represent divergent lineages.

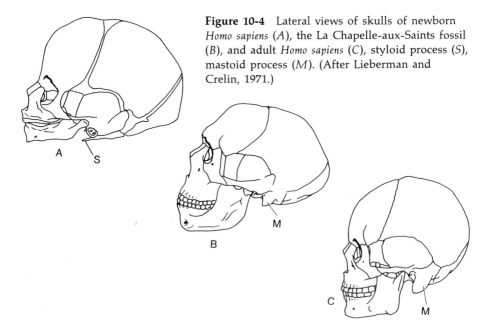

Figure 10-4 Lateral views of skulls of newborn *Homo sapiens* (*A*), the La Chapelle-aux-Saints fossil (*B*), and adult *Homo sapiens* (*C*), styloid process (*S*), mastoid process (*M*). (After Lieberman and Crelin, 1971.)

throughout this period. The skulls in Figure 10-4 have all been drawn to the same approximate size. Note that the newborn human skull in Figure 10-4 and the young Neandertal skulls in Figure 10-3 are virtually identical. The older skulls and adult La Chapelle-aux-Saints skull are still more similar in important features to the human newborn skull than the human newborn is to the adult human skull. The human newborn and Neandertal skulls are relatively more elongated from front to back and relatively more flattened from top to bottom than that of adult *Homo sapiens*. We could present a long list of similar anatomical features, but at the present time we're really concerned with skeletal features that are directly relevant to the reconstruction of the supralaryngeal vocal tract of Neandertal man.

We have to think in terms of the functional anatomy of the vocal tract. If we were to ignore the functional aspects of skeletal morphology we could be led astray, for example, by the fact that the mastoid process[5] is absent in human newborns and relatively small in the La Chapelle-aux-Saints fossil, adding to their similarity compared with the skull of the adult male *Homo sapiens* in Figure 10-4. However, adult human females frequently have small mastoid processes, and children of 3 or 4 years still have almost nonexistent ones. The mastoid process as it develops in *Homo sapiens* is not a formidable structure for the attachment of muscles, but rather a hollowed-out structure lacking compact bone. Although differences can be noted between the mastoid process of adult human males and adult male Neandertal fossil skulls, the differences are not significant with respect to their supralaryngeal vocal tracts.

Most of the unsuccessful attempts at deducing the presence or absence of speech from skeletal structures were based on comparative studies that did not properly assess the functional roles of particular features. Vallois (1961) reviews many of these attempts, which were hampered by the absence of both a quantitative acoustic theory of speech production and suitable anatomical comparisons with living primates that lack the physical basis for human speech. For example, the absence of prominent genial tubercles (small protuberances) in certain fossil mandibles was taken as an absolute sign of the absence of speech, but genial tubercles are sometimes absent in adult humans who speak normally. They play a part in attaching the geniohyoid muscle to the mandible but are not in themselves "crucial" features. Indeed, the notion of looking for "crucial," isolated morphological features is not particularly useful. It's necessary to explore the complete relationship of the skeletal structure of the skull and mandible to the supralaryngeal vocal tract.

Figure 10-5 shows lateral views of the skulls, vertebral columns, and larynges of newborn and adult *Homo sapiens* and the reconstructed La Chapelle-aux-Saints fossil. The Neandertal skull is placed on top of an erect cervical vertebral column instead of on

[5]The term *process* is a broad designation for any prominence or prolongation.

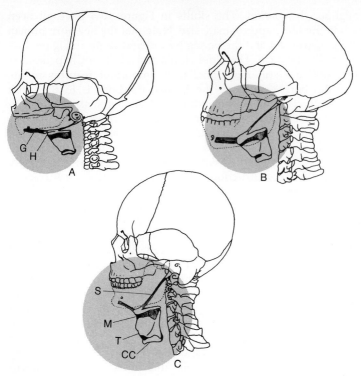

Figure 10-5 Skulls, vertebral columns, and larynges of newborn (*A*) and adult (*C*) *Homo sapiens* and reconstruction of the La Chapelle-aux-Saints fossil (*B*). G, Geniohyoid muscle; H, hyoid bone; S, stylohyoid ligament; M, thyrohyoid membrane; T, thyroid cartilage; CC, cricoid cartilage. The thyroid and cricoid cartilages are the principal outer structure of the larynx. (After Lieberman and Crelin, 1971.)

one sloping forward as depicted by Boule (1911–1913). This is in agreement with Straus and Cave (1957), who determined that the La Chapelle-aux-Saints fossil had suffered from arthritis. However, the arthritic condition of the La Chapelle-aux-Saints fossil could no more have affected his supralaryngeal vocal tract than is the case in modern man, where severe arthritis at advanced ages has virtually no effect on speech. (The La Chapelle-aux-Saints fossil was probably about 40 years old at the time of his death.) Because the second, third, and fourth cervical vertebrae were missing, they were reconstructed to conform with those of adult *Homo sapiens*. The spinous processes (the posterior portion) of the lower cervical vertebrae shown for the adult human in Figure 10-5 are curved slightly upward. They are from a normal vertebral column and were purposely chosen to show that the La Chapelle-aux-Saints vertebrae were not necessarily pongid in form, as Boule (1911–1913) claimed. Crelin's reconstruction (Lieberman and Crelin, 1971) is, in fact, purposely weighted toward making the La Chapelle-aux-Saints fossil more like modern man than an ape. In all cases of doubt, the La Chapelle-aux-Saints supralaryngeal vocal tract reconstruction was modeled on that of the modern human vocal tract. Thus any conclusions that we will draw concerning *limits* on Neandertal phonetic ability are conservative.

Note that the geniohyoid muscle in adult *Homo sapiens* runs down and back from the symphysis of the mandible. (The symphysis is the line of junction at the front of the mandible where the two halves are fused as it develops in the foetal stage.) This is necessarily the case because the hyoid bone is positioned well below the mandible. The two anterior (front) portions of the digastric muscle, which are not shown in Figure 10-5, also run down and back from the mandible for the same reason. When the facets into which these muscles are inserted at the symphysis of the mandible are examined, it is evident that they are likewise inclined to minimize the shear forces for these muscles. Facets are smooth, flat or nearly flat surfaces on bones. Shear forces pose a greater problem than tensile forces in all mechanical systems because the shear strength of most materials is substantially lower than the tensile strength. A stick of blackboard chalk, for example, has great tensile strength and it can't be easily pulled apart lengthwise. However, it has an exceedingly low shear strength so that it can be snapped apart with two fingers. The human chin appears to be a consequence of the inclination of the facets of the muscles that run *down* and *back* to the hyoid. The outward inclination of the chin in some human populations reflects the inclination of the lower part of the inferior (inside) plane of the mandible at the symphysis (Figure 10-2). Muscles are essentially "glued" in place to their facets. In this light, tubercles and fossae may simply be regarded as adaptions that increase the strength of the muscle-to-bone bond by increasing the "glued" surface area. Tubercles essentially are small bumps; fossae are small pits. Their presence or absence is not very critical (DuBrul and Reed, 1960), because the inclination and form of the digastric and geniohyoid facets are the primary elements in increasing the *functional* strength of the muscle-to-bone bond by minimizing shear forces. As Bernard Campbell (1966, p. 2) succinctly notes, "Muscles leave marks where they are attached to bones, and from such marks we assess the form and size of the muscles."

You can easily feel the inclination of the inferior surface of the symphysis of your mandible. Whereas the chin is more prominent in some adult humans than others, the lower part of the inside surface of the mandibular symphysis always is arranged to accommodate muscles that run down and back to a low hyoid position. As DuBrul (1958, p. 42) correctly notes, the human mandible is unique: "The whole lower border of the jaw has swung from a pose leaning inward to one flaring outward." An examination of the collection of skulls at the Musée de l'Homme in Paris indicated that this is true, regardless of race and sex, for normal adult humans. When the corresponding features are examined in newborn

Homo sapiens (Figure 10-5), it is evident that the nearly horizontal inclination of the facets of the geniohyoid and digastric muscles is a concomitant feature of the high position of the hyoid bone (Negus, 1949; Crelin, 1969; Wind, 1970). These muscles are nearly horizontal with respect to the symphysis of the mandible in newborn *Homo sapiens*—and the facets therefore are nearly horizontal to minimize shear forces. Newborn *Homo sapiens* thus lacks a chin because the inferior surface of the symphysis of the mandible is *not* inclined to accommodate muscles that run down and back. When the mandible of the La Chapelle-aux-Saints fossil is examined, it is evident that the facets of these muscles resemble those of newborn *Homo sapiens*. The inclination of the styloid process away from the vertical plane is also a concomitant and coordinated aspect of the skeletal complex that supports a high hyoid position in newborn *Homo sapiens* and the La Chapelle-aux-Saints fossil. The stylohyoid muscle which helps to support the hyoid is attached to the styloid process. There are sufficient fossil remains of the

Figure 10-6 Lateral views of skulls of newborn (*A*) and adult (*C*) *Homo sapiens* and the La Chapelle-aux-Saints fossil (*B*). L, angle of pterygoid lamina; S, angle of styloid process; R, ramus; M, body. (After Lieberman and Crelin, 1971.)

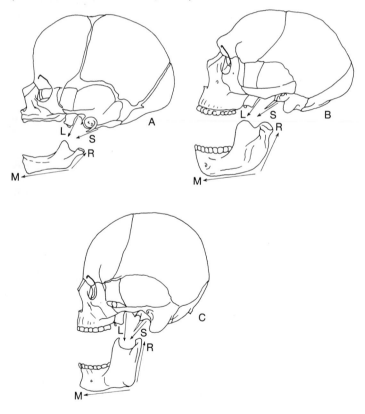

base of the La Chapelle-aux-Saints left styloid process to determine its original approximate size and location.[6]

Figures 10-6 and 10-7 are lateral views and inferior views of the base of the skull of a human newborn, the La Chapelle-aux-Saints fossil, and an adult human. Figures 10-8, 10-9, and 10-10 are photographs of the base (bottom) of the skull and lateral views of the mandibles of the La Chapelle-aux-Saints and La Ferrassie I fossils.

[6]The inclination of the styloid process in modern and fossil skulls can be determined most accurately from the inclination of the base of the styloid process. The thin anterior portion of the styloid process is likely to be distorted from its natural position during life.

Figure 10-7   Inferior (bottom) views of base of skulls of newborn (*A*) and adult (*C*) *Homo sapiens* and the La Chapelle-aux-Saints fossil (*B*). D, dental arch; P, palate; S, distance between palate and foramen magnum; V, vomer bone; SP, exposed sphenoid bone; BO, basilar part of occipital; FM, foramen magnum.

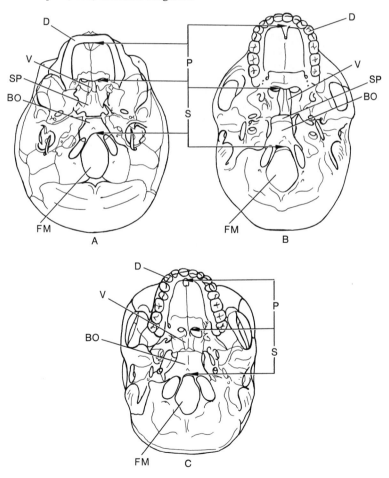

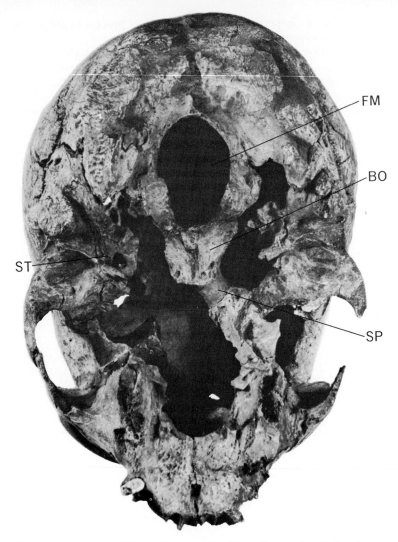

Figure 10-8 Base of the skull of the La Chapelle-aux-Saints fossil. Note the presence of the exposed sphenoid, SP, the base of the left styloid process SF, the basilar part of the occipital BO, and the foramen magnum FM in the fossil. (Courtesy of the Musée de l'Homme.)

The La Ferrassie I fossil, a typical Neandertal fossil, was found in the same region of France as the La Chapelle-aux-Saints fossil and is from the same period. It is evident that the two fossil skulls are quite similar. The total morphological complex of the base of the skull is functionally equivalent in both of these fossils and stands in marked contrast to that typical of adult modern man. Although the mandible of the La Chapelle-aux-Saints fossil is not

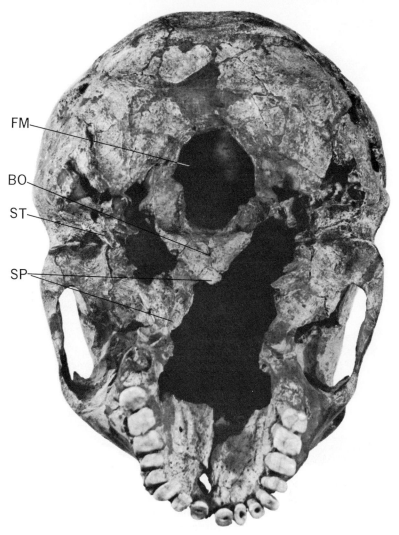

FM

BO

ST

SP

Figure 10-9 Base of the skull of the La Ferrassie I fossil. Note the similarity of this fossil skull to the one in Figure 10-8. Fragments of the exposed sphenoid SP and the base of the left styloid process ST are again present. The foramen magnum FM and basilar part of the occipital BO are evident in the fossil. The reconstruction of the base of the skull of Neandertal fossils thus is based on skeletal evidence rather than on conjecture. (Courtesy of the Musée de l'Homme.)

in a good state of preservation, the mandible of the La Ferrassie I fossil is well preserved.

The detailed skeletal features that support the muscles of the supralaryngeal vocal tract and mandible are all similar in the Neandertal fossil and newborn *Homo sapiens.* For example, the

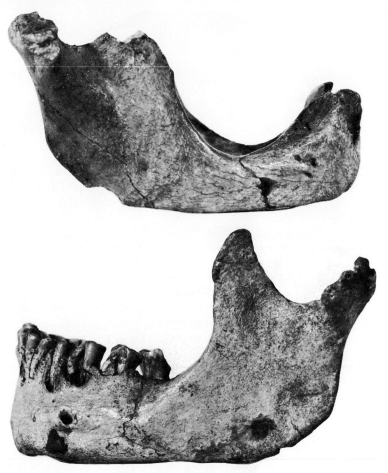

Figure 10-10 Mandibles of La Chapelle-aux-Saints fossil (top) and La Ferrassie I fossil (bottom). Although the La Chapelle mandible is not well preserved, the La Ferrassie mandible can be used as a guide in reconstruction. (Courtesy of the Musée de l'Homme.)

pterygoid process of the sphenoid bone is relatively short and its lateral lamina[7] is more inclined away from the vertical plane in the newborn and the fossil lateral views of Figure 10-6. The medial pterygoid plate, which is one of the points where the superior pharyngeal constrictor muscle is attached, is also similar in the newborn and the fossil. This muscle plays a part in speech production as well as in swallowing.

With respect to the base of the skull (Figure 10-7), it is again apparent that the newborn *Homo sapiens* and fossil forms have many common features that differ from those of adult *Homo sapiens.* These

[7]The term *lamina* describes a thin, flat plate in this context.

differences all are consistent with the morphology of the supra-laryngeal airways of newborn *Homo sapiens,* in which the pharynx and the pharyngeal constrictor muscles lie behind the opening of the larynx. Moreover, the larynx is positioned quite high with respect to the mandible and the cervical vertebrae. This has many skeletal consequences. For example, the sphenoid bone, which is one of the major bones of the skull, is greatly exposed in newborn *Homo sapiens* and fossil Neandertal skulls between the vomer[8] and the basilar part of the occipital bone. This is a skeletal feature that provides room for a larynx positioned high with respect to the mandible. There has to be room for the larynx behind the palate in newborn *Homo sapiens* and in Neandertal fossils. The difference in the morphology of the base of the skull, i.e., the increased exposure of the sphenoid, is a skeletal consequence of this anatomical necessity. The basilar part of the occipital bone between the foramen magnum (the hole into which the vertebral column fits) and the sphenoid is likewise only slightly inclined away from the horizontal toward the vertical plane in newborn *Homo sapiens* and in Neandertal fossil skulls. The "flattened-out" skull base characteristic of Neandertal fossils, newborn *Homo sapiens,* and nonhuman primates can essentially be viewed as the osteological correlate of their "single-tube" (cf. Chapter 9) supralaryngeal vocal tracts. We cannot build an adult human supralaryngeal vocal tract on the Neandertal skull; a structured complex of skeletal features makes it impossible. Everything that we know about the comparative anatomy of primates militates against Neandertal fossils having a "two-tube" supralaryngeal vocal tract in which the two tubes are equal in length and at right angles. The La Chapelle-aux-Saints fossil, for example, would have to be provided with a tongue 16 cm in length if we ignored the skeletal evidence and reconstructed an adult human supralaryngeal vocal tract. The larynx would have to be positioned near the sternum (the breast bone), 13 cm below the base of the occipital, because of the short neck; the tongue length relative to the skull would be more typical of a horse than of a human. Of course, the skeletal structure of the skull works together with the soft tissue. Debetz (1961), in connection with attempts to explain the causes for the appearance of certain characteristics belonging to *Homo sapiens,* notes that "the peculiarities of the skull, whose importance in the evolution of man is not in any case less important than the peculiarities in the structure of the hand and of the entire body, remain inexplicable." The specializations of the *Homo sapiens* skull, in part, appear to relate to the species-specific human supralaryngeal vocal tract.

In Figure 10-11 tongues and pharyngeal musculature are shown for newborn and adult *Homo sapiens* and the Neandertal reconstruction. The larynx in the reconstruction is actually positioned somewhat lower than Crelin judged it to have been in order to "push" the Neandertal reconstruction somewhat closer to the *Homo sapiens*

---

[8]The vomer bone divides the two nasal passages.

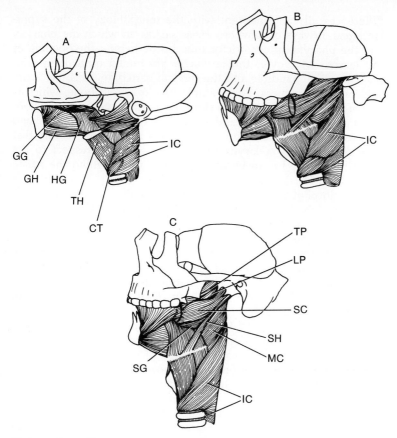

Figure 10-11 Tongues and pharyngeal musculature of newborn
(*A*) and adult (*C*) *Homo sapiens* and reconstruction of the La
Chapelle-aux-Saints fossil (*B*). GG, genioglossus; GH, geniohyoid; HG,
hyoglossus; TH, thyrohyoid; CT, cricothyroid; TP, tensor veli palatini;
LP, levator veli palatini; SC, superior pharyngeal constrictor; MC,
medial pharyngeal constrictor; IC, inferior pharyngeal constrictor; SH,
stylohoid; SG, styloglossus. (After Lieberman and Crelin, 1971.)

side and thereby compensate for any slight errors. Crelin's reconstruction of the supralaryngeal vocal tract appears to be in accord
with an earlier attempt of Keith, which is represented in a diagram
by Negus (1949). Negus, unfortunately, does not provide the details
of Keith's reconstruction. The reconstruction also is essentially in
accord with the inferences of Coon (1966) and DuBrul (1958). In
Figure 10-12 casts of the supralaryngeal vocal tracts of newborn
Homo sapiens, the Neandertal reconstruction, and adult *Homo sapiens*
are shown. Figure 10-13 diagrams these supralaryngeal vocal tracts
in outlines drawn to approximately the same size. The Neandertal
vocal tract, though larger, is essentially the same single-tube vocal
tract as that of newborn *Homo sapiens* and the chimpanzee discussed
in Chapter 9.

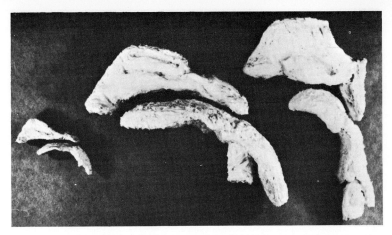

Figure 10-12 Casts of supralaryngeal vocal tracts of newborn (left) and adult (right) *Homo sapiens* and reconstructed La Chapelle-aux-Saints vocal tract (center). The nasal, oral, and pharyngeal air passages are shown. (From Lieberman and Crelin, 1971.)

Figure 10-13 Outlines of supralaryngeal vocal tracts of Figure 10-12 drawn to same size: newborn (*A*) and adult (*C*) *Homo sapiens* and La Chapelle-aux-Saints fossil (*B*). NC, Nasal cavity; V, vomer bone; RN, roof of nasopharynx; P, pharynx; HP, hard palate; SP, soft palate; OC, oral cavity; T, tip of tongue; E, epiglottis; O, opening of larynx into pharynx; VF, level of vocal cords; FC, foramen cecum. (After Lieberman and Crelin, 1971.)

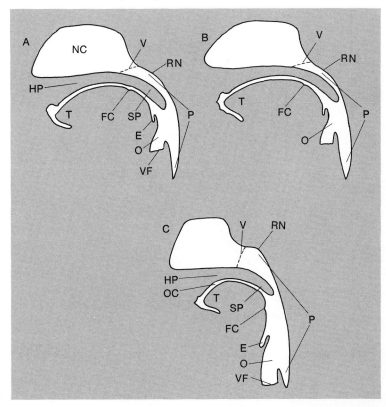

The reconstructed Neandertal supralaryngeal vocal tract was modeled using the computer program developed by Henke (1966) and the technique we discussed in Chapter 9. The same constraints were applied to the possible range of supralaryngeal area function variation as were applied to human newborns except for the possible contribution of variations in larynx height. As we noted in Chapter 8, the vertical mobility of the larynx is limited in newborn *Homo sapiens* and in nonhuman primates. The hyoid body closely approximates the thyroid cartilage in these forms, and the neck is shorter, decreasing the mobility of the larynx. It is probable that

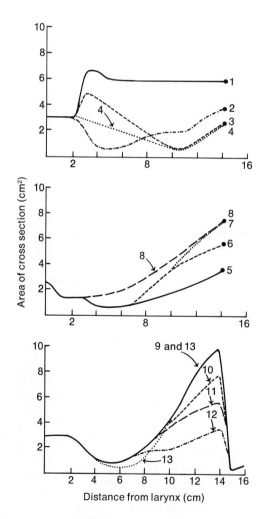

Figure 10-14 Some of the Neandertal supralaryngeal area functions modeled on the computer. Curve 1 is an unperturbed "schwa"-shaped vocal tract. Curves 2–4 are attempts to produce the vowel [i], curves 5–8 are attempts to produce [a], and curves 9–13 are attempts to produce [u]. (After Lieberman and Crelin, 1971.)

the Neandertal larynx also had these same restrictions on its mobility during speech. However, we again decided to "push" the reconstructed vocal tract toward that of adult *Homo sapiens*. We therefore used data derived from measurements on adult *Homo sapiens* (Fant, 1960) that would enhance the phonetic ability of the reconstructed Neandertal vocal tract with respect to cross-sectional area function variations in the region of the larynx.

We sketched a number of area functions into the computer using its light pen and oscilloscope input system. Some of the "best" area functions are plotted in Figure 10-14. These area functions were directed toward producing "best" Neandertal approximations to the human vowels [i], [u], and [a]. Some are probably rather "strained," e.g., functions 3, 9, and 13 in Figure 10-14. The formant frequencies corresponding to these area functions are plotted in Figure 10-15 in the same manner as the chimpanzee and newborn data in Chapter 9. It is apparent that the Neandertal supralaryngeal

Figure 10-15   Formant frequencies calculated for Neandertal vowel production. The numbers refer to the area functions of Figure 10-14. (After Lieberman and Crelin, 1971.)

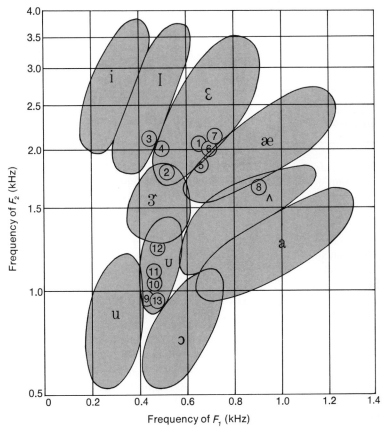

vocal tract has similar phonetic limitations. The larger oral cavity of the Neandertal fossil allows somewhat better [u] approximations than is the case for chimpanzee, but vowels like [i], [u], and [a] cannot be produced.

The calculated range of vowel formant frequencies for the reconstructed Neandertal supralaryngeal vocal tract, like the chimpanzee and newborn *Homo sapiens* vocal tracts discussed in Chapter 9, is subject to the effects of the Neandertal pharynx, which would act as a tube parallel to the direct airway leading out of the larynx. The acoustic effects of this Neandertal pharynx would be similar to the effects of human hyponasality. The second formant frequencies of the [i] approximations (points 2, 3, and 4 in Figure 10-15) would have lower values. The first formant frequency of points 3 and 4 also probably is too low, because we "gave" the Neandertal reconstruction the full range of human laryngeal mobility. The computer modeling of consonantal articulations indicated that the Neandertal vocal tract would not be able to produce velar consonants like the English stops [g] and [k]. However, bilabials like [b], [d], and [t], as well as continuants like [s] and [z], would be possible. Nasal versus nonnasal distinctions might be doubtful because of the effects of the parallel pharyngeal cavity and the gradual, shallow angle of the nasopharynx, which might make it difficult to seal the nasal cavity from the oral cavity. All Neandertal vocalizations thus might have a continual nasal quality, and it would not be possible to produce unnasalized sounds.

STERKFONTEIN 5: *AUSTRALOPITHECUS AFRICANUS*

The Sterkfontein 5 fossil, which was found in South Africa, is a specimen of *Australopithecus africanus* that probably can be assigned a date of between 3 million and 2 million years ago. A lateral view of the cast of this skull is shown in Figure 10-16. Crelin's reconstruction follows from the similarities that exist between this fossil and present-day orangutans and, to a lesser degree, chimpanzees. The relevant anatomical features are similar to those we discussed in connection with Neandertal man plus the pongid aspects of the Sterkfontein fossil. It is evident in Figure 10-17 that the reconstructed vocal tract is virtually identical in form to that of the chimpanzee and would have the same phonetic limitations.

The human "bent" supralaryngeal vocal tract is not a correlate of upright posture. *Australopithecus africanus* was a biped, though perhaps not one identical to later forms (Pilbeam, 1972), yet the vocal tract is essentially pongid. Neandertal fossils like La Chapelle-aux-Saints had a human-like upright posture (Straus and Cave, 1957), yet they also lacked a human "bent" supralaryngeal vocal tract. The descent of the larynx and the evolution of the

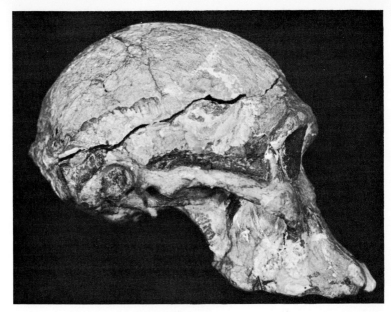

Figure 10-16 Lateral view of a skull (cast) of *Australopithecus africanus* from Sterkfontein. (Courtesy of Wenner-Gren Foundation.)

Figure 10-17 Casts of oral, pharyngeal, and laryngeal cavities of Sterkfontein fossil reconstruction (top) and chimpanzee (bottom). Note that the supralaryngeal airways are almost identical except for their size. The nasal cavities have been omitted to make the similarities in these vocal tracts more apparent.

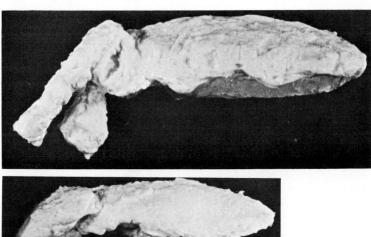

human supralaryngeal vocal tract therefore cannot be associated, as Negus (1949), DuBrul (1958), and Hill (1972) claim, with upright posture.

ES-SKHŪL V AND STEINHEIM

It is useful to group the Es-Skhūl and Steinheim fossils together for our purposes, though they are quite different in many ways. The relevant parameter for this grouping is their supralaryngeal vocal tracts. However, their status with respect to the evolution of human linguistic ability is different as will be apparent after we discuss some of the neural factors that play a part in the perception of human speech and the structure of human language. The Es-Skhūl V fossil was found in a cave near Mount Carmel in Israel. It probably dates from about 50,000 to 40,000 years ago. Despite the presence of moderate brow ridges, which are evident in the photograph of the fossil skull in Figure 10-18, it is essentially modern. The base of the skull and the mandible of the Es-Skhūl V fossil are no different from those encountered in the range of modern adult *Homo sapiens*. This was first observed by McCown and Keith (1939) in their initial description of the Mount Carmel fossil remains and has since been confirmed by every competent

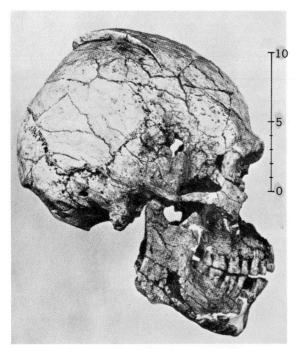

Figure 10-18 Lateral view of the Es-Skhūl V fossil skull. (Courtesy of the trustees of the British Museum, Nat. Hist.)

authority. The statistical analyses of Howells (1970, in press) also support these observations. For example, the symphysis of the mandible and the angulation of the styloid processes are within the range of variation typical of modern *Homo sapiens.* A detailed catalogue of features isn't very worthwhile, because everything is essentially modern in character. The reconstructed supralaryngeal vocal tract is like that of adult *Homo sapiens,* with which it appears in Figure 10-19. It would have imposed no limits on its owner's phonetic repertoire if he attempted to produce the full range of human speech.

The Steinheim fossil belongs to a different period of hominid evolution and poses more problems. We, unfortunately, cannot be very certain as to its age or the exact nature of its supralaryngeal vocal tract. The fossil was found near Stuttgart, Germany, in 1933 and probably dates to between 250,000 and 400,000 years ago. Exact dating is almost impossible because the site in which the skull was found is now "dug out"; faunal and radiometric datings are likely to be less than adequate. The Steinheim skull is quite primitive compared to the Es-Skhūl V skull. Its cranial capacity probably is about 1,200 cm^3, whereas the cranial capacity of Es-Skhūl is about 1,500 cm^3, within the range of modern *Homo sapiens.* The cranial capacity of the La Chapelle-aux-Saints fossil is also about 1,600 cm^3, so the Steinheim skull is more primitive in this regard. A useful additional point of reference is the cranial capacity of *Australopithecus africanus,* which is about 440 cm^3 (Holloway, 1973a).

Direct access to the Steinheim skull is not possible, which is a great pity because photographs show that it is distorted and as yet imperfectly cleaned. The only available material is the cast at the University Museum of the University of Pennsylvania. A first

Figure 10-19 Casts of the oral, pharyngeal, and laryngeal cavities of Es-Skhūl V reconstruction (left), and adult *Homo sapiens* (right).

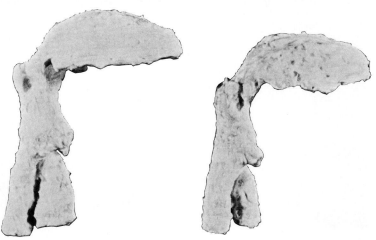

attempt toward a new restoration and reconstruction of the supra-laryngeal vocal tract is described by Crelin (1973). Crelin's restoration was based on casts of the Steinheim skull and the Wenner-Gren Foundation casts of the Swanscombe skull fragments found in England. The Swanscombe skull fragments probably belong to the same period as the Steinheim fossil and are similar to it (Weiner and Campbell, 1964). Crelin's reconstructed Steinheim supralaryngeal vocal tract is functionally equivalent to that of modern *Homo sapiens*. However, Crelin's reconstruction must be viewed as very preliminary, because he was not able to examine the original fossil. Until direct work on the original fossil can be completed, conclusions drawn from its distorted skull base must remain conjectural. However, distorted as casts of the Steinheim fossil may be, they indicate that its supralaryngeal vocal tract may have been more modern in form than that of the La Chapelle-aux-Saints fossil. How modern is the question.

BROKEN HILL (RHODESIAN MAN)

In Figure 10-20 a lateral view of the Broken Hill fossil is shown. The fossil was found in the Broken Hill mine in Zambia in 1921.

Figure 10-20 Lateral view of the Broken Hill fossil skull. (From Day, 1965.)

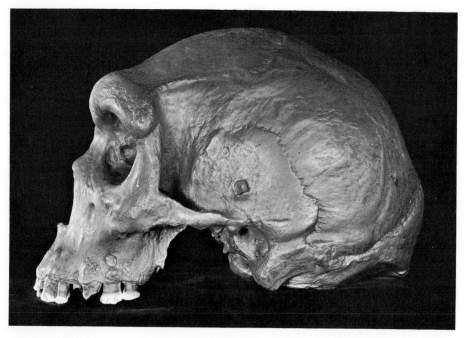

The conditions in which it was found made it difficult to assign a definite date to the fossil, but it was believed to be comparatively recent. New faunal studies (Klein, 1973) and amino acid racemization age determinations (Bada et al., 1974) suggest that it dates to about 100,000 years ago. The Omo II fossil (Day, 1965) from the Kibish formation is similar to the Broken Hill fossil and has a similar tentative age.[9]

The cranial capacity of the Broken Hill fossil is about 1,280 cm^3, and the skull can be differentiated from those of Neandertal man by a number of metrical characteristics (Morant, 1928). The angulation of the base of the occipital bone, which can be seen in Figure 10-20, is modern; the distance between the foramen magnum and hard palate is short compared to that of Neandertal man, and the sphenoid bone is not exposed in the skull base. The supralaryngeal vocal tract of the Broken Hill fossil has a right angle bend in it despite the large size of the palate. Crelin's reconstruction is shown in Figure 10-21 together with the supralaryngeal vocal tract region of adult *Homo sapiens*. The reconstructed Broken Hill supralaryngeal is intermediate between the nonhuman "single-tube" and the human "two-tube" vocal tract. Although it has a right-angle bend, the pharyngeal region is smaller than that of adult modern *Homo sapiens*. When it is modeled it can produce acoustic signals appropriate to the human vowels [i], [u], and [a]. However, the resulting signals are not as stable, i.e., resistant to articulatory sloppiness, as equivalent human vocal tract configurations. The vowels of Broken Hill, therefore, would be intermediate with respect to the functional phonetic feature *acoustic stability*, which we discussed in Chapter 7. Note that the large palate in this fossil form occurs with a bent supralaryngeal vocal tract. Reduction of the palate in forms like Steinheim, Es-Skhūl V, and modern *Homo*

[9]The Omo II fossil was found at a low depth in a formation whose upper level can be dated at 34,000 years, but it may be 100,000 years old or more.

Figure 10-21   Casts of the oral, pharyngeal, and laryngeal cavities of the Broken Hill reconstruction (left) and adult *Homo sapiens* (right).

sapiens therefore cannot, in itself, have caused the larynx to descend, producing the human supralaryngeal vocal tract.

The results of the reconstructions and computer modelings discussed in this chapter demonstrate that the two-tube human supralaryngeal vocal tract was present in some fossil hominids, absent in others, and present in intermediate form in others. The evolution of the human supralaryngeal vocal tract does not appear to have been a direct byproduct of other morphological changes. It is absent in both early and recent bipedal hominids, *Australopithecus africanus* and Neandertal man. Its evolution, moreover, cannot be directly linked to the reduction in palate size, because the Broken Hill fossil also has a supralaryngeal vocal tract with a right-angle bend. As we noted in Chapter 1 (and indeed throughout this work), the speech-producing mechanism is not the only factor that is relevant for the evolution of human speech and language. Neural mechanisms that decode human speech and structure the grammar of human language also are necessary factors. We will discuss some of these factors as they bear on the match between the production and perception of acoustic communications. We'll then return to assess the possible significance of the evolution of the human supralaryngeal vocal tract.

Neural and Cognitive Factors

11

BRAIN SIZE

One of the most obvious facts that emerges from the study of fossil hominids is that cranial capacity tends to increase from earlier to more modern forms. This tendency is true not just for hominids. Lartet (1868) first formulated this biological "law" in connection with the evolution of mammals. He observed that

> The further back that mammals went into geological time, the more was the volume of their brain reduced in relation to the volume of their head and to the overall dimensions of their body.[1]

Recent quantitative studies of mammalian evolution show that

[1] As translated by Jerison (1970).

there are selective advantages associated with large relative cranial capacity. Jerison (1970), for example, has reviewed the fossil evidence on the evolution of brains and bodies during the 60 million years of the evolution of carnivorous and ungulate (hooved) mammals of the northern hemisphere. The data show that

> there has been a progressive increase in relative brain size accompanied by and correlated with increased diversity among species in relative brain size. Small-brained species have also evolved, but more large-brained species have appeared in successive epochs.

Enlarged brains were a selective advantage for most, though not all, mammalian species. Brain size increased relative to body size, and more species evolved with bigger brains. Figure 11-1 is a graph from Jerison's (1970) study. Three facts are apparent. First, archaic carnivores had relatively larger brains than ungulates. Second, diversity evolved. Some species adapted to their environments most successfully by means of behavioral patterns that involved bigger brains. Other species did not; they evolved more efficient teeth, hooves, and so on. Third, average relative brain size increased dramatically over this 60-million-year period.

Figure 11-1 Brain size (endocast weight) as a function of body size in 69 fossil ungulates and carnivores. Paleogene fossils lived from about 70 million to 25 million years ago. Neogene fossils are those who lived from 25 million years ago to the present time. (Redrawn from H. J. Jerison, "Brain Evolution: New Light on Old Principles," *Science, 170,* 1224–1225, 1970. Copyright 1970 by the American Association for the Advancement of Science.)

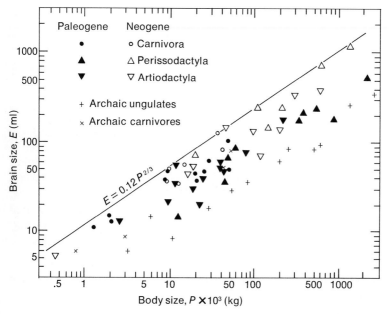

The facts of hominid evolution do not seem startling or unique when we discover that many other mammalian species have also evolved larger cranial capacities. Figure 11-2 is based on Tobias's (1973) diagram of the probable sequence of early hominid evolution. The ancestral population of hominids appears to be *Australopithecus africanus*. The Sterkfontein fossil discussed in Chapter 10 is a good example of this relatively unspecialized hominid. Tobias (1973) believes that about 3 million years ago a branch of *Australopithecus africanus* underwent strong selection for cerebral enlargement, out of proportion to body size. This branch is represented

Figure 11-2 Populations of early hominids identified systematically and arranged chronologically. The horizontal distance between any pair of population ovals is approximately proportional to the morphological and taxonomic distance between the taxa represented by the ovals. (After Tobias, 1973.)

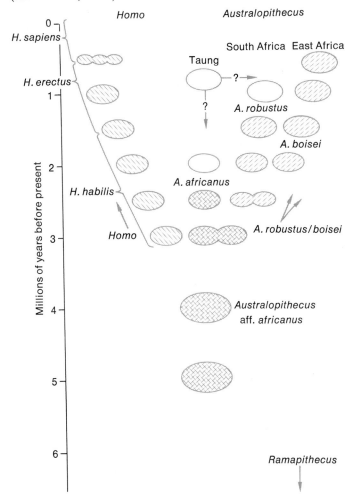

in Figure 11-2 by the *Homo* lineage. Perhaps the earliest known member of this lineage is the large-brained cranium found at East Rudolf, Kenya, by Richard Leakey (1973). This *Homo* lineage was characterized from an early period by strong association with tool use and toolmaking. Tobias notes that

> Some populations of *A. africanus* continued with relatively little change, after the emergence of the *Homo* lineage. Yet others underwent a series of dental specializations, developing an increasingly robust body, under dietary or behavioral influences, thus giving rise to the robuster lineages of *Australopithecus*. In South Africa this produced the moderately large *A. robustus* and in East Africa the excessively robust *A. boisei.* . . . These lines of specialization diverged away from the *Homo* lineage and were, it seems, not characterized by strong dependence on implemental activities. Having spawned two derivative lineages, *Homo* and *A. robustus/A. boisei, A. africanus* largely disappeared from the scene. (1973, p. 24)

All of the more recent hominids in the *Homo erectus/Homo sapiens* lineage evolved toward larger cranial capacities. The evolution of the *Homo* lineage some 3 million years ago was marked by an increase in average cranial capacity to over 600 cm³ (*Homo habilis*) from the 440 cm³ average cranial capacity of *Australopithecus africanus*. The average volume of the modern human brain is about 1400 cm³. Cranial capacity, in itself, is not that crucial a factor. In closely related species, a heavier mean body weight is generally associated with a proportionately greater brain weight (Stephan, 1972). Cranial capacity relative to weight and stature is more relevant. The size and weight of *Homo habilis* and *Australopithecus africanus*, however, appear to have been rather similar. The change in

Figure 11-3 Cranial capacities of early hominids with approximate sample limits (data supplied by D. Pilbeam).

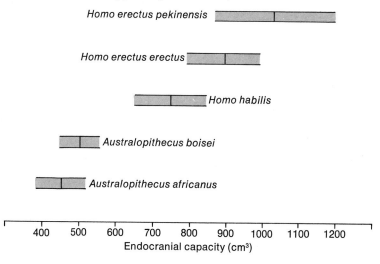

cranial capacity for these early hominids can be seen in Figure 11-3. Note that the average cranial capacities don't reveal the full measure of the difference between *Australopithecus africanus* and *Homo habilis;* the spread is much greater for *Homo habilis.*

Differences in cranial capacity, of course, don't necessarily reveal differences in the organization of the brain. It is difficult to make too many inferences from the surface morphology of endocasts of fossil skulls. However, there are differences in the external shape of the brains of early fossils in the *Homo* lineage that differentiate them from australopithecine brains. In brief, there is evidence for further cerebral development in *Homo erectus* and *Homo habilis* (Holloway, 1973a; Tobias, 1973). Australopithecine brains, in turn, are quite different from those of apes (Holloway, 1972; Tobias, 1973).

LATERALITY, CEREBRAL DOMINANCE, AND LANGUAGE

In Chapter 7 we discussed the "decoding" of human speech. Human listeners when they perceive speech take into account the size of the supralaryngeal vocal tract that produced the acoustic signal. The neural processing that underlies the perception of speech appears to critically involve the left, dominant hemisphere of the brain. Pierre Broca brought to the attention of the scientific world the specialization of the left hemisphere of the human brain for speech. Broca's observations, communicated to the Anthropological Society of Paris in 1861, concerning the site of damage to the brain that results in the loss of speech, initiated the modern era of brain research. Broca's area is sketched in Figure 11-4, which is itself the product of research involving the study of lesions and brain stimulation (Penfield and Roberts, 1959). Studies of the effects of brain lesions (summarized in Chapter 2) consistently demonstrate that the left, dominant hemisphere is more involved in the perception of speech than in the perception of nonspeech sounds. Listeners who have suffered various traumas in their left hemispheres have difficulty in perceiving the consonant–vowel sequences that form the syllables of human speech. When normal human listeners hear speech sounds, greater electrical potentials are recorded by electrodes positioned over their left hemispheres (over Broca's area) than over their right hemispheres. In contrast, no differences in electrical activity can be noted by the same electrode array when the subjects listen to musical sounds (McAdam and Whitaker, 1971; Wood et al., 1971).

The results of hundreds of experiments with dichotically presented speech (Shankweiler and Studdert-Kennedy, 1967; Liberman et al., 1967) again demonstrate that the left hemisphere of the brain is somehow crucially involved in the perception of human speech. The dichotic experiments involve the simultaneous pre-

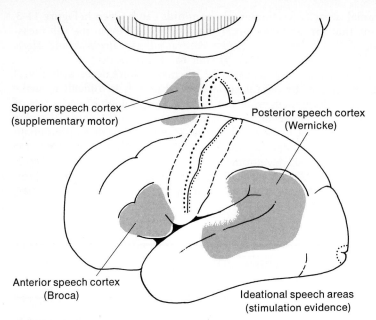

Figure 11-4 Areas of the brain that are especially connected with speech and language. (Redrawn from Wilder Penfield and Lamar Roberts, *Speech and Brain-Mechanisms*, Figure 4, p. 201. Copyright © 1959 by Princeton University Press. Reprinted by permission of Princeton University Press.)

sentation of two different speech sounds to a listener. One sound is presented to the subject's right ear through one headphone. The other, "competing" sound is presented to the subject's left ear via a second headphone channel. Under these conditions, encoded consonant–vowel syllables presented to the subject's right ear tend to be heard. The listener doesn't blend the two different sounds; he simply doesn't hear the competing left ear sound. However, the effect is manifested statistically; that is, subjects do sometimes hear instead the sound presented to their left ears. But as long as they are listening to encoded consonant–vowel stimuli, they tend to hear the sounds presented to their right ears more often. The effect disappears when musical or music-like sounds are used. Its basis seems to be the fact that the right ear is connected to the dominant, left hemisphere of the brain by a major contralateral pathway. This results in a speech sound presented to the right ear having an advantage over the left ear signal with respect to the left hemisphere speech processor. The ipsilateral connections of both ears to the right and left hemispheres prevent the effect from being total.

Many other language impairments can be traced to traumas involving the left hemisphere of the brain (Jakobson, 1968). The development of the neural mechanisms for speech processing and language that appear to involve this hemisphere therefore has served as a point of departure for studies of brain function and the evolution of human language (Geschwind and Levitsky, 1968; Lancaster, 1968). However, it is difficult to assess the presence of left hemisphere dominance from the endocast of a fossil brain. Although it is possible to show that the left hemisphere of the brain is more developed in contemporary *Homo sapiens* (Geschwind and Levitsky, 1968; LeMay and Culebras, 1972), it so far has not been possible to do this with most of the available fossil hominid materials. Holloway (1963b) notes the unsuitability of the endocasts existing so far for the australopithecines and the fossils designated *Homo habilis.* Some of the *Homo erectus* fossils may be more suitable. The interpretations of more recent fossils like La Chapelle-aux-Saints are still subject to debate, and we shall have to wait for more definitive answers concerning lateralization in fossil hominids.

In any event, the "mechanism" of the brain is not understood. We are beginning to appreciate the complexity of the brain. Cortical development, in itself, probably is not the only factor involved in the evolution of the neural prerequisites of human language. As Holloway (1972) notes, there are cortical–cortical and subcortical–cortical pathway differences in primates that make meaningful functional comparisons of the involvement of cortical function in human language quite difficult. We cannot assume that the communications of other primates are "emotional" and that human language involves mostly cerebral operations (Geschwind and Levitsky, 1968). These negative, or rather cautionary, statements should not be misinterpreted. Comparative studies of fossil hominid endocasts are certainly useful, but we have to be careful.

MATCHED SIGNALING SYSTEMS

In recent years a number of electrophysiological and behavioral studies have demonstrated that various animals have auditory detectors "tuned" to signals that are of interest to them. Even "simple" animals like crickets appear to have neural units that code information about the rhythmic elements of their mating songs: the calling songs of male crickets consist of stereotyped rhythmic pulse intervals and females respond to conspecific males by their songs (Hoy and Paul, 1973).

Similar results have been obtained in the squirrel monkey (*Saimiri sciureus*). Wollberg and Newman (1972) recorded the electrical activity of single cells in the auditory cortex of awake monkeys during the presentation of recorded monkey vocalizations and other acoustic signals. Eleven calls, representing the major classes of this species' vocal repertoire, were presented, as well as tone bursts, clicks, and a variety of acoustic signals designed to explore the total auditory range of these animals. Extracellular unit discharges were recorded from 213 neurons in the superior temporal gyrus of the monkeys. More than 80 per cent of the neurons responded to the tape-recorded vocalizations. Some cells responded to many of the calls that had complex acoustic properties. Other cells, however, responded to only a few calls. One cell responded with a high probability only to one specific signal, the "isolation peep" call of the monkey.

The experimental techniques that are necessary in these electrophysiological studies demand great care and great patience. Microelectrodes that can isolate the electrical signal from a single neuron must be prepared and accurately positioned. The electrical signals must be amplified and recorded. Most importantly, the experimenters must present the animals with a set of acoustic signals that explore the range of sounds they would encounter in their natural state. Demonstrating the presence of "neural mechanisms" matched to the constraints of the sound-producing systems of particular animals is therefore a difficult undertaking. The sound-producing possibilities and behavioral responses of most "higher" animals make comprehensive statements on the relationship between perception and production difficult. We can explore only part of the total system of signaling and behavior. However, "simpler" animals are useful in this respect because we can see the whole pattern of their behavior.

The behavioral experiments of Capranica (1965) and the electrophysiological experiments of Frishkopf and Goldstein (1963), for example, demonstrate that the auditory system of the bullfrog (*Rana catesbeiana*) has single units that are matched to the formant frequencies of the species-specific mating call. Bullfrogs are members of the class Amphibia. Frogs and toads compose the order Anura. They are the simplest living animals that produce sound by means of a laryngeal source and a supralaryngeal vocal tract (Stuart, 1958). The supralaryngeal vocal tract consists of a mouth, a pharynx, and a vocal sac that opens into the floor of the mouth in the male. Vocalizations are produced in the same manner as in primates; the vocal folds of the larynx open and close rapidly, emitting "puffs" of air into the supralaryngeal vocal tract, which acts as an acoustic filter. Frogs can make a number of different calls (Bogert, 1960), including mating calls, release calls, territorial calls that serve as warnings to intruding frogs, rain calls, distress calls, and warning calls. The different calls have distinct acoustic properties, and there are obvious differences in the manner in which frogs produce some calls. For example, the distress call is made with the frog's mouth wide open, whereas all other calls are made with the mouth closed. The articulatory distinctions that underlie the other calls are not as obvious. A feature analysis of these calls, like that proposed in Chapter 8 for primate calls, would be somewhat premature. Capranica (1965) has, however, analyzed the acoustic properties of the bullfrog mating call in detail.

The mating call of the bullfrog consists of a series of croaks. The duration of a croak varies from 0.6 to 1.5 sec and the interval between croaks varies from 0.5 to 1.0 sec. The fundamental frequency of the bullfrog croak is about 100 Hz. The formant frequencies of the croak are about 0.2 and 1.4 kHz. Capranica generated synthetic frog croaks by means of a POVO speech synthesizer (Stevens et al., 1955), a fixed speech synthesizer designed to produce human vowels that serves equally well for the synthesis of bullfrog croaks. In a behavioral experiment Capranica showed that bullfrogs responded to synthesized croaks so long as there were energy concentrations at either or both of these frequencies. The presence of acoustic energy at other frequencies inhibited the bullfrogs' responses. (The bullfrogs' responses consisted of joining in a croak chorus.)

Frishkopf and Goldstein (1963), in their electrophysiological study of the bullfrog's auditory system, found two types of auditory units. They found cells in units in the eighth cranial nerve of the anesthetized bullfrog that had maximum sensitivity to frequencies between 1.0 and 2.0 kHz and other units that had maximum sensitivity to frequencies between 0.2 and 0.7 kHz. However, the units that responded to the lower frequency range were inhibited by appropriate acoustic signals. Maximum response occurred when the two units responded to time-locked pulse trains at rates of 50 and 100 pulses per second that had energy concentrations at, or near, the formant frequencies of bullfrog mating calls. Adding acoustic energy between the two formant frequencies at 0.5 kHz inhibited the responses of the low-frequency single units.

The electrophysiological, behavioral, and acoustic data all complement each other. Bullfrogs have auditory mechanisms that are structured to specifically respond to the bullfrog mating call. Bullfrogs don't respond to any sort of acoustic signal as though it were a mating call; they respond to particular calls that have the acoustic properties of those that can be made only by male bullfrogs, and they have neural mechanisms structured in terms of the species-specific constraints of the bullfrog sound-producing mechanism. Capranica tested his bullfrogs with the mating calls of 34 other species of frog, and they responded only to bullfrog calls, ignoring all others. The croaks have to have energy concentrations equivalent to those that would be produced by both formant frequencies of the bullfrogs' supralaryngeal vocal tract. The stimuli furthermore have to have the appropriate fundamental frequency.

The bullfrog has one of the simplest forms of sound-making system that can be characterized by the source-filter theory of sound production. Its perceptual apparatus is demonstrably structured in terms of the constraints of its sound-producing apparatus and the acoustic parameters of the source-filter theory, the fundamental frequency and formant frequencies.

PLASTICITY AND THE EVOLUTION OF HUMAN SPEECH

Frogs are rather simple animals, but they nonetheless have evolved different species-specific calls. Some of the 34 species whose mating calls failed to elicit responses from *Rana catesbeiana* were closely related; others were more distantly related. It is obvious that natural selection has produced changes in the mating calls of anuran species. The neural mechanisms for the perception of frog calls are at the periphery of the auditory system, and they apparently are not very plastic, because Capranica was not able to modify the bullfrogs' responses over the course of an 18-month interval. Despite this lack of plasticity, frogs have evolved different calls in the course of their evolutionary development.

Primates have more flexible and plastic neural mechanisms for the perception of their vocalizations. Recent electrophysiological data (Miller et al., 1972) show that primates such as the rhesus monkey (*Macaca mulatta*) will develop neural detectors that identify important signals. Receptors in the auditory cortex responsive to a 200-Hz sine wave were discovered after the animals were trained by the classic methods of conditioning to respond behaviorally to this acoustic signal. These neural detectors could not be found in the auditory cortex of untrained animals. The auditory system of these primates thus appears to be "plastic." These results are in accord with behavioral experiments that involve human subjects, where "categorical" responses to arbitrary acoustic signals can be produced by means of operant conditioning techniques (Lane, 1965). They are also in accord with the results of classic conditioning experiments like those reported by Pavlov, whose dogs learned to identify and respond decisively to the sound of a bell, an "unnatural" sound for them. The dogs obviously had to "learn" to identify the bell.

The first hominid "languages" probably evolved from communication systems that resembled those of present-day apes. The social interactions of chimpanzees are marked by exchanges of facial and body gestures as well as vocalizations (Goodall, 1968). The recent successful efforts establishing "linguistic" communications between humans and chimpanzees by means of either visual symbols or sign language (discussed in Chapter 2) demonstrate that apes have the cognitive foundations for analytic thought; they also use tools, make tools, and engage in cooperative behavior (e.g., hunting). All of these activities have been identified as factors that may have placed a selective advantage on the evolution of enhanced linguistic ability (Washburn, 1968; Hill, 1972).

Australopithecus africanus, as we noted in Chapter 10, essentially had the same supralaryngeal vocal tract as present-day apes. However, this still would allow *Australopithecus africanus* to establish a vocal language that made use of the long list of phonetic features we discussed in Chapter 8 *if* other prerequisites were also present. *Australopithecus africanus* would have had to have had the motor skills and automatization to produce the coordinated articulatory maneuvers that are necessary for the production of phonetic features like *phonation onset* and also would have to have had the neural ability to perceive the differences in sound quality that characterize these features. Both of these prerequisites probably were met. As we noted in Chapter 2, present-day rhesus monkeys can automatize motor activity (electrophysiological data; Evarts, 1973). Although chimpanzees throw stones, only humans can make the complex calculations and rapid automatized coordinations that are necessary to forcefully hit both moving and stationary targets (Holloway, 1972). Australopithecines were more advanced in relative brain size than any present-day ape. Quantities of shaped stones have been recovered associated with early hominids that probably were used as projectiles (Leakey, 1971). The transference of patterns of "automatized" behavior that we discussed in Chapter 2 from activities like toolmaking and hunting would have facilitated the acquisition of the motor skill necessary to make these sounds. Enhanced communicative ability would in turn have facilitated the use of tools. The process would be circular, a "positive" feedback loop in which each step enhances the adaptive value of the next step. Particular neural capacities may initially not have been "innately" present; that is, they may not have been in place at birth like the auditory detectors of frogs, which don't appear to involve much, if any, "learning." However, the plasticity of the australopithecine auditory system surely would have been at least as great as that of present-day rhesus monkeys, not to mention that of dogs.

The initial language of the australopithecines thus may have had a phonetic level that relied on both gestural and vocal components. The system may have become more elaborate as factors such as tool use, toolmaking, and social interaction became more important. The ability to control rage and sexual behavior is one of the factors that makes human society possible (Hamburg, 1963), and language is probably one of the most important factors in reducing the level of aggressive behavior in human society. Social control was as important a factor as hunting in the evolution of human society (Washburn, 1969). The level of interaction between mother and child that can be noted in the vocal and gestural communications of chimpanzees, in which the mother is the primary agent of socialization (Goodall, 1971), is a good example of this source for the increased selective advantage of communication. As hominid evolution diversified and larger-brained hominids appeared in the *Homo habilis/Homo erectus* lineage, the selective advantages of linguistic ability would have increased.

The final crucial stage in the evolution of *human* language would appear to have been the development of the "bent two-tube" supralaryngeal vocal tract of modern man. Table 11-1 shows a divergence in the paths of evolution. Some hominids appear to have retained the communication system that was typical of the australopithecines, perhaps elaborating the system but retaining a mixed phonetic level that relied on both gestural and vocal components. Other hominids appear to have followed an evolutionary path that has resulted in almost complete dependence on the vocal component for language, relegating the gestural component to a secondary "paralinguistic" function. The process would have been gradual, following from the prior existence of vocal signals in the linguistic communication of earlier hominids.

TABLE 11-1 FOSSIL HOMINIDS CLASSIFIED WITH RESPECT TO SUPRALARYNGEAL VOCAL TRACT	
−Human Supralaryngeal Vocal Tract	**+Human Supralaryngeal Vocal Tract**
Australopithecines: *africanus*	
robustus	
boisei	
Saccopastore I	Steinheim?
Monte Circeo	
Teschik-Tasch (infant)	
La Ferrassie I	
La Chapelle-aux-Saints	
La Quina (infant)	Broken Hill
Pech-de-l'Azé	
	Es-Skhūl V
	Djebel Kafzeh
Solo II	
Shanidar I	Cro-Magnon

(The bracket at left is labeled "Neandertal" spanning from Saccopastore I through Shanidar I.)

After Lieberman (1973).

As we've noted before, the bent supralaryngeal vocal tract that appears in forms like present-day *Homo sapiens* and the Es-Skhūl V fossil allows its possessors to generate acoustic signals that (1) have very distinct acoustic properties and (2) are easy to produce, being *acoustically stable.* These signals are in a sense optimal acoustic signals (Lieberman, 1970). If vocal communications were already part of the linguistic system of early hominids, the mutations that extended either the range or efficiency of the signaling process would have been retained. The process undoubtedly would have been gradual, and the presence of an early intermediate form of supralaryngeal vocal tract in the Broken Hill fossil is to be expected. The reconstructed supralaryngeal vocal tract of the Broken Hill fossil will generate acoustic signals that have property (1), they have more distinct acoustic properties than other vowels. Property (2), acoustic stability, is present in forms like Es-Skhūl V. The initial adaptive value of the bent two-tube supralaryngeal vocal tract would have been to increase the inventory of vocal signals and provide more efficient vocal signals. The plasticity of the primate auditory system would have provided the initial mechanism for "learning" these new sounds; hominids who had the potential to make "new" acoustic signals would also have had the ability to "learn" to respond to these sounds in an automatized way.

Later stages in the evolution of human language probably involved the retention of mutations that had innately determined the neural mechanisms "tuned" to these new sounds. As we noted in

Chapter 2, by *innately determined* we do *not* mean to imply that the organism needs no interaction with the environment to "learn" to perceive these sounds. The evidence instead suggests that humans are innately predisposed to "learn" to respond to the sounds of speech. The responses of 4-week-old infants to the phonetic feature *phonation onset,* which we discussed in Chapter 6, show that they recognize the acoustic cues that differentiate sounds like [b] and [p] in the same manner that adults do. These acoustic distinctions involve 20-msec differences in the timing of the delay between the start of the acoustic signal that occurs when a human speaker opens his lips and the start of phonation. It is most improbable that 4-week-old infants could "learn" to respond to these signals unless there were some innate predisposition for this sound contrast to be perceived. This surely is not surprising. Human infants really do not "learn" the complex physiological maneuvers associated with normal respiration; they have built-in "knowledge." The case for the neural mechanisms involved in the perception of human speech is not as simple as that for respiration. Some contact with a speech environment appears to be necessary. For example, deaf children, though they at first produce the vocalizations of normal children, become quiet after 6 months of age (Lenneberg, 1967). Nottebohm (1970) has shown similar effects in birds: some aspects of a bird's vocal behavior are manifested even when it is raised in isolation, whereas other important aspects develop only when it is exposed to a "normal" communicative environment.

At some later stage, i.e., later with respect to the initial appearance of the bent two-tube supralaryngeal vocal tract, the neural mechanisms that are necessary for the process of speech encoding would have evolved. The human-like supralaryngeal vocal tract would have initially been retained for the acoustically distinct and articulatory stable signals that it could generate. The acoustic properties of the vowels [i] and [u] and the glides [y] and [w], which allow a listener to determine the size of a speaker's supralaryngeal vocal tract, would have preadapted the communication system for speech encoding.

The process of speech decoding, which we discussed in Chapter 7, appears to crucially involve the left hemisphere of the brain. For example, when isolated vowels are presented dichotically to a human listener there is no right-ear advantage so long as he is responding to vowel stimuli that could have been produced by a single, unique vocal tract but there is a strong right-ear advantage if the stimuli are instead derived from a set of different vocal tracts (Darwin, 1971). The listener has to make use of a perceptual recognition routine that normalizes the incoming signals in terms of the supralaryngeal vocal tracts that could have produced the particular stimuli. The neural modeling of this recognition routine apparently involves the left, dominant hemisphere of the listener's brain. The traditional mapping of areas like Broca's and Wernicke's areas in the left hemisphere reflects the existence of a coherent evolutionary process in which the human brain evolved special, unique mechanisms structured in terms of the matched requirements of speech production and speech perception.

THE UNIQUENESS OF ENCODING

Although the speech of modern *Homo sapiens* is a fully encoded system, we can't dogmatically assert that the vocal communications system of fossil hominids was completely unencoded or that other animals have completely unencoded systems. The acoustic basis of speech encoding rests in the fact that the pattern of formant frequency variation of the supralaryngeal vocal tract must inherently involve transitions; the shape of the supralaryngeal vocal tract cannot change instantaneously. If a speaker utters a syllable that starts with the consonant [b] and ends with the vowel [æ], his vocal tract must first produce the shape necessary for [b] and then gradually move toward the [æ] shape. Formant transitions thus have to occur in the [æ] segment that reflect the initial [b] configuration. The transitions would be quite different if the initial consonant were a [d]. The nonhuman supralaryngeal vocal tract can, in fact, produce consonants like [b] and [d], and simple encoding could be established using only bilabial and dental consonant contrasts. The formant transitions would either all be rising in frequency in the case of [bæ] or falling in frequency for [dæ]. It probably would be quite difficult, if not impossible, to sort the various intermediate vowel contrasts that are possible with the nonhuman vocal tract, but a simple encoding system could be built up using rising and falling formant transitions imposed on a general, unspecified vowel [V]. The resulting language would have only one vowel (a claim that has often been made for the supposed ancestral language of *Homo sapiens;* Kuipers, 1960). The process of speech encoding and decoding and the elaboration of the vowel repertoire could build on vocal tract normalization schemes that made use of sounds like [s], which also can provide a listener, or a digital computer program, with information about the size of the speaker's vocal tract. Vocal tract normalizing information could perhaps be derived by listening to a fairly long stretch of speech and then computing the average formant frequency range. The process would be slower than simply hearing a token of [i] or [u], but it would be possible. There might have been a gradual path toward more and more encoding for all hominid populations as social structure and technology became more complex. If this were true, the preadaption of the bent two-tube supralaryngeal vocal tract in some hominid populations would have provided an enormous selective advantage.

In other words, there may not have been any single path toward the evolution of encoded speech. Fossil hominids like Neandertal man may have had cognitive abilities equal to those of hominids like Es-Skhūl V. However, the absence of a preadapted bent two-tube vocal tract would have prevented them from generalizing the encoding principle.

TOOL USE, GRAMMAR, AND ENCODING

Table 11-1 groups a number of fossils into two categories, those who lacked and those who had a bent two-tube supralaryngeal vocal tract. We will discuss the significance of this categorization with respect to various theories of human evolution in Chapter 12. For the moment we want to note that this categorization would not hold if we ignored the differences in supralaryngeal vocal tract anatomy and instead looked at the cultural remains associated with these fossils.

The earlier hominids such as the australopithecines, who lacked human-like vocal tracts, had a primitive culture, but Neandertal man had a fairly complex culture not substantially different from that associated with fossils like Es-Skhūl V. For example, the La Chapelle-aux-Saints fossil was buried in a grave dug in the cave floor. His body had been placed in a crouched position and ceremonial grave goods were included. The La Ferrassie fossil also was buried in a crouched position. The Monte Circeo and Teschik-Tasch fossils probably had been buried. Ritual goods have been found at Neandertal burial sites, e.g., goat horns at Teschik-Tasch, bear bones at the Regourdou site in France (Bonifay and Vandermeersch, 1962), and perhaps flower pollen at the Shanidar site (Solecki, 1971). Elaborate funeral pits are typical of Neandertal burials. Bordes describes the excavation of a typical pit:

> It was roughly circular, and about 0.90 meters wide. It was filled with reddish dirt, in which were flint and bones, none of them specially remarkable. At 0.15 meters below the top layer 50, we found a series of flat stones. . . . Under the big flat stone on the right were two smaller stones, vertically placed. The other stones were arranged in a line. (1972, p. 134)

It is evident that Neandertal culture must have included elements of mysticism or religion. Language in a broad sense must have been present. Neandertal culture also had other fairly complex elements. Fires were lit in well-defined hearths (Bordes, 1972). The stone tools are complex, and include flakes produced by the Levallois technique.

As we noted early in this book, linguists often tend to view human language as though it were disjoint from all other aspects of human behavior. A linguistic grammar is essentially a formal description, or rather a formal abstraction, of certain aspects of language. In general, linguists would not think of applying the formal apparatus of a linguistic grammar to some other kind of human behavior. However, it is apparent that other aspects of human, and indeed nonhuman, behavior can be described with it. For example, Reynolds (1972) has studied the play activity of young rhesus monkeys and found that they have a number of stylized basic gestural patterns. These patterns are all quite short, each consisting of a particular body posture and facial expression. Some of the basic patterns involve movements and vocalizations. The basic play patterns are essentially "atomic" units that combine in certain regular ways to form play sequences. Some, the "initiators," occur only at the start of play sequences. Others, the "terminators," can occur only at the end of a sequence. Still other basic patterns occur within play sequences. The monkeys will break off play whenever a basic pattern occurs in the wrong position. There are, if we borrow the terminology of linguistics, "grammatical" play sequences, and we can describe these sequences by means of "grammatical" rules.

The "grammatical" rules that appear to be appropriate for the description of rhesus monkey play sequences are those usually associated with constituent analysis, i.e., sentence parsing. Let's consider the following short example of sentence parsing, which is drawn from Chomsky (1957). Consider the following set of grammatical "rules":

(1) $S \rightarrow NP + VP$

(2) $NP \rightarrow T + N$

(3) $VP \rightarrow V + NP$

(4) $T \rightarrow the$

(5a) $N \rightarrow man$ (5b) $N \rightarrow house$ (5c) $N \rightarrow ball$

(6a) $V \rightarrow hit$ (6b) $V \rightarrow lost$

where each rule, $X \rightarrow Y$, is to be interpreted as the instruction "rewrite X as Y." We can call the sequence of operations that follows a "derivation" of the sentence *The man hit the ball* where the number at the right of each line in the derivation refers to the "rule" of the grammar used in constructing that line from the previous line.

S

NP + VP	(1)
T + N + VP	(2)
T + N + V + NP	(3)
the + N + V + NP	(4)
the + man + V + NP	(5a)
the + man + hit + NP	(6a)
the + man + hit + T + N	(2)
the + man + hit + the + N	(4)
the + man + hit + the + ball	(5c)

Thus the second line of the derivation is formed from the first line by rewriting S (*sentence*) as NP + VP in accordance with rule (1), the third line is formed from the second line by using rule (2), and so on. We could represent the derivation by means of the diagram in Figure 11-5. If we add a "filter" condition to the rules of the grammar, it will mechanically derive a number of "grammatical" English sentences, e.g., *The man lost the house, The man hit the house.* The "filter" condition states that no derivation shall be considered complete unless all of the alphabetic symbols are replaced by English words. The application of a particular rule in this grammar is contingent on only one fact; the left-hand symbol of a rule must be present on the last line of the derivation.

The grammar that we have discussed is what linguists call a "phrase structure" grammar. It's the formal embodiment of traditional sentence "parsing." Phrase structure grammars in themselves cannot capture the encoded nature of the syntax of human language, which we discussed in Chapter 2 (Chomsky, 1957); however, phrase structure rules do have a role as a component of the grammar of human language (Chomsky, 1957, 1964). They have one formal property that, though it superficially appears trivial, is an important limitation of their explanatory power. A phrase structure rule can be applied in a derivation whenever the alphabetic symbol on the left of the rule appears on the line of the derivation being considered. *A phrase structure rule thus can apply to a line of a derivation without considering its past history.*

We can now return to look more critically at the question of Neandertal culture after this "digression" on the play activity of rhesus monkeys and phrase structure rules. In fact, we have not really been digressing, because the point is that we can apply the "rules" of grammar to the analysis of one aspect of Neandertal culture, stone-tool-making techniques, as revealed by the artifacts that have been found.

Stone-tool-making techniques

The paleolithic period, or old stone age, encompassed perhaps almost 3 million years, and there are important differences in the types of stone tools from different times during this period. The first tools, associated with the australopithecines, were either unshaped stones or stones that had a flake or two taken off them. The tools became progressively more complex, and their manufac-

Figure 11-5 Diagram of syntactic relationships in *The man hit the ball.*

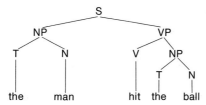

ture ultimately involved taking many, many chips out of the piece of stone that the toolmaker started with. We might think of the process as one in which toolmakers continued to refine the technique of tool fabrication, making the chips smaller and more numerous as time went on. The basic technique would be unchanged, though new modifications would be introduced. In fact, this is probably how toolmaking did develop. The three handaxes sketched in Figure 11-6 represent progressive refinements of essentially the same technique. The first two (*A* and *B*) are handaxes unearthed at Olduvai Gorge in Africa by Mary Leakey and are very early ones. The third (*C*) is a middle Acheulean handaxe from Swanscombe in England. The progressive nature of the develop-

Figure 11-6 Development of the handaxe. *A* is a primitive type from Olduvai, and *B* a more evolved type. They are typical of tools that are at least a million years old. *C* is from Swanscombe, England, and is probably no more than 400,000 years old. (Redrawn from *The Old Stone Age* by F. Bordes. Copyright 1968. Used with permission of McGraw-Hill Book Company.)

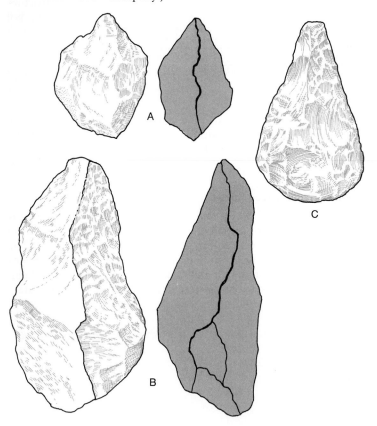

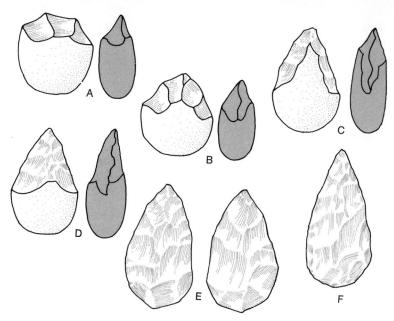

Figure 11-7 Evolution from the chopping tool to the handaxe by the technique of bifacial retouch. (Redrawn from *The Old Stone Age* by F. Bordes. Copyright 1968. Used with permission of McGraw-Hill Book Company.)

ment of toolmaking by this process can be seen in Figure 11-7. All of these illustrations are based on Bordes (1968).[2]

The technique involved in making these tools is conceptually similar to the process of whittling on a stick. You start by making an initial chip, then a second, a third, and so on. In making a particular chip you have to keep only two things in mind: (1) the last chip that you made and (2) the final form of the tool that you're trying to make. The process formally reduces to the phrase structure grammar with a filter condition that we just discussed. The filter condition is formally equivalent to stating that you know what sort of tool you're aiming for. The phrase structure grammar formally embodies the fact that you only need to know the last "line of the derivation," i.e., the state of the tool blank at the instant that you chip it. You don't need to have a memory of the operations involved in getting to that stage.

It doesn't take much time to learn about the process and theory of making tools in this manner. It's a single-stage operation and there really are no intermediate steps or restructuring. How difficult

---

[2] A comprehensive study of stone tools, dating, and nomenclature can be found in Bordes, *The Old Stone Age* (1968).

is it to learn this technique? Washburn describes the efforts of present-day graduate students:

> Let me give you an example of how much skill this takes. Dr. Desmond Clark at Berkeley runs an archeological laboratory and in order to get students to appreciate the problems of early man, he imports lots of stones and lets the students make tools. Now, in the first afternoon a reasonably intelligent graduate student can learn to make this kind of tool. It's just a matter, then, of an hour's work. Of course, one is given the stone and told how to do it, but it's very simple. It could easily be learned by copying. I don't think this involves any use of language or anything like that. (1969, p. 175)

We would be wrong in thinking that all stone tools involved the same technology. About 600,000 years ago, a radically different stoneworking technology began: the Levallois flake tools shown in Figure 11-8 are the result of a multistage process. The toolmaker first made a "core," the preparation of which itself involved a number of steps. The core, which can be seen positioned on the anvil stone in Figure 11-9A and between the toolmaker's legs in Figure 11-9B, was formed by making successive small chips, using the ancient techniques that gradually developed through the paleolithic. Once the core was ready, the toolmaker changed his technique and chipped out large flakes, each of which could serve as a complete tool, with every blow of his hammer (Figure 11-9A) or every push of his chest rod (Figure 11-9B).

Figure 11-8 Flint implements of the typical Mousterian. *A:* Convex side-scraper. *B:* Levallois point. *C:* Mousterian point. *D:* Canted scraper. *E:* Convergent scraper. *F:* Double scraper. (Combe-Grenal, Dordogne, layer 29, except *B,* from Houppeville, Normandy.) (Redrawn from *The Old Stone Age* by F. Bordes. Copyright 1968. Used with permission of McGraw-Hill Book Company.)

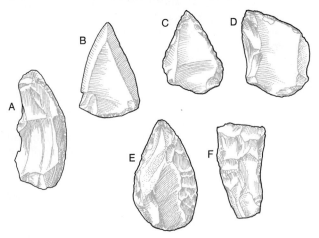

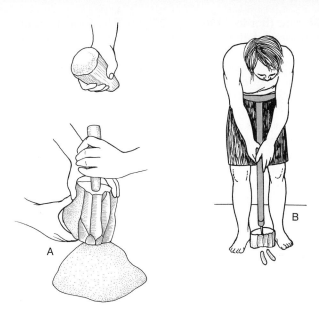

Figure 11-9   An advanced version of the Levalloisian stoneworking technique. The toolmaker first prepares the "core." The core can be seen in sketch (*A*) positioned on an "anvil" stone. Blade tools may be obtained either by striking the core by the indirect percussion (punch) technique shown in sketch (*A*) or by the chest-pressure technique shown in sketch (*B*). (Redrawn from *The Old Stone Age* by F. Bordes. Copyright 1968. Used with permission of McGraw-Hill Book Company.)

How difficult is it to learn this technique? Washburn describes the efforts of present-day graduate students:

> no student has yet succeeded in making one of these in a one-semester course. Given the material, given the object to copy, having a professor tell you how to do it—and Dr. Clark, by the way, is pretty good at this—it still takes much more practice than can be put in a reasonable semester. People who really put a lot of time into this do just as well as the ancient man did, but it takes a great deal of time and skill. (1969, p. 175)

The Levallois toolmaking technique cannot be reasonably described by means of a phrase structure grammar. A transformational grammar, which formally incorporates a memory, is necessary. There was no simple invariant "last chip" at which the toolmaker abruptly stopped preparing the core and switched to flaking off the final products; rather, he had to keep in mind a particular functional attribute of the striking platform that involved the entire upper surface of the core (Bordes, 1968, pp. 27, 28). The formal "grammatical" description of the process must also reflect this degree of abstraction, which cannot be keyed to the appearance of a single "alphabetic" symbol that represents a particular chip of stone.

Phrase structure grammars cannot formally account for the syntax of human language (Chomsky, 1957, 1964); they also cannot serve as grammars of the Levalloisian tool technique, which was one of the characteristics of the culture of Neandertal man. Transformational grammars, as we noted in Chapter 2, introduce the concept of encoding into syntax. Although we cannot positively conclude that the grammar of the syntax of Neandertal language had a transformational component, their stone tools suggest a degree of cognitive development that formally calls for a transformational grammar. Many other aspects of the culture of modern human populations need transformational descriptions if we attempt to derive a formal description. For example, marriage customs involve constraints on the lineages of both bride and groom that involve a memory component. Death rituals involving funeral goods also implicitly involve some knowledge of the former life and habits of the corpse. In contrast, the play activity of rhesus monkey does not appear to involve a transformational grammar with its demands on memory. In Chapter 2 we wondered whether nonverbal communications that have been established between chimpanzees and humans required a transformational syntax. We don't yet know the answer to that question, but it is evident that transformational grammars, with their concomitant encoding properties, are relevant for the description of Neandertal culture.

The most likely assessment of the encoding abilities of Neandertal man thus would be that his language was encoded but not nearly so much as that of modern *Homo sapiens,* because the Neandertal supralaryngeal vocal tract was not suitable for fully encoded speech. The neural structures of the brain that play so crucial a role in the perception of encoded speech in the dominant, left hemisphere of the brain therefore may not have been as well developed in Neandertal man. This is, of course, consistent with the view of Edinger (1948) and Washburn (1968) that "the majority of the unique features of the human brain evolved long after the fundamental patterns of the human way of life. . . . The brain follows in evolution" (Washburn, 1968, p. 37).

Conclusion 12

In this book we've discussed a number of "problems" related to the many different factors that probably have played a part in the evolution of language. These different factors, as Darwin noted, relate to selectional advantages of

> any variation, however slight and from whatever cause
> proceeding, if it be in any degree profitable to an individual
> of any species, in its infinitely complex relations to other
> organic beings and to external nature. . . . (1859, p. 61)

Many of these problems can be explicated in terms of the theory that we've developed for the evolution of language. The "explanatory" power of this theory is, of course, that of any scientific theory, the relating of facts that hitherto were thought to be unrelated.

In Chapter 10 we commented on the claims that Neandertal man cannot be regarded as a separate species, or even a separate variety, distinct from *Homo sapiens*—in other words, that there is no valid basis for regarding fossil hominids like La Chapelle-aux-Saints as being significantly different from modern man (Brace, 1964; Brose and Wolpoff, 1971). The key to this view is the definition of "Neandertal man" that's being used. The term *Neandertal* has been broadened (Brose and Wolpoff, 1971) to include all premodern, late Pleistocene fossils,[1] roughly all the fossils listed in Table 11-1 with the exception of the australopithecine and Steinheim fossils. This classification produces, as Howells puts it,

> a monster of which the morphological character is merely large cranial size and large brows, and of which the range of variations is simply illegitimate. (in press)

Brace and his colleagues have fixated their attention on the brow ridges of various early hominid populations, ignoring the rest of the skull. When the total skull morphologies of these middle and late Pleistocene fossils are examined and compared, it is evident that at least two different hominid populations coexisted. As Howells (1970, in press) demonstrates by means of statistical analyses, the term *Neandertal* has a precise meaning only when it is restricted to

> specimens of the European Würm,[2] usually called "classic," plus certain Near Eastern ones: Tabun, Shanidar, Amud. (in press)

This class of fossils, which in Table 11-1 is labeled "Neandertal," represents a specialization that diverged from the line (or lines) that are more direct ancestors of modern *Homo sapiens*. Fossils like Es-Skhūl V and Djebel Kafzeh are functionally distinct from the Neandertal fossils; they exhibit the anatomical specializations necessary for human speech. Neandertal fossils lack these specializations. A general overlap with modern man is conceivable only if forms like Es-Skhūl V are put into the same class as, e.g., La Chapelle-aux-Saints, La Ferrassie, and Monte Circeo. Hominids who could have produced human speech would have to be classified with hominids who could not have produced human speech.

---

[1]Hominid fossils can be dated in terms of clearly defined geological phenomena such as glaciations, by the animal remains associated with the fossils, or by radiometric methods that involve determining the balance of various isotopes of radioactive materials. Pilbeam (1972) presents a concise introduction to the techniques and problems of dating fossils as well as the general framework of hominid evolution.

[2]The Würm glaciation, which lasted from about 70,000 to about 50,000 years ago.

This would be equivalent to putting forms that had the anatomical prerequisites for bipedal posture into the same class as forms that lacked this ability.

The question immediately arises, is this category, i.e., set of fossils labeled "Neandertal," a separate species? Although modern research has provided genetic criteria that differentiate species, the basic problem remains. Where does one draw the species boundary? It is useful to remember Darwin's definition of the term *species*

> as one arbitrarily given for the sake of convenience to a set of individuals closely resembling each other, . . . it does not essentially differ from the term *variety*, which is given to less distinct and more fluctuating forms. (1859, p. 52)

Darwin also noted that

> the only distinction between species and well-marked varieties is that the latter are known, or believed, to be connected at the present day by intermediate gradations, whereas species were formerly thus connected. (1859, p. 485)

It is evident that fossil forms like Broken Hill bridge the gap between classic Neandertal man and modern *Homo sapiens*. We do not know, and we probably never will be able to know, all the traits that may have differentiated various hominid populations that are now extinct. We do not know, for example, whether viable progeny would have resulted from the mating of forms like Cro-Magnon and La Quina. Even if we did know that viable progeny would result from the mating of Neandertal and early *Homo sapiens* populations, we would not necessarily conclude that these forms were members of the same species. The term *species,* as Darwin noted, is simply a labeling device. *Canis lupus* and *Canis familiaris* are considered to be separate species even though they may freely mate and have viable progeny. The behavioral attributes of wolves and dogs make it important for people, particularly shepherds, to place these animals in different species, even though some dogs, e.g., chihuahuas and St. Bernards, are more distinct morphologically and behaviorally and can't mate with each other. The question of separate, genetically significant, species labels for Neandertal and other fossil hominid populations is thus probably unanswerable and really not very crucial. We can simply note that different types of hominids apparently lived until comparatively recent times.

The use of the term *species* is different, however, for the paleontologist and the biologist. Fossils have to be grouped into species on the basis of morphology, even though the paleontologist hopes that morphological similarity reflects genetical similarity. Neandertal fossils could be labeled *Homo neanderthalensis* if we felt that the ability to produce the full range of sounds of human speech is the defining characteristic of the species *Homo sapiens*. This would essentially be an extreme Cartesian position, making present-day human language the defining characteristic. This seems, to me, to be too narrow a distinction. Though Neandertal hominids may not have had the speech-producing ability of modern humans they must have employed language. Even if we wanted to state that language is the defining characteristic of *Homo sapiens* we would have to admit the possibility of forms of language other than those characteristic of modern humans. *Human* language, the possible language of present-day humans, should not be regarded as the "critical" factor that determines the question of speciation. The classification *Homo sapiens neanderthalensis* thus is more reasonable. But the question of whether Neandertal fossils should be labeled *Homo neanderthalensis* or *Homo sapiens neanderthalensis* is itself not very productive, because we cannot deduce the range of biological and behavioral data that would make either label meaningfully distinctive.

Figure 12-1 is a very tentative "family tree" that represents a hypothetical hominid lineage for the recent past. The fossils in the right branching lineage represent the hominids who retained specializations that ultimately formed the bases of human language. The uppermost group of fossils represent a sampling of hominids who are generally considered representative of archaic forms of modern *Homo sapiens*. We have listed some of the fossils so classified by Howells (in press). The fossils listed below this group in the lineage have modern supralaryngeal vocal tracts and skulls that are modern in most respects (Howells, 1970, in press). They have the brow ridges that probably led Brace (1964) to classify them as "Neandertal," but this is a fairly trivial reason for putting them into the same class as the fossils in the left branching lineage. (We'll return to the brow ridge question later.)

The list of fossils grouped together in the Neandertal lineage also could be expanded. The Neandertal fossils discussed in Chapter 10 obviously fit into this grouping. So do many of the fossils listed by Oakley et al. (1971) as well as those classified as Neandertal by Howells (1970, in press). These late Neandertal fossils appear to be descendants of fossils like the Arago fossils recently discovered by the deLumleys (deLumley, in press). The adult Arago fossil looks very much like the adolescent Neandertal fossils discussed by Vlček (1970); for example, it has a mandible that resembles a longer version of the mandible of a very young Neandertal fossil or a newborn human, lacking the massiveness of the adult Neandertal mandible[3] (Figures 10-6 and 10-10). The details of this hypothetical lineage, from the Arago fossil to the late Neandertal fossils, have been left indeterminate. It would be foolish, given the present absence of intermediate fossil remains, to draw up a detailed family tree. What does seem evident is that there was a sustained selective pressure that ultimately resulted in the "classic"

---

[3]These resemblances are first impressions, and we must wait for a more systematic quantitative investigation of the affinities of late Neandertal fossils to this earlier fossil. However, the deLumleys' initial classification of these fossils as "Anteneanderthaliens" appears to be reasonable.

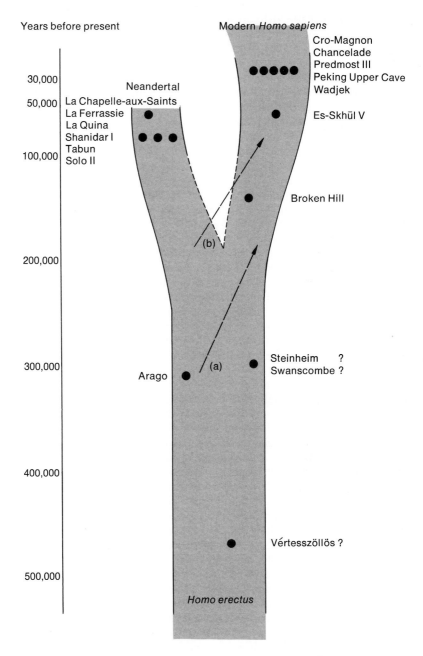

Figure 12-1 Tentative "family tree" of recent hominid evolution.

Neandertal skull with its extreme prognathism and supraorbital brow ridges.[4]

What selective value might the special characteristics of Neandertal man have had? Virtually all appraisals of the functional value of the prognathous Neandertal face agree that the large teeth it supported would be very effective for chewing (Boule and Vallois, 1957). Brace (1964) has elaborated on this theme, claiming that the Neandertal front teeth were regularly used to grasp objects. The massive brow ridge, in this light, would be simply a concomitant skeletal feature supporting the temporal muscles, which can exert an upward force on the mandible. Whether Neandertal men or women actually used their teeth as a set of living pliers is irrelevant. We can account for the selective advantage of the prognathous Neandertal face in a far simpler manner by taking account of the factors that influence the efficiency of chewing in hominids and the relation of chewing to the absorption of nutrients.

Dental studies (Manley and Braley, 1950; Manley and Shiere, 1950; Manley and Vinton, 1951) show that chewing efficiency in *Homo sapiens* is solely a function of the surface area of the teeth that is in contact in the act of chewing—in other words, the "swept" tooth area. Boule and Vallois (1957) pointed out the larger tooth area of Neandertal fossils. The effect of efficient mastication of food is to increase the absorption of nutrients about 10 per cent in *Homo sapiens.* Mutations that resulted in an increase in chewing efficiency therefore would have had a selective advantage and would have been retained. Hominid forms that have smaller tooth areas have less efficient chewing. The reduction of the mandible in modern *Homo sapiens,* therefore, cannot be ascribed to enhancing chewing efficiency. Neandertal man probably represents the end point of a hominid lineage specialized for chewing.

The evolution of the bent two-tube vocal tract that is apparent in forms like Es-Skhūl V is the result of a different selective pressure, specialization for enhanced vocal communication. Es-Skhūl V and other late forms in this lineage have reduced mandibles, which, in turn, probably reflect the evolution of the arched roof of the human pharynx. David Pilbeam and Edmund S. Crelin, for example, have both independently proposed that the evolution of the human pharynx may have restructured the hominid skull: as the larynx descended, the base of the skull gradually shortened. If the starting point for this process were a long, low skull like the Arago fossil, the shortening of the skull base would have caused the facial region to pull inward from its outthrust position. With the face thus pulled in, the cranium would have had to become higher in order to contain the same amount of brain tissue. As this happened, the brow and sides of the skull would have become more vertical. The starting point could also have been a later Neandertal skull or an earlier, less specialized *Homo erectus* skull.

[4]Depending on the particular skeletal measures involved, the Neandertal dimensions are 4 to 6 standard deviations from similar dimensions derived from measurements of the total range of modern *Homo sapiens* (Howells, in press).

The process may have occurred independently several times. The arrows labeled (a) and (b) on Figure 12-1 point to this possibility. All we can say, given the "Imperfection of the Geological Record" that Darwin noted, is that two lines of specialization appear to have occurred, derived from the *Homo erectus* skull. Anatomical specializations were retained that conferred selective advantages with regard either to chewing or to vocal communication. Some fossil hominids, such as Broken Hill, may indeed represent either transitions or compromises. In less technical cultures the selective advantages of enhanced vocal communication might not have outweighed the advantages of being able to chew more efficiently.

The gradual development of hominid culture and technology would have placed a greater and greater selective advantage on enhanced linguistic ability. The effect of being able to talk ten times faster, a consequence of fully encoded human speech, would be more apparent when there was more to talk about and when fires and access to many cutting tools (a consequence of improved tool-making technology) placed less value on chewing. The human-like supralaryngeal vocal tract is also less efficient for respiration. The right-angle bend in the adult human supralaryngeal airway increases its flow resistance, making it less efficient than the newborn infant's airway (Kirchner, 1970). The nonhuman supralaryngeal anatomy allows the oral cavity to be sealed from the rest of the airway during inspiration, which aids the sense of smell (Negus, 1949) and allows an animal to breathe while its mouth contains a liquid (e.g., when a dog laps water). The adult human supralaryngeal airways also increase the possibility of asphyxiation; food lodged in the pharynx can block the entrance to the larynx. This is not possible in the nonhuman supralaryngeal airways, because the supralaryngeal pharynx serves as a common pathway for both food and air only in adult *Homo sapiens*. The selective advantages of communication would be overwhelming only when the value of communication in the total hominid culture outweighed these disadvantages. Complete encoding, as we noted in Chapter 11, thus may have occurred very late in the course of hominid evolution, and some of the fossil hominids whom we have labeled Neandertal may have been among the direct ancestors of *Homo sapiens*. However, the Neandertal hominids who retained the "classic" Neandertal skull presumably became extinct. As Darwin noted,

> the extinction of old forms and the production of new and improved forms are intimately connected together. (1859, p. 317)

There are bound to be extinct hominid forms just as there are extinct ungulates, carnivores, and so on.

If the process of anatomical specialization for enhanced vocal communication started at a late period, it would have proceeded rapidly. The sounds of human speech coupled with the neural mechanisms of speech encoding and decoding would have exerted a strong selective pressure. Natural selection would have insured the survival of faster talkers. The presence or absence of particular sounds in the vocal communications of hominid populations in an earlier period, without the coeval occurrence of the neural mechanisms for decoding and encoding, also would have channeled hominid evolution into at least two lineages. Animal studies, such as the ones relating to frogs and birds that we discussed earlier, have established the role of vocalizations in courtship and mating. The presence or absence of human-like speech would have served as a powerful influence in assortative mating. In the present population of *Homo sapiens* it is evident that linguistic differences and affinities play a strong role in mate selection (Neel and Ward, 1970; Ward, 1972). We would expect this phenomenon to be accentuated when different hominid populations were inherently unable to produce the sounds of other groups. Sexual selection determined by speech patterns may thus have played a significant role in the divergence of groups like the late Neandertals from other kinds of hominids. Human languages never have as many nasal sounds as they might have. For example, one of the "universals" of human language is the fact that in a given language the frequency of occurrence of nasal vowels is always less than that of nonnasal vowels (Ferguson, 1963, p. 58). Nasal vowels also appear to have been less frequent in earlier Indo-European languages. This relative absence of nasalization may simply reflect an earlier situation when modern forms of *Homo sapiens* coexisted with hominids who could not produce unnasalized speech. Producing unnasalized sounds would have resulted in speech that was maximally distinct from that of the Neandertal population.

Humans often tend to enhance differences that relate to sexual selection. Normal speakers of American English, for example, emphasize the formant frequency differences that differentiate adult males and females. Men tend to speak as though they had larger and longer supralaryngeal tracts than they actually have, and the distinctions appear to be learned by small children (Sachs et al., 1973). There also actually are systematic differences between the supralaryngeal vocal tracts of males and females. The rate of mandibular growth abruptly increases at the onset of puberty in males[5] (Walker and Kowalski, 1972), and the adult male supralaryngeal vocal tract typically is longer than the adult female vocal tract (Fant, 1960). Humans enhance this difference to signal their "desired" sexual role.

NEOTENY AND VARIATION

It is clear that the skeletal features of adult *Homo sapiens* do not particularly resemble those of newborn *Homo sapiens*. The infantile

---

[5] The longer mandibles of males also are associated with slightly larger brow ridges in some populations. This is in accord with the presumed correlation of mandible and supraorbital brow ridge that we discussed in connection with chewing.

forms of primates often do not resemble their adult forms (Schultz, 1969). Moreover, Schultz (1944, 1968) has shown that the infantile forms of various newborn primates resemble newborn *Homo sapiens,* whereas the adult forms of these nonhuman primates diverge markedly from adult *Homo sapiens.* However, this does not mean that adult *Homo sapiens* has evolved by preserving neonatal features (Montagu, 1962). If this were the case, adult *Homo sapiens* would not be able to speak. The theory of neoteny, which claims that humans have evolved by retaining juvenile characteristics, is viable only if one ignores the morphology and ontogenetic development of *Homo sapiens.*

A related problem that becomes clear in the light of the skeletal similarities that exist between newborn *Homo sapiens* and adult Neandertal fossil skulls is the variation in certain isolated skeletal features within the adult population of *Homo sapiens.* Many of the skeletal features characteristic of the adult Neandertal skull can often be noted in "normal" adult human skulls. For example, the foramen magnum sometimes is shaped like that of Neandertal skulls, the auditory meatus, which fixes the ear's position, is sometimes positioned low on the skull, and the dental arch sometimes is shaped like the adult Neandertal dental arch. Physical anthropologists sometimes compile long lists of these similarities to support the claim that Neandertal man cannot be differentiated from modern *Homo sapiens.* These variations simply demonstrate that the course of human ontogenetic development is not uniform, that variations may exist, and that some individual adult humans or adult human populations may retain one or more of the anatomical features characteristic of newborn humans—anatomical features that are common to human newborns, infant Neandertals, and adult Neandertals (Vlček, 1970). What is not "normal" is for the general anatomical development to retain what Legros Clark called "the total morphological pattern" characteristic of newborn *Homo sapiens.* This condition is considered pathological. Down's syndrome, as we noted earlier, results in the retention of all, or some, of the morphological characteristics of the newborn to the point where it interferes with normal behavior (Benda, 1969). Down's syndrome is recognized as pathological because the development of major anatomical and neurological complexes is arrested. Deviations in the rate of development of individual anatomical features in the "normal" population can and must be expected. That is why we can find isolated anatomical features of Neandertal fossils in the "normal" adult human population.

PROBLEMS AND QUESTIONS

It is always refreshing to close the discussion of a theory by pointing out some of the questions and problems that the theory raises—what Darwin (1859, Chapter VI) termed the "Difficulties on Theory." Like Darwin, we are still at the mercy of the "Imperfection of the Geological Record" (1859, Chapter IX). The "family tree" in Figure 12-1 is rather sketchy. Fossils like Vértesszöllös cranium lack intact skull bases, and we cannot reconstruct their supralaryngeal vocal tracts. It is provisionally listed in the right branching lineage because the back of its skull is consistent with the skulls of hominids who did have human-like supralaryngeal vocal tracts. There are so few fossil remains from this period of time that one looks at anything that's available. We also lack *Homo erectus* skulls with well-preserved skull bases. The Steinheim skull still has to be restored. These gaps hopefully will be filled in.

There are many other things that we don't know. For instance, the presence or absence of encoding in the general behavior and in the communications of nonhuman primates is an open question. The presence of a system of sound contrasts analogous to human phonetic features in the vocal communications of nonhuman primates also is a relevant question. Indeed, the whole question of "language" in animals and what its syntax might be is of interest with respect to the evolution of language and the possible forms that language may be realized in. Language does not necessarily have to involve all of the factors that have structured human language. The probable absence of speech encoding equivalent to that of modern *Homo sapiens* and the presence of a highly developed culture both point to the presence of a different language in Neandertal culture. Conversely, birds have the potential for producing encoded speech signals. Birds such as the mynah (Klatt and Stefanski, 1974) can imitate human speech using a sound-producing mechanism that does not involve either a larynx or a supralaryngeal vocal tract, although they lack the cognitive ability that is also a necessary factor in language. It is most unlikely that birds could develop a language unless they had larger brains.

MODERN *HOMO SAPIENS*

One of the great "mysteries" of human evolution is the sudden acceleration in the rate of change of human culture that occurred between 40,000 and 30,000 years ago. In Figure 12-1 some of the earlier forms of modern *Homo sapiens* are listed at the top of the right branching lineage. Although the stone tools and toolworking techniques associated with these fossils are linked to earlier techniques and earlier tools (Bordes, 1968), there are immense changes. Tool types became more varied; new materials were utilized; finely detailed bone implements like needles became common; new techniques for stoneworking appeared, including use of long, narrow flakes with parallel sides as blades for making tools; grinding and

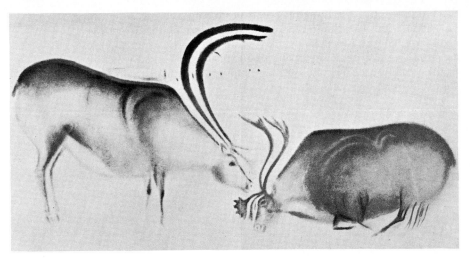

Figure 12-2 Abbé Breuil's drawing of the Font de Gaume reindeer. (From Ucko and Rosenfeld, 1967.)

polishing ultimately became commonplace. The appearance of art was sudden (Ucko and Rosenfeld, 1967). The drawings of the upper paleolithic, which were executed on cave walls, have been equaled but never surpassed in human history. In Figure 12-2 a paleolithic cave drawing of reindeer found at the cave of Font de Gaume in the Dordogne region of France is reproduced. The drawing was made by the Abbé Breuil in 1901. Over a hundred decorated caves have been found since the first discoveries over a century ago. The art of the paleolithic also includes engravings and sculpture. Accompanying the art is the first evidence of the use of technology to expand human cognitive abilities. Orthographic systems can be viewed as devices that overcome the limits of human memory, whether the orthography is numerical, alphabetic, or syllabic. Alexander Marshack's (1972) studies of the apparent engraved patterns found on mobilary objects, e.g., batons and spear throwers, perhaps demonstrate the existence of complex notational systems. The exact nature of what was being recorded is not always clear. However, the startling thing is that notational systems were in use 30,000 years ago. Human morphology, cognitive ability, and language probably were fully evolved.

Human language is thus the result of the convergence of many factors: automatization, cognitive ability, encoding. But the particular form that human language has taken appears to be the result of the evolution of the human supralaryngeal vocal apparatus. It and the concomitant changes in the morphology of the skull that differentiate present-day *Homo sapiens* from all other living animals were thus factors as important in the late stages of hominid evolution as dentition and bipedal posture were in early stages. However, the uniqueness of the human speech-producing apparatus should not distract our attention from the aspects of human language that are more general and that we may share with other species. We are what we are because of our linguistic ability, and the study of the evolution of that ability may help us understand both how we came to be and what we really are.

Bibliography

Andrew, R. J., 1963, Trends apparent in the evolution of vocalization in the Old World monkeys and apes, *Symp. Zool. Soc. Lond., 10,* 89–101.

Atkinson, J. R., 1973, *Aspects of intonation in speech: Implications from an experimental study of fundamental frequency,* unpublished Ph.D. dissertation, University of Connecticut.

Bacon, F., 1620, Magna instauratio [The great instauration], IN *Essays, advancement of learning, New Atlantis and other pieces,* ed. R. Jones, Odyssey Press (1937).

Bada, J. L., Schroeder, R. A., Trotsch, R., and Berger, R., 1974, Concordance of collagen-based radiocarbon and aspartic acid racemization ages, *Proc. Natl. Acad. Sci., 71,* 914–917.

Bastian, J., 1965, Primate signalling systems and human languages, IN *Primate behavior: Field studies of monkeys and apes,* ed. I. Devore, Holt, Rinehart and Winston.

Beck, B. B., in press, Primate tool behavior, IN *Proceedings of the IXth international congress of anthropological and ethnological science, Chicago, Ill.,* Mouton.

Bell, C., 1844, *Anatomy and philosophy of expression,* 3rd ed., G. Bell and Sons.

Bell, C. G., Fujisaki, H., Heinz, J. M., Stevens, K. N., and House, A. S., 1961, Reduction of speech spectra by analysis-by-synthesis techniques, *J. Acoust. Soc. Amer., 33,* 1725–1736.

Bell-Berti, F., 1973, *The velopharyngeal mechanism: An electromyographic study,* unpublished Ph.D. thesis, City University of New York (also *Haskins Lab. Status rep. speech res. Suppl.,* Haskins Laboratories, 270 Crown Street, New Haven, Conn. 06510).

Benda, C. E., 1969, *Down's syndrome, mongolism and its management,* Grune and Stratton.

Beranek, L. L., 1954, *Acoustics,* McGraw-Hill.

Bloomfield, L., 1933, *Language,* Holt.

Bogert, C. M., 1960, The influence of sound on the behavior of amphibians and reptiles, IN *Animal sounds and communication,* eds. W. E. Lanyon and W. N. Tavolga, American Institute of Biological Sciences.

Bonifay, E., and Vandermeersch, B., 1962, Dépots rituels d'ossements d'ours dans le gisement moustérien du Regourdu (Montignac, Dordogne), *Compt. Rend. Hebd. Seanc. Acad. Sci. Paris, 255,* 1635–1636.

Bordes, F., 1968, *The old stone age*, World University Library, McGraw-Hill.

———,1972, *A Tale of two caves*, Harper and Row.

Bosma, J. F., and Fletcher, S. G., 1961, The upper pharynx, a review. Part I: Embroyology and anatomy, *Ann. Otol. Rhinol. Laryngol., 70*, 935–973.

Boule, M., 1911–1913, L'homme fosille de la Chapelle-aux-Saints, *Ann. Paleontol., 6,* 109; *7, 21, 85; 8,* 1.

———, and Vallois, H. V., 1957, *Fossil men*, Dryden Press.

Brace, C. L., 1964, The fate of the "classic" Neanderthals: A consideration of hominid catastrophism, *Curr. Anthropol., 5,* 3–43.

Broca, P., 1861, Nouvelle observation d'aphemie produite par une lesion de la moitie posterieure des deuxieme et troisieme ciconvolutions frontales, *Bull. Soc. Anat. Paris, 6* (series 2), 398–407.

Brodie, A. G., 1949, On the growth pattern of the human head from three months to eight years of life, *Amer. J. Anat., 68,* 209–259.

Brose, D. S., and Wolpoff, M. H., 1971, Early upper paleolithic man and late middle paleolithic tools, *Amer. Anthropologist, 73,* 1156–1194.

Campbell, B., 1966, *Human evolution: An introduction to man's adaptions*, Aldine.

Camper, P., 1779, Account of the organs of speech of the orang outang, *Phil. Trans., 69,* 139–150.

Capranica, R. R., 1965, *The evoked vocal response of the bullfrog*, MIT Press.

Chiba, T., and M. Kajiyama, 1958, *The vowel: Its nature and structure*, Phonetic Society of Japan.

Chomsky, N., 1957, *Syntactic structures*, Mouton.

———, 1964, *Aspects of the theory of syntax*, MIT Press.

———, 1968, *Language and mind*, Harcourt.

———, and Halle, M., 1968, *The sound pattern of English*, Harper.

Coon, C. S., 1966, *The origin of races*, Knopf.

Cooper, F. S., Liberman, A. M., Borst, J. M., and Gerstman, L. J., 1952, Some experiments on the perception of synthetic speech sounds, *J. Acoust. Soc. Amer., 24,* 597–606.

Crelin, E. S., 1969, *Anatomy of the newborn: An atlas*, Lea and Febiger.

———, 1973, The Steinheim skull: A linguistic link, *Yale Scientific, 48,* 10–14.

Darwin, C., 1859, *On the origin of species* (facsimile ed.), Atheneum.

———, 1872, *The expression of emotion in man and animals*, J. Murray.

Darwin, C. J., 1971, Ear differences in the recall of fricatives and vowels, *Quart. J. Exptl. Psychol., 23,* 386–392.

Day, M., 1965, *Guide to fossil man*, World.

Debetz, G. F., 1961, Soviet anthropological theory, IN *Social life of early man*, ed. S. L. Washburn, Aldine.

Delattre, P. C., Liberman, A. M., and Cooper, F. S., 1955, Acoustic loci and transitional cues for consonants, *J. Acoust. Soc. Amer., 27,* 769–773.

deLumley, H., and deLumley, M. A., 1971, Découverte de restes humains anténéandertaliens datés du début du Riss à la Caune de l'Arago (Tautavel, Pyrénées-Orientales), *Compt. Rend. Acad. Sci. Paris, 272,* 1739–1742.

deLumley, M. A., in press, Les anteneanderthaliens de l'ouest de l'Europe, In *Proceedings of the IXth international congress of anthropological and ethnological science, Chicago, Ill.,* Mouton.

Descartes, R., 1892, Correspondence, IN *The philosophy of Descartes*, trans. H. A. P. Torrey, Holt.

Descartes, R., 1955, *The philosophical works of Descartes*, trans. E. S. Haldane and R. T. Ross, Dover.

DuBrul, E. L., 1958, *Evolution of the speech apparatus*, Charles C Thomas.

———, and Reed, C. A., 1960, Skeletal evidence of speech? *Amer. J. Phys. Anthropol., 18,* 153–156.

Edinger, T., 1948, Evolution of the horse brain, *Mem. Geol. Soc. Amer., 25,* 1–777.

Eimas, P. D., and Corbit, J. D., 1973, Selective adaption of linguistic feature detectors, *Cog. Psychol., 4,* 99–109.

———, Siqueland, E. R., Jusczyk, P., and Vigorito, J., 1971, Speech perception in infants, *Science, 171,* 303–306.

Evarts, E. V., 1973, Motor cortex reflexes associated with learned movement, *Science, 179,* 501–503.

Fant, G., 1960, *Acoustic theory of speech production*, Mouton.

Farnsworth, D. W., 1940, High-speed motion pictures of the human vocal cords, *Bell Lab. Rec., 18,* 203–208.

Ferguson, C. A., 1963, Assumptions about nasals, IN *Univerals of language*, 2nd ed., MIT Press.

Ferrein, C. J., 1741, *Mem. Acad. Paris,* 409–432 (Nov. 15).

Flanagan, J. L., 1955, A difference limen for vowel formant frequency, *J. Acoust. Soc. Amer., 27,* 613–617.

————, 1972, *Speech analysis, synthesis and perception,* 2nd ed., Springer.

Fodor, J., Bever, T. B., and Garrett, M. F., 1974, *The psychology of language: An introduction to psycholinguistics and generative grammar,* McGraw-Hill.

Fouts, R. S., 1973, Acquisition and testing of gestural signs in four young chimpanzees, *Science, 180,* 978–980.

Frishkopf, L. S., and Goldstein, M. H., Jr., 1963, Responses to acoustic stimuli from single units in the eighth nerve of the bullfrog, *J. Acoust. Soc. Amer., 35,* 1219–1228.

Gardner, R. A., and Gardner, B. T., 1969, Teaching sign language to a chimpanzee, *Science, 165,* 664–672.

Gerstman, L., 1967, Classification of self-normalized vowels, IN *Proceedings of IEEE conference on speech communication and processing,* pp. 97–100.

Geschwind, N., 1970, The organization of language and the brain, *Science, 170,* 940–944.

————, and Levitsky, W., 1968, Human brain: Left-right asymmetries in temporal speech region, *Science, 161,* 186–187.

Gold, B., 1962, Computer program for pitch extraction, *J. Acoust. Soc. Amer., 34,* 916–921.

Goodall, J., 1965, Chimpanzees of the Gombe Stream reserve, IN *Primate behavior,* ed. I. DeVore, Holt, Rinehart and Winston.

———— (van Lawick-Goodall), 1968, A preliminary report on expressive movements and communication in the Gombe Stream chimpanzees, IN *Primates: Studies in adaption and variability,* ed. P. Jay, Holt, Rinehart and Winston.

———— (van Lawick-Goodall), 1971, *In the shadow of man,* Dell.

Green, S., 1973, Physiological control of vocalizations in the Japanese monkey: Inferences from a field study, *J. Acoust. Soc. Amer., 53,* 310 (abstract).

Grenewalt, C. A., 1967, *Bird song: Acoustics and physiology,* Smithsonian Institution.

Haeckel, E., 1866, *Generelle Morphologie der Organismen,* Vol. 2 of *Allgemeine Entwicklungsgeschichte der Organismen,* Reimer.

Halle, M., 1957, In defense of the number two, IN *Studies presented to Joshua Whatmough on his sixtieth birthday,* ed. E. Pulgram, Mouton.

Hamburg, D. A., 1963, Emotions in the perspective of human evolution, IN *Expression of the emotions in man,* ed. P. Knapp, International Universities Press.

Hayes, C., 1952, *The ape in our house,* Harper.

Heinz, J. M., 1962, Reduction of speech spectra to descriptions in terms of vocal tract area functions, Sc.D. thesis, Massachusetts Institute of Technology.

Helmholtz, H. L., 1863, *Die Tonempfindung,* Berlin (reprinted in translation as *On the sensations of tone,* Dover, 1954).

Henke, W. L., 1966, *Dynamic articulatory model of speech production using computer simulation,* Ph.D. dissertation, Massachusetts Institute of Technology (Appendix B).

Hewes, G. W., 1973, Primate communication and the gestural origin of language, *Curr. Anthropol., 14,* 5–24.

Hill, J. H., 1972, On the evolutionary foundations of language, *Amer. Anthropologist, 74,* 308–317.

Hirsch, I. J., 1959, Auditory perception of temporal order, *J. Acoust. Soc. Amer., 31,* 759–767.

————, and Sherrick, C. E., Jr., 1961, Perceived order in different sense modalities, *J. Exptl. Psychol., 62,* 423–432.

Hockett, C. F., and Ascher, R., 1964, The human revolution, *Curr. Anthropol., 5,* 135–168.

Hollien, H., Moore, P., Wendahl, R. W., and Michel, J. F., 1966, On the nature of vocal fry, *J. Speech Hearing Res., 9,* 245–247.

Holloway, R. L., 1972, Australopithecine endocasts, brain evolution in the Hominoidea, and a model of hominid evolution, IN *The functional and evolutionary biology of primates,* ed. R. Tuttle, Aldine-Atherton.

————, 1973a, New endocranial values for the East African early hominids, *Nature, 243,* 97–99.

————, 1973b, Endocranial capacities of the early African hominids and the role of the brain in human mosaic evolution, *J. Human Evol.*

Howells, W. W., 1970, Mount Carmel man: Morphological relationships, IN *Proceedings of the VIIIth international congress of anthropological and ethnological science, Tokyo, Vol. I: Anthropology,* pp. 269–272.

————, in press, Neanderthal man: Facts and figures, IN *Proceedings of the IXth international congress of anthropological and ethnological science, Chicago, Ill.,* Mouton.

Hoy, R. R., and Paul, R. C., **1973,** Genetic control of song specificity in crickets, *Science, 180,* 82–83.

✓ **Huxley, T. H., 1863,** *Evidence as to man's place in nature,* Williams and Norgate.

Irwin, O. C., 1948, Infant speech: Development of vowel sounds, *J. Speech Hearing Disorders, 13,* 31–34.

✓ **Jakobson, R., 1968,** *Child language aphasia and phonological universals,* Mouton.

Jakobson, R. C., Fant, G. M., and Halle, 1952, *Preliminaries to speech analysis,* MIT Press.

✓ **Jerison, H. J., 1970,** Brain evolution: New light on old principles, *Science, 170,* 1224–1225.

Jones, T. B., and Kamil, A. C., 1973, Tool-making and tool-use in the northern blue jay, *Science, 180,* 1076–1077.

Kelemen, G., 1948, The anatomical basis of phonation in the chimpanzee, *J. Morphol., 82,* 229–256.

———, **1958,** Physiology of phonation in primates, *Logos, 1,* 32–35.

———, **1961,** Anatomy of the larynx as a vocal organ: Evolutionary aspects, *Logos, 4,* 46–55.

✓ ———, **1969,** Anatomy of the larynx and the anatomical basis of vocal performance, *Chimpanzee, 1,* 165–186.

✓ **Kellogg, W. N., 1968,** Communication and language in the home-raised chimpanzee, *Science, 162,* 423–427.

Kenyon, K. W., 1969, *The sea otter in the eastern Pacific Ocean,* Government Printing Office.

Kiang, N. Y.-S., and Peake, W. T., 1960, Components of electrical responses recorded from the cochlea, *Ann. Otol. Rhinol. Laryngol., 69,* 448–458.

Kimura, D., 1964, Left-right differences: The perception of melodies, *Quart. J. Exptl. Psychol., 16,* 355–358.

✓ ———, **1973,** The asymmetry of the human brain, *Sci. American, 228,* 70–78.

Kirchner, J. A., 1970, *Pressman and Kelemen's physiology of the larynx,* rev. ed., American Academy of Ophthalmology and Otolaryngology.

Klatt, D. H., and Stefanski, R. A., 1974, How does a mynah bird imitate human speech? *J. Acoust. Soc. Amer.* (in press).

———, **Stevens, K. N., and Mead, J., 1968,** Studies of articulatory activity and airflow during speech, *Ann. N.Y. Acad. Sci., 155,* 42–54.

Klein, R. G., 1973, Geologic antiquity of Rhodesian man, *Nature, 244,* 311–312.

Koenig, W. H., Dunn, H. K., and Lacey, L. Y., 1946, The sound spectrograph, *J. Acoust. Soc. Amer., 18,* 19–49.

Kratzenstein, C. G., 1780, Sur la naissance de la formation des voyelles, *J. Phys. Chim. Hist. Nat. Arts, 21 (1782),* 358–381 (translated from *Acta Acad. Petrograd,* 1780).

Kuipers, A. H., 1960, *Phoneme and morpheme in Kabardian,* Mouton.

Ladefoged, P., and Broadbent, D. E., 1957, Information conveyed by vowels, *J. Acoust. Soc. Amer., 29,* 98–104.

———, **DeClerk, J., Lindau, M., and Papcun, G., 1972,** An auditory motor theory of speech production, *UCLA Working Papers Phonet., 22,* 48–75.

La Mettrie, J. O., 1747, *De l'homme-machine,* ed. A. Vartanian (critical ed., 1960), Princeton University Press.

✓ **Lancaster, J. B., 1968,** Primate communication systems and the emergence of human language, IN *Primates,* ed. P. C. Jay, Holt, Rinehart and Winston.

✓ **Lane, H., 1965,** Motor theory of speech perception: A critical review, *Psychol. Rev., 72,* 175–309.

Lartet, E., 1868, De quelques cas de progression organique vérifiables dans la succession des temps, géologiques sur des mammifères de même famille et de même genre, *Compt. Rend. Acad. Sci. Paris, 66,* 1119–1122.

Leakey, M. D., 1971, *Olduvai gorge,* Vol. III, University Press.

✓ **Leakey, R. E. F., 1973,** Evidence for an advanced Plio-Pleistocene hominid from East Rundolf, Kenya, *Nature, 242,* 447–450.

LeMay, M., and Culebras, A., 1972, Human brain—Morphological differences in the hemispheres demonstrable by cartoid arteriography, *New Engl. J. Med., 287,* 168–170.

✓ **Lenneberg, E. H., 1967,** *Biological foundations of language,* Wiley.

✓ **Liberman, A. M., 1970,** The grammars of speech and language, *Cog. Psychol., 1,* 301–323.

✓ ———, **Cooper, F. S., Shankweiler, D. P., and Studdert-Kennedy, M., 1967,** Perception of the speech code, *Psychol. Rev., 74,* 431–461.

Lieberman, P., 1960, Perturbations in vocal pitch, *J. Acoust. Soc. Amer., 33,* 597–603.

———, **1963a,** Some acoustic measures of the periodicity of normal and pathologic laryngea, *J. Acoust. Soc. Amer., 35,* 334–353.

———, **1963b,** Some effects of semantic and grammatical context on the production and perception of speech, *Lang. Speech, 6,* 172–187.

———, **1967,** *Intonation, perception, and language,* MIT Press.

———, **1968,** Primate vocalizations and human linguistic ability, *J. Acoust. Soc. Amer., 44,* 1574–1584.

———, **1970,** Towards a unified phonetic theory, *Linguist. Inquiry, 1,* 307–322.

———, **1972,** *The speech of primates,* Mouton.

———, **1973,** On the evolution of human language: A unified view, *Cognition, 2,* 59–94.

———, **and Crelin, E. S., 1971,** On the speech of Neanderthal man, *Linguist. Inquiry, 2,* 203–222.

———, **Klatt, D. H., and Wilson, W. A., 1969,** Vocal tract limitations on the vowel repertoires of rhesus monkey and other nonhuman primates, *Science, 164,* 1185–1187.

———, **Harris, K. S., Wolff, P., and Russell, L. H., 1972a,** Newborn infant cry and nonhuman primate vocalizations, *J. Speech Hearing Res., 14,* 718–727 (also in *Hoskins Lab. Status Rep. 17/18,* 1968).

———, **Crelin, E. S., and Klatt, D. H., 1972b,** Phonetic ability and related anatomy of the newborn, adult human, Neanderthal man, and the chimpanzee, *Amer. Anthropologist, 74,* 287–307.

Liljencrants, J., and Lindblom, B., 1972, Numerical simulation of vowel quality systems: The role of perceptual contrast, *Language, 48,* 839–862.

Lindblom, B., 1963, Spectrographic study of vowel reduction, *J. Acoust. Soc. Amer., 35,* 1773–1781.

———, **and Sundberg, J., 1969,** A quantitative model of vowel production and the distinctive features of Swedish vowels, *Speech Transmission Lab. Rep., 1.* Royal Institute of Technology, Stockholm, Sweden.

Lisker, L., and Abramson, A. S., 1964, A cross-language study of voicing in initial stops: Acoustical measurements, *Word, 20,* 384–422.

———, **1971,** Distinctive features and laryngeal control, *Language, 47,* 767–785.

Lynip, A. W., 1951, The uses of magnetic devices in the collection and analysis of the preverbal utterances of an infant, *Genet. Psychol. Monogr., 44,* 221–262.

MacNeilage, P. F., and Sholes, G. N., 1964, An electromyographic study of the tongue during vowel production, *J. Speech Hearing Res., 7,* 209–232.

Manley, R. S., and Braley, L. C., 1950, Masticatory performance and efficiency, *J. Dent. Res., 29,* 448–462.

———, **and Shiere, F. R., 1950,** The effect of dental efficiency on mastication and food preference, *Oral Surg. Oral Med. Oral Pathol., 3,* 674–685.

———, **and Vinton, P., 1951,** A survey of the chewing ability of denture wearers, *J. Dent. Res., 30,* 314–321.

Markel, N. M., in press, Converbal behavior associated with conversation turns, IN *Proceedings of a conference on the organisation of behavior in face-to-face interaction, IXth international congress of anthropological and ethnological science, Chicago, Ill.,* Mouton.

Marshack, A., 1972, *The roots of civilization: The cognitive beginnings of man's first art, symbol, and notation,* McGraw-Hill.

Mayr, E., 1964, Introduction to facsimile edition of Darwin's *On the origin of species,* Atheneum.

McAdam, D. W., and Whitaker, H. A., 1971, Language production: Electroencephalic localization in the normal human brain, *Science, 172,* 499–502.

McCown, T. D., and Keith, A., 1939, *The stone age of Mount Carmel,* Vol. II of *The fossil human remains from the Levalloiso-Mousterian,* Clarendon Press.

Mead, J., and Agostoni, E., 1964, Dynamics of breathing, IN *Handbook of physiology, Part I: Respiration,* eds. I. W. O. Fenn and H. Sahn, American Physiological Society.

Miller, G. A., 1956, The magical number seven, plus or minus two: Some limits on our capacity for processing information, *Psychol. Rev., 63,* 81–97.

Miller, J. M., Sutton, D., Pfingst, B., Ryan, A., and Beaton, R., 1972, Single cell activity in the auditory cortex of rhesus monkeys: Behavioral dependency, *Science, 177,* 449–451.

Montagu, M. F. A., 1962, Time, morphology and neoteny in the evolution of man, IN *Culture and the evolution of man,* ed. M. F. A. Montagu, Oxford University Press, pp. 324–342.

Montaigne, M. E., 1580, Apology for Raymond Sebond, IN *Selections from the essays of Montaigne,* ed. and trans. D. M. Frame, Appleton-Century-Crofts, 1948.

Morant, G. M., 1928, Studies of paleolithic man. III. The Rhodesian skull and its relations to Neanderthaloid and modern types, *Ann. Eugen., 3,* 337–360.

Mpitsos, G. J., and Davis, W. J., 1973,

Learning: Classical and avoidance conditioning in the mollusk *Pleurobranchaea, Science, 180,* 317–323.

Müller, J., 1848, *The physiology of the senses, voice and muscular motion with the mental faculties,* trans. W. Baly, Walton and Maberly.

Neel, J. V., and Ward, R. H., 1970, Village and tribal genetic distance among American Indians, and the possible implications for human evolution, *Proc. Amer. Acad. Sci., 65,* 323–330.

Negus, V. E., 1929, *The mechanism of the larynx,* Heinemann.

———, 1949, *The comparative anatomy and physiology of the larynx,* Hafner.

Noback, G. J., 1923, The developmental topography of the larynx, trachea, and lungs in fetus, new-born, infant and child, *Amer. J. Dis. Child., 26,* 515–533.

Nottebohm, F., 1970, Ontogeny of bird song, *Science, 167,* 950–956.

Oakley, K. P., Campbell, B. G., and Molleson, T. I., eds., 1971, *Catalogue of fossil hominids,* Part II: *Europe,* Trustees of the British Museum (Natural History).

Osgood, C. E., 1953, *Method and theory in experimental psychology,* Oxford University Press.

Penfield, W., and Roberts, L., 1959, *Speech and brain-mechanisms,* Princeton University Press.

Perkell, J. S., 1969, *Physiology of speech production: Results and implications of a quantitative cineradiographic study,* MIT Press.

Perrault, C., 1676, *Mémoires pur servir à l'histoire naturelle des animaux,* L'Imprimerie Royale.

Peterson, G. E., and Barney, H. L., 1952, Control methods used in a study of the vowels, *J. Acoust. Soc. Amer., 24,* 175–184.

———, Wang, W. S.-Y., and Sivertsen, E., 1958, Segmentation techniques in speech synthesis, *J. Acoust. Soc. Amer., 30,* 739–742.

Pilbeam, D., 1972, *The ascent of man: An introduction to human evolution,* Macmillan.

———, 1974, personal communication.

Postal, P. M., 1968, *Aspects of phonological theory,* Harper and Row.

Premack, D., 1972, Language in chimpanzee? *Science, 172,* 808–822.

Purkinje, K., 1836, *Badania w przedmiocie fizyologil mowy Ludzkiej,* Krakow.

Rand, T. C., 1971, Vocal tract size normalization in the perception of stop consonants, *Haskins Lab. Status Rep. Speech Res., SR-25/26,* 141–146.

Reynolds, P. C., 1972, Play, language and human evolution, paper presented at 1972 meeting of the American Association for the Advancement of Science, Washington, D.C.

Reynolds, V., and Reynolds, F., 1965, Chimpanzees of the Budongo forest, IN *Primate behavior,* ed. I. DeVore, Holt, Rinehart and Winston.

Rothenberg, M., 1968, *The breath-stream dynamics of simple-released-plosive production,* Karger.

Rowell, T. E., and Hinde, R. A., 1962, Vocal communication by the rhesus monkey (*Macacca mulatta*), *Proc. Zool. Soc. Lond., 138,* 279–294.

Rozin, P., Poritsky, S., and Sotsky, R., 1971, American children with reading problems can easily learn to read English represented by Chinese characters, *Science, 171,* 1264–1267.

Rumbaugh, D. M., 1973, Reading and sentence completion by a chimpanzee, *Science, 182,* 731–733.

Sachs, J., Lieberman, P., and Erickson, D., 1973, Anatomical and cultural determinants of male and female speech, IN *Language attitudes: Current trends and prospects,* eds. R. Shuy and R. Fasold, Georgetown University Press.

Scammon, R., 1923, A summary of the anatomy of the infant and child, IN *Pediatrics,* Vol. I, Chap. III, ed. I. Apt, Saunders, pp. 296–297.

Schultz, A. H., 1944, Age changes and variability in gibbons, *Amer. J. Phys. Anthropol.,* n.s. 2, 1–129.

———, 1968, The recent hominoid primates, IN *Perspectives on human evolution,* Vol. I, eds. S. L. Washburn and P. C. Jay, Holt, Rinehart and Winston, pp. 122–195.

———, 1969, *The life of primates,* Universe Books.

Shankweiler, D., and Studdert-Kennedy, M., 1967, Identification of consonants and vowels presented to left and right ears, *Quart. J. Exptl. Psychol., 19,* 59–63.

———, Verbrugge, R., and Strange, W., 1974, Measuring the increment in ambiguity of spoken vowels attributable to talker differences, *J. Acoust. Soc. Amer., 55,* 553.

Siebert, W. M., 1973, Signals and noise in sensory systems, *Technol. Rev.,* 23–29 (May).

Simpson, G. G., 1966, The biological nature of man, *Science, 152,* 472–478.

Sobotta, J., and Figge, F. H. J., 1965, *Atlas of human anatomy,* Vol. II, Hafner.

Solecki, R. S., 1971, *Shanidar, the first flower people,* Knopf.

Stephan, H., 1972, Evolution of primate brains: A comparative anatomical investigation, IN *The functional and evolutionary biology of primates,* ed. E. Tuttle, Aldine, pp. 155–174.

Stevens, K. N., 1972, Quantal nature of speech, IN *Human communication: A unified view,* eds. E. E. David and P. B. Denes, McGraw-Hill.

———, and House, A. S., 1955, Development of a quantitative description of vowel articulation, *J. Acoust. Soc. Amer., 27,* 484–493.

———, Bastide, R. P., and Smith, C. P., 1955, Electrical synthesizer of continuous speech, *J. Acoust. Soc. Amer., 27,* 207.

Stokoe, W. C., Jr., 1960, *Sign language structure: An outline of the visual communication system of the deaf,* Studies in Linguistics Occasional Paper 8, University of Buffalo.

Straus, W. L., Jr., and Cave, A. J. E., 1957, Pathology and posture of Neanderthal man, *Quart. Rev. Biol., 32,* 348–363.

Stuart, R. R., 1958, *The anatomy of the bullfrog,* Denoyer-Geppert.

Tobias, P. V., 1973, Implications of the new age estimates of the early South African hominids, *Nature, 246,* 79–83.

———, in press, Brain evolution in the Hominoidea, IN *Proceedings of the IXth international congress of anthropological and ethnological science, Chicago, Ill.,* Mouton.

Troubetzkoy, N. S., 1969, *Principles of phonology,* trans. C. Baltaxe, University of California Press.

Truby, H. M., Bosma, J. F., and Lind, J., 1965, *Newborn infant cry,* Almqvist and Wiksell.

Tyson, E., 1699, *Orang-outang, sive homo sylvestris: Or, the anatomy of a pygmie compared with that of a monkey, an ape, and a man,* Thomas Bennet and Daniel Brown.

Ucko, P. J., and Rosenfeld, A., 1967, *Paleolithic cave art,* World University Library, McGraw-Hill.

Vallois, H. V., 1961, The evidence of skeletons, IN *Social life of early man,* ed. S. L. Washburn, Aldine.

Van den Berg, J. W., 1960, Vocal ligaments versus registers, *Curr. Probl. Phoniat. Logoped., 1,* 19–34.

Virchow, R., 1872, Untersuchung des Neanderthal-Schädels, *Z. Ethnog., 4,* 157–165.

Vlček, E., 1970, Étude comparative onto-phylogénétique de l'enfant du Pech-de-l'Azé par rapport à d'autres enfants néandertaliens, IN *L'enfant du Pech-de-l'Azé,* ed. D. Feremback et al., Masson, pp. 149–186.

von Kempelen, W. R., 1791, *Mechanismum der menschlichen Sprache nebst der Beschreibung seiner sprechenden Maschine,* J. B. Degen.

Walker, G. F., and Kowalski, C. J., 1972, On the growth of the mandible, *Amer. J. Phys. Anthropol., 36,* 111–118.

Ward, R. H., 1972, personal communication.

Washburn, S. L., 1968, *The study of human evolution,* Oregon State System of Higher Education.

———, 1969, The evolution of human behavior, IN *The uniqueness of man,* ed. J. D. Roslansky, North-Holland.

Weiner, J. S., and Campbell, B. G., 1964, The taxonomic status of the Swanscombe skull, IN *The Swanscombe skull,* ed. C. D. Ovey, Royal Anthropological Institute of Great Britain.

Wernicke, C., 1874, *Der aphasische Symptomen-complex,* Franck and Weigert.

Williams, J. T., 1965, *A static model of the tongue during vowel articulation,* M.S. thesis, Massachusetts Institute of Technology.

Willis, R., 1828, On the vowel sounds, and on reed organ pipes, *Trans. Cambridge Phil. Soc., 3,* 10.

Wind, J., 1970, *On the phylogeny and ontogeny of the human larynx,* Wolters-Noordhoff.

Winitz, H., 1960, Spectrographic investigation of infant vowels, *J. Genet. Psychol., 96,* 171–181.

Wollberg, Z., and Newman, J. D., 1972, Auditory cortex of squirrel monkey: Response patterns of single cells to species-specific vocalizations, *Science, 175,* 212–214.

Wood, C. C., Goff, W. R., and Day, R. S., 1971, Auditory evoked potentials during speech perception, *Science, 173,* 1248–1251.

Woodward, A. S., 1921, A new cave man from Rhodesia, South Africa, *Nature, 108,* 371–372.

Yerkes, R. M., and Learned, D. W., 1925, *Chimpanzee intelligence and its vocal expressions,* Williams and Wilkins.

Zelazo, P. R., Zelazo, N. A., and Kolb, S., 1972, "Walking" in the newborn, *Science, 176,* 314–315.

Zhinkin, N. I., 1963, An application of the theory of algorithms to the study of animal speech—Methods of vocal intercommunication between monkeys, IN *Acoustic behavior of animals,* ed. R. G. Busnel, Elsevier.

Index